When Faith and Reason Meet:
The Legacy of John Zahm, CSC

When Faith and Reason Meet:
The Legacy of John Zahm, CSC

David B. Burrell, C.S.C.
With historical sketch by
Ralph Weber

ABOUT THE AUTHOR:

DAVID B. BURRELL, C.S.C. is Theodore M. Hesburgh Professor Emeritus of Philosophy and Theology at the University of Notre Dame. He is internationally regarded as an eminent scholar, in Philosophy, Theology and Islamic Studies and the author of numerous articles and 12 books.

WHEN FAITH AND REASON MEET:
The Legacy of John Zahm, C.S.C.
by David B. Burrell, C.S.C..

Copyright © 2009 by David B. Burrell

10 9 8 7 6 5 4 3 2 1

ISBN 978-0-9776458-9-3

Published by
CORBY BOOKS
A Division of Corby Publishing, L.P.

P.O. Box 93
Notre Dame, IN 46556
Editorial Office: 11961 Tyler Rd., Lakeville, IN 46536
Website: corbypublishing.com

MANUFACTURED IN THE UNITED STATES OF AMERICA

CONTENTS

Preface:
Perspectives on a Subject

Introduction
(with historical sketch by Ralph Weber)

1
Bible, Science, and Faith..................................... 1

2
Evolution and Dogma.. 15

3
Accomplistments of a Provincial
and Prelude to a New Life.................................... 37

4
[J.H. Mozans] *Following the Conquistadores –*
a Trilogy on South America................................ 55

5
[J.H. Mozans] *Women in Science*
and *Great Inspirers*..117

6
From Berlin to Baghdad to Babylon.............................137

Epilogue:
Assessment of John Zahm in a Larger Context...........173

ACKNOWLEDGMENTS

As one who undertook an historical study with trepidation, I called upon the resources of my confreres in Holy Cross whose *métier* this is: Tom Blantz, Jim Connelly, Rick Gribble, and Bill Miscamble, though I am principally indebted to Ralph Weber, whose doctoral dissertation in history at Notre Dame (1956) served as the basis for his biographical study, *Notre Dame's John Zahm* (Notre Dame IN: University of Notre Dame Press, 1961), and who has been unstinting in his enthusiasm for the project and his suggestions for its improvement—most of which I tried to execute. The personal and intellectual environment of Tantur Ecumenical Institute in Jerusalem made this work possible, through its rector, Michael McGarry, C.S.P., with Mrs. Vivi Siniora, the house matron of seventeen years, and now vice-rector, Bridget Tighe, F.M.D.M., who together create a home for students and scholars of all ages and nationalities, in a thirty-five acre oasis at a checkpoint, so the realities of the Holy Land are never far away. This notable "imaginary" led me to focus what John Zahm regarded as his signal endeavor: the work introducing Western readers to what we have come to call "the Middle East," though it is only 'middle' or 'east' from London!

The other motivation for undertaking this work has been a sense of "genealogy" of my religious family, the Congregation of Holy Cross, and the conviction that as much as founders are to be venerated (as ours has recently been formally recognized as "blessed"), those who carry forward the legacy deserve special recognition as well. For it is the intermediaries who give a tradition the shape it has assumed, and Zahm's dedication to study with teaching has come to characterize Holy Cross education at all levels in this country and the Asian, African, and South American venues where Holy Cross "missions" inevitably gravitated to education. For that reason I dedicate this attempt to retrieve one of our "fathers in faith" to his companions who have instilled in students worldwide a sense of "faith seeking understanding," notably those in scientific endeavors, like Richard Timm, C.S.C. in Bangladesh, as well as dedicated teachers and researchers in north and south America.

My profound gratitude to the competent staff of the archives of the Indiana Province of the Congregation of Holy Cross, notably Jackie Dougherty and her able successor, Deb Buzzard. A chance encounter with my colleague, Marvin O'Connell, the distinguished biographer of Edward Sorin and John Ireland—both friends and mentors of Zahm, precipitated a reading of the manuscript on his part, which helped me to add some clarifying material.

PREFACE:
Perspectives on a Subject

WHEN THE LIBRARY OF CONGRESS, which serves as a national library and repository of books published in the United States, began planning its millennial symposium in 1999, librarian James Billington consulted the agenda for the previous centenary celebration only to find no representative of religion or the arts. The mindset prevailing in 1899 apparently trusted that "science" would suffice to lead humankind along the march of progress so evident since reason had displaced obscurantism. And if romanticism's widespread reaction to reason's incapacity to respond to the yearnings of the human soul had failed to move these representatives of the Enlightenment to include the arts, the complementary stirrings of the "great awakening" would doubtless have elicited yet more formidable fears of the specter of religion. As Billington invited people to reflect on a century in which it is calculated that more people have lost their lives to pseudo-scientific ideologies than the rest of human history, he moved to correct both lacunae. The person whom he chose for religion—the current archbishop of Chicago, Francis George, O.M.I.—would allow himself but one prognosis for the upcoming twenty-first century, which will highlight the relevance of our subject even more decisively, but let us first focus on the climate in 1899, when Notre Dame's John Zahm had found a persuasive voice for articulating the integrity of rational inquiry in scientific investigation while expounding the complementary guidance of faith as well.[1] In retrospect, while his presence could have proved illuminating to that august gathering, Notre Dame was then far from the university which he would prod it to become, and of course a Catholic priest could only have spoiled the party. Yet already in 1887, Zahm's presentation on "the Catholic church and modern science" to Indiana University, at the invitation of president Louis Jordan, had so impressed the local press reviewer as to inspire a dig at the religion he encountered in southern Indiana, while praising Zahm's scholarship as well as the excellent training provided for Catholic priests: "unlike many a Protestant minister, Father Zahm knew what he believed, where he got his belief, and how to sustain himself in the same."[2] But not only was Indiana far from Washington; one also suspects such trenchant criticism of the de facto religious establishment would have been even less tolerated in the center of American power, so omission proved a more suitable strategy for the representatives of the intellectual elite at the Library of Congress in 1899.

Yet much as Vatican Council II provided Catholics a needed corrective for Vatican Council I a century earlier, the inclusion of religion and the arts in the 1999 Library of Congress symposium offers us a way to articulate the decided relevance of John Zahm to our time, even more than to his own. For if his work had failed to catch the attention of the Librarian of Congress in 1899, his writings on evolution and Catholic doctrine

---

[1] His most original work is *Evolution and Dogma* (Chicago: D.H. McBride & Co., 1896), supplemented by a collection of essays, most originating in a Chatauqua-like "Catholic Summer School" series: *Bible, Science and Faith* (Baltimore: John Murphy & Co., 1894), *Science and the Church* (Chicago: D.H. McBride & Co., 1896), *Scientific Theory and Catholic Doctrine* (Chicago: D.H. McBride & Co., 1896).

[2] Bloomington *Progress*, as reprinted in the Notre Dame *Scholastic* 19 February 1887; cited in Ralph Weber, *Notre Dame's John Zahm: American Catholic Apologist and Educator* (Notre Dame IN: University of Notre Dame Press, 1961) 45 [henceforward: Weber].

(translated into Italian) had negatively captured that of the Vatican, just as he was given the opportunity to initiate a sustained campaign to upgrade the educational valence of his fledgling Catholic university in northern Indiana. Yet those efforts would prove no less unwelcome to influential contemporaries of his own religious community than his writings on evolution to Vatican defenders of the faith. A century later, however, his views reconciling Catholic faith with evolution have received confirmation from Pope John Paul II, while the university for which he expended his life has vigorously pursued the trajectory he limned. The manner in which his educational dream for Notre Dame became realized will prove instructive in exploring the politics peculiar to those Catholic universities animated by religious congregations, yet the way his intellectual and moral stamina continued to sustain and direct him, once his aspirations for both church and university had been blocked, may offer a story even more illuminating than the institutional one.

For as Jung remarked, conscious individuals live out their times as well as their lives, and John Zahm's reflections during his travels subsequent to Rome's rejection of his theoretical reconciliations regarding religion and science, as well as his own community's resistance to practical proposals for Notre Dame's achieving university status, reveal just that. In penetrating the inner reaches of South America, he managed to combine his talents as a naturalist with his zeal as a Catholic priest to come to a critical appraisal of the way the Catholic faith had been transplanted there (with a keen ear for the plaintive voice of Bartolomeo de las Casas), as well as a stunning appreciation of the rich natural beauty of that vast continent.[3] But even these three groundbreaking works of reflective exploration pale before the prescient

---

[3] *Following the Conquistadores: Up the Orinoco and Down the Magdelena* (New York: D. Appleton, 1910), *Following the Conquistadores: Along the Andes and Down the Amazon* (New York: D. Appleton, 1911), *Following the Conquistadores: Through South America's Southland* (New York: D. Appleton, 1916).

account he offers Westerners on the eve of his anticipated journey from Berlin to Baghdad, posthumously published in 1922.[4] These reflections display a mind trained in Greek and Latin classics in an 1870s Notre Dame, desirous now of sharing with us the amplitude to which life had tempered both his mind and his heart to accept and learn from cultural and religious "others." The most telling chapter in this regard—"Islam Past and Present"—will return us to the 1999 Library of Congress symposium, where Cardinal George permitted himself but one prognosis for the century into which we have entered: that nothing would prove to be more salient religiously than the dialogue between Christianity and Islam. For in this chapter Zahm employs one example after another, framed as personal encounters via train and raft from Istanbul to Baghdad, to studiously correct western misapprehensions and fears of Islam. Depressingly enough for contemporary readers, those misapprehensions not only continue to prevail, but have succeeded in reinforcing a western hubris become destructive as it is oblivious to the dignity of difference.[5] How the contours of his initial education and his subsequent life could have shaped a Catholic priest born in Ohio in 1851 to so prescient an appreciation of Islam is a story worth telling.

Yet the larger story is one limned by the work of Bernard Lonergan, S.J., whose seminal work, *Insight* (1958), celebrates the "unrestricted desire to know," reminding us of the saving *eros* of intelligence. For that is what John Zahm's life—his ambitions, reversals, and sustained recovery—teaches us in an inescapable manner. Lonergan's astute appropriation of Catholic tradition (inspired by John Henry Newman), together with his experience teaching theology in Rome in the 1950s and '60s,

---

[4] *From Berlin to Baghdad and Babylon* (New York and London: D. Appleton, 1922).

[5] Jonathan Sacks: *Dignity of Difference* (New York: Continuum, 2002).

led him to divide those who "search for understanding" from those "who need certitude." John Zahm clearly exemplified the first, as his inquiring mind led him to explore the interface between faith and scientific inquiry, between new and old worlds, between a Catholic subculture and a wider academic world. Temperamentally, he was an adventurer, a *Grenzganger* [boundary-crosser], who undertook exploratory travel when his proposals for exploring the frontiers between science and faith were thwarted by ecclesiastical authorities, and his ambitions for advancing his nascent university, Notre Dame, into full-fledged university status was blocked by members of his own religious community who were administering it.

Yet we shall see how his presence in and to that same community (of Holy Cross) would bear the fruit he desired nearly a quarter-century after his death in 1921. That community dynamic will form the subtext emerging from our assessment of his own intellectual and spiritual journey, undertaken in the wake of severe reversals. And for some, notably men and women whose lives are shaped by and who themselves help to shape such religious communities, the subtext may even prove more instructive than the testimony of Zahm's own life as an intellectual and a person of faith. Yet perhaps the most illuminating fact is that all of us are who and what we are in virtue of the nourishing contexts of family and sustaining communities, so again, it is the interface which counts. In fact, I have been moved to attempt this appreciation of John Zahm as a younger member of the family of Holy Cross, realizing after fifty years of religious profession how much this family (with my original family) has contributed to what I have become. We are all so beholden to the legacies that sustain us that appreciations like this offer us a way to extend that legacy, enriched, to those who come after us.

My indebtedness to Ralph Weber's *Notre Dame's John Zahm* (Notre Dame IN: University of Notre Dame Press, 1961)—to be referred to as 'Weber'—will be evident throughout. Researched as only a history doctoral candidate knows how to do, his skilled account makes up for my deficiencies in archival research. Yet at the same time, it makes possible an appreciation of this sort, which can reliably depend on his careful scrutiny of extensive source. And even extend his inaugural work (a half-century later), as his title gives the focus of that work: "John Zahm and Notre Dame," allowing us to marvel at all this talented young Holy Cross priest was able to contribute to that fledgling institution from his ordination in 1875, coincident with being appointed professor of chemistry and physics, co-chair of the science department, and director of library and curator of the museum, as well as a member of the board of trustees, until his departure from Notre Dame in 1906! Handpicked by the founder of the University, Edward Sorin, C.S.C., to be "vice-president" of Notre Dame in 1885 (at the age of 34), John Zahm became Sorin's traveling companion as well, as they visited the Holy Land together in 1887.

In the spirit of a young religious congregation (Holy Cross dates its origination from 1841 in LeMans in France), a few of whom were transplanted a year later into a pioneer country, Zahm found himself involved in a burgeoning set of initiatives, centering on the foundation at Notre Dame du Lac in northern Indiana. Early on, he traveled the American southwest, in search of Catholic heritage in the new world, attracting students to the new university via chartered railroad cars. His talent for science and technology, coupled with his penchant for travel, led him on an inspection tour of European science facilities in 1878 and (in a more practical vein) to electrify the campus in the early 1880s. Throughout this period, he was intent on communicating the extensive discoveries of scientific inquiry to students and yet wider publics. By 1883 he had begun his public probe into evolution from the perspective of faith. Beginning in 1893, Zahm began his association with the Catholic Summer School, a Chautauqua-like movement for adult education, with five lectures in Plattsburg, New York on "Science and Revealed Religion" (Weber, 55). It is that spirit of inquiry which this appreciation will highlight, tempered and interiorized in response to criticism from ecclesiastical authorities and confreres resistant to his visionary call. We shall review the stages of his personal intellectual inquiry as they are punctuated by his major published works, recalling that he had anticipated an extensive study of Dante in his later years—a project cut short by influenza, but continued, as so many of his initiatives, in the Notre Dame of today in the Devers Program of Dante Studies.

INTRODUCTION

with Historical Sketch by Ralph Weber

WHO WAS JOHN ZAHM, and why explore his life and work? While Ralph Weber, his original biographer, will fill in the details, what moved me to undertake this study, and presumably will move readers to engage it, is this man's abiding need and ability to imagine "the other," yet do so in an American climate rather preoccupied with itself. From his earliest days on an Ohio farm in the mid-nineteenth century, we can say he lusted to learn, and that yearning was soon directed into arenas often neglected by others. When empirical science was burgeoning he immersed himself in that subject, with its technological appurtenances. At the same time, a remarkably competent philosophical and theological education equipped him to focus on the interface between science and his religious faith, where he proved unwilling to court either simple opposition or facile juxtapositions. He had to probe apparent contradictions to determine what deeper conciliances might be hidden there. That is why his works on religion and science, published at the turn of the century—from 1890 to 1905—have received the abiding attention of historians of science. Yet when Vatican suspicions closed off further inquiry in that direction, his ceaselessly inquiring mind moved into cultural and historical domains, seeking to delineate the multiple dimensions of the Latin American continent for his North American colleagues. These forays into Latin American topography, culture, and politics piqued the attention of the adventuresome naturalist and former president, Theodore Roosevelt, who enlisted his services for what was to be Zahm's third and last South American exploration. Physical forays were followed by landmark historical inquiries into "women in science," complemented by two vignettes on women in history who were "great inspirers." So if gender difference is the most pervasive "difference" we all know, Zahm probed that as well. Finally, in a veritable *coup de grace*, his final work, whose editing was cut short by the flu epidemic in Munich in 1921, re-created the world of biblical "near east," with prescient reflections on the Islam of his day—composed in its entirety before undertaking the actual voyage, inhibited as he was from sailing for the duration of the Great War.

He carried out these ground-breaking inquiries in the context of a religious congregation recently translated from France to northern Indiana, whose leader, Edward Sorin, C.S.C. boldly inaugurated a "university" on their arrival in northern Indiana in 1841, calling it "Notre Dame." Born soon after, in 1851, on an Ohio farm, John Zahm brought both German and English to the education he sought at this fledgling university, where he soon imbibed Greek, Latin, and French. Though his interests turned quickly to science, this classical training left an abiding taste for Homer, which he read in the original for recreation, as well as prepared him to revel in the poetry of Dante's Divine Comedy, which was to give him lifelong inspiration. The Congregation of Holy Cross was intended by its founder to be a religious "family," a microcosm of the community of faith and the human family, with priests, brothers and sisters working side by side. Zahm joined this family soon after enrolling in Notre Dame, and was then afforded a fitting philosophical and theological education, after undergoing a period of testing, or novitiate. He was immediately given multiple responsibilities, befitting his talents as well as the pressing needs of the new institution. Yet none of these would stand in the way of that probing habit of inquiry which had become second-nature to him. Eager to attract Hispanic students to Notre Dame in the 1880s, he travelled to the American southwest, engaging railroad cars to bring them to Indiana, as well as devoting himself to a Chautauqua-like "Catholic Summer School," where his brief would be "science and religion." Utterly engaged as teacher and publicist, he turned the summer lectures into copiously annotated books which lost none of their spontaneous flavor. The most controversial was his 1896 *Evolution and Dogma*, in which he contended (much the same as Pope John Paul II would in 1996) that the biblical creator, understood via the rich developments of Christian philosophical theology, was certainly "big enough" to employ chance as a secondary cause in sustaining the universe which the creator originates and sustains.

Yet the fallout of that work, once translated into Italian and French by well-meaning European friends, would presage a momentous shift in Zahm's relation to Notre Dame and to his religious congregation of Holy Cross. His manner of negotiating that crisis, however, will constitute the warp and woof of this study: to show that the same uncanny capacity to imagine "the other," drawn as he ever was by difference, leads him to be an adventurous "border-crosser," whether that be literally in his South American ventures; intellectually, in his study of women in science and in literary life; or culturally, in exploring the lands of the bible in ancient and contemporary "near East," yet finally, in his own person, as he came to inspire future leaders of Notre Dame to carry it over the threshold of a genuine university. The plot of this appreciation will follow the sinuous interlacing of these intellectual voyages, to the point where a decidedly contemporary person emerges, attuned to "the other" with no need or desire to colonize what is different, but able to explicate that difference in a way designed to nourish his compatriots. A real teacher, certainly, and one whose adventuresome spirit at the outset of the twentieth century should inspire a cognate sense of adventure in those who face the incipient century following. In the face of media stereotypes, the capacity to enter into the imaginary of "the other" sounds like the gift our century needs above all. So in the spirit of appreciation, we shall offer excerpts of Zahm's own writings to spice each chapter, letting the sequence of his writings unfold the lineaments of the story. But first a detailed itinerary from an Indiana farm to the plethora of taxing projects designed to make a university of the "University of Notre Dame du Lac."

From an Indiana Farm to Notre Dame: an Enthusiast in Education
(Historical Sketch by Ralph E. Weber)

The occasion was the golden jubilee, in 1888, of Father Edward Sorin, founder of the University of Notre Dame; the speaker, as reported in the June 2 Notre Dame *Scholastic*, was Father John A. Zahm, Vice-President of the University:

> I love to see in our Notre Dame of to-day the promise of the potency of a Padua or a Bologna, a Bonn or a Heidelberg, an Oxford or a Cambridge, a Salamanca or a Valladolid. It may be that this view will be regarded as one proceeding from my own enthusiasm, but it matters not. I consider it a compliment to be called an enthusiast. Turn over the pages of history and you will find that all those who have left a name and a fame have been enthusiasts, and it is because our venerable Founder has been an enthusiast – I use the word in its primary signification – that he has been able to achieve so much.

To the conservative mind the word "enthusiast" may connote too much of the impetuous and irresponsible. There were not a few present at the dinner who would have been more comfortable had it not been used to describe their ageing Superior General. But, all agreed that in speaking of himself, Zahm had chosen the right word.

The second of fourteen children, John Zahm was born June 11, 1851. His father, Jacob, had been brought as a child to America when his grandparents emigrated from Alsace in the 1820s. His mother, Mary Ellen, daughter of John Braddock and grandniece of Major General Edward Braddock, was born in Pennsylvania and later moved to New Lexington, Ohio, where she and Jacob Zahm met and married. John Zahm's boyhood in New Lexington until the age of twelve was characterized by strict discipline, thrift, perseverance, and a love for literature. His formal schooling began in a one-room log school where elementary studies were taught at times which did not conflict with farm chores. One of Zahm's classmates during these early years was Januarius Aloysius McGahn who later became a famous war correspondent before the turn of the century. Like their parents before them, Jacob and Mary Ellen Zahm, with their eight children migrated westward and in 1863 settled on a two-acre plot of fertile soil a few miles north of Huntington, Indiana. Gradually the venturesome family prospered, which enabled the father, a carpenter-farmer by trade, to buy additional acreage. John, the oldest son, was never idle, and here too he continued his formal schooling at SS. Peter and Paul School.

In 1867, then fifteen years old, John decided to resolve his thoughts concerning a vocation to the priesthood. Writing in mid-October to his aunt, Sister M. Praxedes, who had become a Holy Cross Sister a few years earlier at St. Mary's College near Notre Dame, he inquired about the religious life and asked that she give his letter to Father Sorin at Notre Dame. Sorin replied promptly and asked Zahm how far he was in his Latin studies, what studies he had taken in English and German, and finally, what sum his parents could pay yearly for his education at Notre Dame.[6] Zahm's answers were satisfactory, for a short time later Sorin wrote: "As you seem so anxious to come & try yourself here, I am willing to accept your offer viz.: on your paying $50 to keep you for five months in the College. You may come anytime your parents will deem it expedient."[7] Relieved, after months of indecision, Zahm began the hundred mile journey northward soon after fall harvest. His luggage filled with the required clothing and the "1 table-knife, 1 fork, 1 teaspoon, 1 tablespoon" specified in the *Catalogue*,[8] he arrived on campus, December 3, 1867. The cluster of yellow brick buildings bordering the lake appeared imposing, especially the Main Building which served as classroom building and dormitory. The campus appeared busy too as students dashed hither and yon shortly before the annual holy-day, the Feast of the Immaculate Conception. It was fitting that Notre Dame's future inspirer should begin his college education at this time.

The University, not much older than Zahm at the time, was still under the dynamic leadership of Sorin. This missionary priest, born at La Roche, France, in 1814 and ordained in 1838 at Le Mans, France, joined the newly formed Auxiliary Priests of Father Moreau in 1840. At the urgent request of Bishop de la Hailandière, Sorin with six Brothers sailed on the *Iowa* for America one year later and arrived at Vincennes, Indiana. Some months later, the bishop gave Sorin money and Father Stephen Badin's former Indian mission

---

[6] Sorin to Zahm, October 20, 1867. Albert Zahm Collection, UNDA.
[7] *Ibid.*, November 14, 1867. Albert Zahm Collection, UNDA.
[8] *Twenty-Fourth Annual Catalogue of Notre Dame University, 1867-68* (Notre Dame, 1868), p. 14.

property near South Bend, Indiana, in order to found a college. By November 1842, the Holy Cross members took over their new property near the south bend of the St. Joseph River and began the difficult job of establishing a school. Our Lady's University developed rapidly in the years that followed as brick buildings arose on the wilderness campus: in 1844, the State of Indiana gave Sorin a university charter. So well did the institution expand its enrollment, buildings, and financial programs, that Sorin, fifteen years after the founding, assessed Notre Dame's monetary value at $159,047.15.

St. Louis University provided the model for the University's plan of studies as Sorin instituted a simple but thoroughly practical curriculum under two departments in 1848 – the Classic and Commercial. The two programs were theoretically identical except for the fact that Commercial students substituted bookkeeping and commerce courses for Latin and Greek. By the spring of 1868, University officials listed thirty-one subjects with ninety-one classes.[9] In addition, they reported that their program of studies, in which each subject was taught separately and each class divided according to one or more divisions (based upon the enrollment and students' proficiency), surpassed the European program of eight invariable classes and was done with a view to saving American students the useless review of matters already studied, together with time and money. These French religious had become Americanized quickly!

Recognizing the heightened interest in the physical and natural sciences, Notre Dame authorities added a physical and natural science program to the curriculum during the Civil War, and assumed a position of leadership among American Catholic colleges after Appomattox. A survey of sixty Catholic colleges

---

[9] Notre Dame *Scholastic*, May 23, 1868.

in 1866 shows that thirty-five others taught natural philosophy; thirty-four others, chemistry; thirteen, geology; and twelve others, botany.[10] Notre Dame taught all these subjects. By modern standards, Notre Dame was a small school. Its grammar, high school, and college departments, during the school year 1867-1868, numbered a faculty of 39 and a student body of 448. At commencement that year, three A.B. degrees, three B.S. degrees, thirty Commercial and five Medical certificates were awarded.[11] Tuition costs fluctuated during the Civil War; however by 1867, they were set at one hundred and fifty dollars per semester (five months) for board, bed, bedding and tuition. Fringe services such as washing and mending of linens, doctor's fees, medicine, and nursing care were also included in this fee. Primarily for the benefit of prospective students' parents, school authorities emphasized that the University was located at some distance from the nearest town and hence the students were not distracted; furthermore, the "stern though mild" discipline riveted the students' attention to their studies. Although the semester began in the first week of September, a new student was welcome whenever he could come – the Director of Studies discussed his previous schooling with each applicant and assigned the proper sequence of courses.

Because of his interest in the priesthood, Zahm enrolled in the Classical Course, which involved a program of studies similar to that still pursued in B.A. programs in many present day Catholic colleges and universities. The scholarly progress Zahm exhibited was recorded in the Honorable Mention Table, a kind of scholar's bulletin board, which was published in almost every issue of the Notre Dame *Scholastic*, a

---

[10] Sebastian Anthony Erbacher, *Catholic Higher Education in the United States, 1850-1866* (Washington, 1937), pg. 8g. Only thirty-five of them had charters with permission to grant degrees. Burns and Kohlbrenner, *A History of Catholic Education* (New York, 1937), p. 266.

[11] Burns Collection, PA.

weekly student newspaper. Shortly after his arrival he received mention for fourth algebra, and during the remainder of the school year he took honors in first grammar, third German, and seventh Latin. In the May 16 issue he was honored for having obtained six certificates for improvement in studies during the previous two months. His rhetoric notebook, now in the Provincial Archives, reveals the wide variety of his compositions: "The Crusades," "Discovery of America," "Concerning the Right of Young People to Judge Their Elders," "The Blessings of Christianity," and "Do Savage Nations Possess a Right to the Soil." His essay on wealth, "The Safest Way to Become Wealthy," reflected America's optimism about capitalistic enterprise so current after the Civil War. He wrote that the desire of becoming wealthy was so strong and widespread that it must have been intended by God for man's greater good. To become wealthy, he continued, a man must be honest, orderly, thrifty, and friendly with his neighbors. In this manner, a man could become rich enjoyably and with a clear conscience. Thus, too, tranquility of soul would be his highest happiness and "worth more than all the riches that he could possess."

Zahm's semester examination grades in the middle of his sophomore year, published in the *Scholastic*, February 6, 1869, gave little indication of a great academic future for he failed mathematics and German! The problem was reflected in a letter he received from Sister M. Praxedes in which she said she was pleased he would stay on longer in college and urged him to persevere.[12] The temporary indecision over, he achieved a coveted place at the Table of Honor by the end of the semester.[13] A better picture of Zahm's intellectual and personal development is drawn from his extra-curricular

---

[12] Sister M. Praxedes to Zahm, January 12, 1869. Albert Zahm Collection, UNDA.

[13] The personal approach to education was emphasized, for at weekly faculty meetings honor students were chosen for special seats of honor in the refectory.

activities. The St. Aloysius Philodemic Society, the Scientific Association, the Archconfraternity, the Student Choir and the Juanita Baseball Club were important to his education. The St. Aloysius group publicized in the *Scholastic* of June 11, 1870, that it had sponsored debates on sixteen questions, two lectures, and twenty-one declamations during the preceding year; and that the library for its twenty members numbered over one thousand books, magazines, pamphlets, and newspapers. Soon after his arrival on campus, Zahm became an officer and librarian of this stimulating group. In debates, his earnestness and logic brought him student respect. More than this, however, Zahm mastered the art of public speaking on popular topics which ranged from "That Poland has suffered more from oppression than Ireland" to the necessity for Latin language study. A fellow student wrote the best description of Zahm during these years when he commented that Zahm's essay on "Truth" was like its author, "quiet, scholarly, and correct."[14]

Founded a few months after Zahm's arrival, the United Scientific Association, restricted in its membership to honor students, became an energetic organization under the directorship of Father Joseph C. Carrier. This man exerted a great influence on Zahm.[15] Born circa 1833 in France, Carrier was teaching physics at Ferney College near Geneva when Bishop Joseph Cretin of St. Paul, Minnesota, encouraged him to leave in 1855 and study for the priesthood at St. Paul. Following the death of Cretin, Carrier transferred to Notre Dame in 1860 and was ordained a priest in the Congregation of Holy Cross in

---

[14] *Loc. cit.*, December 3, 1870.

[15] Years later, Carrier confided to Professor James Edwards that Zahm failed to give him sufficient credit for the science department – "I am afraid that Fr. Zahm is not over unselfish, nor over just in his appreciation of what he may owe to me – little as that may have been. The disciple is now made famous by the conspiracy of – no doubt, well deserved – world-wide publicity; while the master . . . is content to remain ignored, or well-nigh so." Carrier to Edwards, March 3, 1895. Edwards Collection, UNDA.

1861. After a chaplaincy in Sherman's army, Carrier returned to Notre Dame's science department. As director of the Science Museum and Professor of Chemistry and Physics, Carrier developed the science curriculum despite the hesitant acceptance of his curriculum by some Notre Dame professors. One of these men, Joseph A. Lyons, carried the controversy into print when he wrote that scientific studies claimed an undue preference to the harm of classical studies. The former, he said, afforded little mental discipline and "open the mind to no knowledge of human nature and social duties."[16]   Notre Dame, he admitted, had a scientific course for those whom divine Providence had given a special aptitude for science; however, "she prefers the classical and, as much as in her lies, exhorts her children to the same preference."[17]   Carrier had a different view for he explained in the columns of the *Scholastic*, January 30, 1869, that a study of science, especially zoology, trains the intellectual powers and is therefore, "worthy of the reverent exercise of the highest faculties of the human mind." He also emphasized in his lectures that the first chapter of the Book of Genesis did not conflict with historical geology.[18]

Zahm worked closely with Carrier in the Scientific Association as his essay reprinted in the *Scholastic* on May 27, 1871, indicates. Entitled "Thoughts on Science and the Age in which we live," Zahm noted that progress and general enlightenment characterized the nineteenth century for the ancient philosophers studied theoretical rather than practical science. In declaring Watt's steam engine, Morse's telegraph, and the invention of printing the truly great discoveries, Zahm sounded much like John Quincy Adams, who had said twenty-five years earlier: "Fulton and Morse have done more by their discoveries, for

---

[16] Joseph A. Lyons, *Silver Jubilee of the University of Notre Dame* (Chicago, 1869), p. 49.

[17] *Ibid.* p. 50.

[18] *Loc. cit.*, February 11, 1871.

their country and the human race, than any two hundred Presidents in succession could be expected to accomplish."[19] Zahm's essay ended on a typically late nineteenth-century American glorification of Progress by declaring science "is now and deservedly so, regarded as the only talisman of wealth, prosperity and happiness; as the highest exponent of power and intellectual superiority; as the primary index of the material and social condition of mankind, and as the most reliable touchstone of the progress and tendency of the age in which we live."

Commencement marked the end of college studies for Zahm, not quite four years after his enrollment, on June 21, 1871, when he received his Bachelor of Arts degree in a graduating class which numbered one other A.B. student, three LL.D., one M.S. and one M.A., thirty Master of Accounts and four Medical Certificate students. For Zahm, the graduation ceremonies terminated only one phase of his formal schooling since he had finally resolved his doubts concerning the priesthood. Consequently, on September 11, 1871, he was received into the Congregation of Holy Cross and entered the novitiate at Notre Dame. Because of financial reasons and a shortage of staff, the Congregation assigned its seminarians to teach in the college in addition to pursuing their studies in the seminary. Practically every other Catholic college with a source of seminarians available followed this practice.[20] During the first year Zahm taught regular classes in Greek and grammar. A year later, he became Carrier's Assistant in the Science Department and the *Twenty-ninth Annual Catalogue* listed him as Assistant Librarian, Curator of the Museum, Assistant in Chemistry, Physics, and Natural Science! In spite of the manifold duties, Zahm found the life satisfying and therefore made his

---

[19] As quoted in Carleton Mabee, *The American Leonardo, A Life of Samuel F.B. Morse* (New York, 1943), p. 186.

[20] Edward J. Power, *A History of Catholic Higher Education in the United States* (Milwaukee, 1958), pp. 92-93.

religious vows on November 1, 1872. At the end of that school year he received his Master of Arts degree.

When Carrier was appointed president of St. Mary's College, Galveston, Texas, in 1875, Zahm, a subdeacon and only twenty-three years old, became Professor of Chemistry and Physics, and Co-Director of the College Library (which opened at 3:45 p.m. each day), Curator of the Museum and a member of the Board of Trustees. With typical enthusiasm, Zahm followed in the footsteps of Carrier in many ways. For example, on October 25, 1874, the *Scholastic* reported his purchase of several hundred dollars' worth of physics equipment with the comment, "It is quite a sight to see this gentlemen's room with instruments and machines of all kinds in it." Succeeding Carrier to the directorship of the St. Aloysius Society in 1874, Zahm, according to the students, gave the group "tone and dignity by his presence, as well as edification by his wise and instructive counsel."[21]   He became president of the Scientific Association in 1875. The Minims, Notre Dame's grade school students and Sorin's favorite young friends, shared Zahm's enthusiasm as he thrilled them with sparks of fire from a Leyden jar and lantern views of Rome.

As June 4, 1875, and ordination to the priesthood approached, Zahm could reflect on a busy seven and one-half years at Notre Dame. Still outwardly serious and formal, a notable characteristic in his public life, he presented a youthful physical appearance. He was of medium height and slender, with light brown hair, a high forehead and oval face. His physical characteristics contributed only a fair indication of tremendous nervous energy. The youth from rural Huntington, Indiana, had matured quickly during these years. His deep interest in classical studies combined with fine ability in scientific work gave promise of

---

[21]*Loc. cit.*, January 17, 1874.

a well-balanced teacher. Many extra-curricular responsibilities developed his administrative talents while the busy "jack-of-all-trades" seminary years prepared him for the future role of developing a young religious congregation and an expanding American Catholic university. That these were pioneering days in Catholic education, he personally realized. Elevated to the priesthood on June 4, Zahm accepted the responsibilities of the future. Scholarly, outwardly quiet, enthusiastic, he was anxious to develop a congregation and university of saints and scholars.

Writing a personal note to Orestes A. Brownson in the fall of 1875, Zahm revealed his concern over the future education of English-speaking Catholic students as he urged Brownson to publish the various articles from the *Review* in book form:

> As yet English-speaking Catholics have but few volumes of Essays & Criticisms by Catholic authors. The Protestants are far ahead of us in this department of literature, and it is a pity that our youth should be obligated to have recourse to such works on similar subjects by Catholic writers. I for one particularly felt this want during my college course; not only myself but many also of my Catholic fellow students . . . certainly nothing is more needed, or better calculated to supply the want so long felt by our more advanced students in philosophy & general literature.[22]

In a sense Zahm was writing a platform for his own activities during the years following his ordination as he sought to improve Catholic higher education by exceptional teaching and superior science facilities at Notre Dame. Finally, his apologetical essays on a wide range of topics reached a large audience.

His educational crusade in the decade after ordination included Carrier's practice of giving popular science lectures for students at Notre Dame and at St. Mary's College, a school for young ladies conducted by the Holy Cross Sisters, located a mile

---

[22] Zahm to Brownson, October 14, 1875. John Zahm Collection, UNDA.

west of Notre Dame. In addition to the duties of Librarian, Curator of the Museum, Professor of Chemistry and Physics in the academic year, 1876-1877, he also held the posts of Vice-Chancellor, Vice-President, Director of students, director of the St. Aloysius Philodemic Society, assistant director of the St. Cecilia Philomatheon Association, president of the Scientific Association and president of the Lemonnier Boating Club! Lectures with experiments, or science education with visual aids, had been inaugurated successfully at Harvard in 1850 by Professor Josiah Parsons Cooke, a master in this form of education.[23] As their popularity increased during the next two decades, others followed his leadership. In March, 1876, Zahm presented the first chemistry lecture in the Scientific Series, inaugurated by him, on "Water." In it, he demonstrated with an electric battery that water was composed of oxygen and hydrogen; moreover, he exhibited an oxy-hydrogen blowpipe, the electric arc, and suggested that machinery might be run off power from the latter.

The audience termed his lecture brilliant and the *Scholastic* on March 11, urged its readers to procure their tickets for the next five lectures immediately, since they would never have such a fine opportunity for learning about Physics and Chemistry. Pleased with the reception, Zahm continued the Series with lectures on heat, light, chemical affinity, sound transmission, static electricity, magnetism, and optics. That this activity was becoming an integral part of Notre Dame's education may be inferred from the statement in the *Thirty-fourth Annual Catalogue*: "They are intended mainly for those students who cannot or do not wish to take up the Scientific Course, but who nevertheless desire to have a general knowledge of the leading facts and principles of the Physical and Natural Sciences." Using the magic lantern, he presented travel lectures periodically to the

---

[23] Charles Loring Jackson, "Chemistry 1865-1929," in Samuel Eliot Morison, ed., *The Development of Harvard University* (Cambridge, 1930), p. 259.

campus audience. Scenes of ancient and modern Europe rang-
ing from the ruins of Pompeii and Egypt to St. Peter's Basili-
ca in Rome were shown. With showmanship and a rather rare
display of humor, he delighted the students with slides of the
faculty and ended a typical program with comical illustrations
such as "the bad effects of getting up at half-past 5 o'clock" in
the morning and "coffee as a cure for fits."

Acquisitions for the Science Department and science shows
continued. Like Carrier, Zahm believed a knowledge of science was indispensable to an educated man; and good equipment was absolutely necessary for the study of science. As a
result of the buying trip along the Atlantic seaboard in 1876,
Zahm added equipment for the Physics Department such as a
stereopticon, a microscope for projection, a galvanometer and
self-condensing gas cylinders. However, the prize purchase he
made during the tour of the Philadelphia Centennial Exposition
was Rudolph Koenig's device which graphically illustrated the
tone of sound by means of manometric flames.[24] An historian of education has said the Philadelphia Exposition gave new
vigor to science education:[25] this proved exceptionally true at
Notre Dame. Again during the eastern tour the following summer, Zahm purchased additional equipment: optical devices
for studying double refraction and polarized light together with
Helmholtz and Lissajous sound machines. In 1876 he bought
expensive microphones and a phonograph – the students were
amazed when he demonstrated the latter machine at a campus
convocation.

Notre Dame's museum, by 1876, contained four thousand species of birds, stuffed quadrupeds, and color lithoes of
animals, plants and minerals. They had been collected under

---

[24] *Scholastic*, November 11, 1876.
[25] Ellwood P. Cubberly, *The History of Education* (New York, 1920), p. 799.

the direction of Carrier. Zahm, eager to develop a first-rate collection, purchased quantities of shells, minerals and salt-water fish during one of his eastern tours. Upon his request, Father William Corby, President of Notre Dame, authorized the purchase in 1877 of an extraordinary collection of specimens which had been exhibited at the Chicago Exposition. After convincing the University council that the Science Department should be expanded, Zahm had little difficulty in urging them that this collection of skeletons – human, monkeys, horse, wolf, birds – should be purchased for $5,000.[26] A few months later, again at Zahm's request, the Council voted to exchange a house in Chicago for a J. M. Veasey collection of zoological and mineral specimens valued at $6,000.[27] This collection of Rocky Mountain animals, including buffaloes, mountain sheep, and antelope, prompted the South Bend *Tribune* to report:

> In securing this collection Notre Dame has shown her enterprise, as in other things, and her knowledge of the wants of the present generation – the facilities for acquiring a thorough scientific education . . . we can, without being a prophet, foretell, that the scientific department of Notre Dame will at no distant future be recognized as one of the centers of science in our country.[28]

With the addition of the Veasey collection, which required ten large wagons for the transfer from the railroad station to the campus, the natural history museum was moved from Phelan Hall to the fourth floor of the Main Building – a move dictated by space requirements but regretted when the latter building was destroyed by fire less than a year later. Meanwhile Zahm promised the students in the pages of the *Scholastic*, May 11, 1878, that Notre Dame would have one of the nation's best

---

[26] The asking price was $8,000 but Notre Dame offered $5,000. University Report, PA.

[27] *Ibid.*

[28] As reprinted in *loc. cit.*, April 6, 1878.

museums: "It will not be a mere repository of curiosities, but a systematic working collection of such specimens, preparations, etc. as will be of most value to the student in the prosecution of his scientific studies."

In accord with the administration's decision the previous fall to expand the Science Department, Zahm left on June 4, 1878, for a careful inspection tour of European science laboratories preparatory to constructing a new science building on campus. After an unpleasant voyage, because of seasickness, Zahm stopped off in Liverpool, England. While exploring the Museum of Natural History there he recorded in his diary in great detail the room dimensions and the precise measurements of the display cases, and noted as well that the various specimens were grouped artistically.[29] Traveling on, he inspected the Royal Museum at The Hague, and noted incidentally, that the Dutch were plain, quiet and industrious. Turning southward, he toured Cologne before going on to Bonn University. At Bonn and eager to learn the latest scientific advances, he attended the physics lectures of Professor Kelleler and Professor Schliiger in paleontology: very precise notes and sketches of the University's mineralogical cabinets, physical and chemical lecture rooms and equipment were faithfully recorded during the ten-day visit. The boat ride down the Rhine River valley and a tour through Coblentz and Mayence provided a pleasant interlude before he resumed his intellectual pursuits at Heidelberg. There he attended lectures on theoretical Chemistry and electro-magnetism and discovered that Heidelberg's collection of scientific materials was not as complete as that at Bonn. A week later, he arrived at Karlsruhe and the Royal Polytechnic School, famous for its physics equipment. Following tours of Oldsberg, Holzem, and Brussels, he turned southward to Paris

---

[29] Zahm's diary is in the Provincial Archives.

and visited the Exposition during the latter days of July. He was surprised to find that the equipment on display did not equal that shown at the Philadelphia Exposition.

The young, relatively unknown priest visited Rudolph Koenig in Paris and worked with him on some acoustical experiments. Moreover, he attended a meeting of the French Society of Physics and observed carefully the electrical apparatus on display. With unconcealed pleasure, he accepted its invitation to membership.[30] Too, the electric lights strung along the Rue de l'Opera gave him further enthusiasm for future Notre Dame projects. After a Baedecker-type tour through Paris, its environs, and the discovery of the *Père La Chaise,* "the most wonderful cemetery in the world – a real *ville des morts,*" he returned to England and studied the facilities of the British Museum before embarking at Liverpool for the return voyage by way of Southern Ireland. In a characteristic style, begun as a reporter on the Notre Dame *Scholastic,* Zahm described the visit to the "Greenland of Catholicism" in a manner which pleased the Irish-American readers of the *Catholic Columbian.* In this account, the first of his "newspaper letters," he predicted that Ireland's great moral power and the force of public opinion would effect what fire and the sword had hitherto failed – independence.[31]

Zahm's European tour proved to be a "growth" investment for Notre Dame as his imagination and project-planning took on new proportions. When he returned to the class room in the third week of September, he was enthusiastic with new plans for Notre Dame's development. Also he had reason to be proud of the advances in equipment and facilities his department had made in the three previous years. His desire to provide a superior science education was finding fulfillment; and gradually

---

[30] *Loc. cit.,* September 21, 1878; May 7, 1892.
[31] Clipping from the *Catholic Columbian* for 1878. PA.

the museum was becoming first rate. The *Scholastic* on April 19, 1879, journalistically patted Zahm on the back by stating that the numerous additions to the museum collection were excellent. Four days after this report appeared, the total museum, except for three stuffed specimens, was destroyed in the "Great Calamity!"

This $200,000 conflagration, lasting three turbulent hours, began in the Main Building at eleven o'clock on Wednesday morning. Hastily-formed bucket brigades had little effect as the fire destroyed the main Building, Minim Hall, Music Hall, the Old Men's Home, and most of the Infirmary. The following day's Chicago *Times* described the destruction succinctly: "Hot Havoc – Vast Libraries and Innumerable Scientific Treasures Consumed or Ruined." The University closed its college year one day later, transferred the Minims to Phelan Hall, and began reconstruction. Friends, alumni, and students were urged to send donations for the new Notre Dame. Zahm went to Fort Wayne on one of the fund-raising tours; this visit together with the others he made, netted the building fund over two thousand dollars in cash and pledges.[32] He personally began rebuilding the museum collection by requesting friends and former students, especially those living in mining districts, to send specimens of minerals, fossils, stuffed animals, skeleton, shells, coins, corals, and Indian relics.

The fire of '79 failed to diminish Notre Dame's progressive spirit; in fact, witnesses reported that Father Sorin looked years younger and more energetic in building the University a second time! Indicative of this resurgence, the new Main Building opened for classes in September, five months later! Zahm, a major force in this new drive, enlarged his program for rebuilding the science facilities and equipment. His request for specimens

---

[32] A few of Zahm's notebooks which list the amount of money and/or work promised for rebuilding the college are in the Provincial Archives.

was answered with large shipments of minerals from South Dakota and the Rocky Mountain region, copper from the Lake Superior region, minerals and shells from Iowa, coins from South Bend, and quartz crystals from Alabama. Despite the recent extraordinary expense, he secured Sorin's permission to begin a construction fund for a new Science Hall. In a letter dated October 23, 1879, Sorin stated: "Our Father Zahm is hereby fully authorized to keep for the building of the eastern wing, as marked in the place, for a Scientific Hall, all donations and moneys he may, from this day, solicit and receive for that purpose".[33]

Characterized by strong determination, Zahm began new ventures for acquiring funds for the proposed building. With an eight-hundred-pound electro-magnet built according to his specifications by Charles Reitz, he commenced a lecture tour which opened at Notre Dame shortly after Christmas. The next stop on his schedule, a few weeks later, was the South Bend Opera House. The South Bend *Daily Register* reported on January 8, 1880:

> Father Zahm is youthful in appearance as he is in years, but a man of fine presence, and carries a head on his shoulders that rises to an intellectual dome of unusual height. His language was well suited to the popular style of lecturing, through its simplicity and succinctness, and the lecture was so profusely illustrated by experiments that the audience was kept awake to every point introduced.

Determined to prevent another fire, University authorities appointed Zahm campus fire chief, shortly after the Main Building was completed. Under his direction, a fire pump was installed which filled strategically-located water tanks around the perimeter of the campus. A cautious and competent man, he installed still another fire pump in the basement of the boiler

---

[33] As quoted in Patrick J. Carroll, "Mind in Action," *Ave Maria*, 63 (January, 1946), 82.

house, and this pump, by drawing water from the lake, could fill the cistern and four tanks in the college and surrounding buildings in one hour–a job which previously required a full day. Two years after the fire, the installation of hydrants and outlets within the buildings completed the fire insurance program. In June, 1881, a fire drill was held and eight heavy streams of water were directed on the Main Building within five minutes. Apparently his new fire-fighting system encouraged a certain lethargy, for the "Council Minute Book" noted on November 17, 1882, that a fire department would be organized, and one month later, "It was decided . . . to get the fire company to practice."

The *Scholastic* reported on October 29, 1881, that Zahm had purchased a dynamo-electric machine which, when connected to the steam plant, powered a lamp of 2,500 candles. This arrangement permitted the Sorin Cadets to drill at night in the Junior Yard; and a few evenings after this unprecedented innovation, the Minims played a game of night football. For Commencement ceremonies the following June, he used the equipment for spotlighting the Main Building, the Academy of Music and the college grounds. A few months later Zahm made arrangements with the Vanderpoel Electric Light Company of Chicago to build a new Notre Dame electric light plant which would be used for outdoor lighting. All this activity prompted one newspaper to comment:

> It seems to us that the learned gentlemen at Notre Dame are making scientific advancement pretty rapidly for people who are supposed to live mainly in the mists of the middle ages.[34]

The first phase of campus electrification ended with the installation of an electric crown on the sixteen-foot statue of the Blessed Virgin on top of the Golden Dome in 1884.

Zahm's fund raising took on a new aspect with his trip to Columbus, Ohio, in the summer of 1880 as he began recruiting

---

[34] *Ypsilanti Sentinel* as reprinted in *loc. cit.*, December 16, 1882.

students for Notre Dame. Moreover, he secured reduced rates from the Pennsylvania Railroad for the new students' trip to Notre Dame. The next summer, he again advertised the University in southern Ohio and returned with a student contingent in the fall. In 1882, Zahm turned westward and spent the first of many summers in the West – Mexico, New Mexico, Colorado, and Wyoming – in exploration for museum specimens and new students. His diary of the journey, now in the Provincial Archives, lists the promises by Albuquerque parents to send their sons to Notre Dame and their daughters to St. Mary's. Discounts of 10 per cent less than catalogue prices were promised for two students from the same family and 15 per cent, for three or more. Railroad fares were set at one-half the usual rate. Although in 1870 Notre Dame had only one student from New Mexico and none from Colorado, approximately twenty-five new students from the Denver area returned with Zahm on a special palace car in 1882. His diary listed precise feeding instructions, and also financial ones, for some of his charges. The contingent's arrival in South Bend was declared one of the most picturesque events of the season as the eager students and their two lively burros left the train. Without question, the priest-promoter had a shrewd eye for publicity and money-raising projects. He had learned, as he told his brother Albert, "Keep yourself before the public always – if you wish the public to remember you or do anything for you."

Zahm returned in the summer of 1883 to the Southwest and after exploring the Rocky Mountain area with his brother Albert, went south into Chihuahua, Mexico, to study the Zuni and Accoma Indian customs and gather rare mineral specimens. Albert enjoyed serving as assistant to his brother for the two respected each other. Albert, eleven years younger, enrolled at Notre Dame in 1878 and like his brother, although registered in the Classical Course, took great interest in the study of science, especially

aeronautical research. Eager for Albert's advancement and recognizing his brother's inventive ability, Zahm encouraged Albert
to use the science laboratory during the evenings and weekends.
The Zahm brothers were a spirited team on Notre Dame's campus as they complemented each other's study and personality.
As Albert remarked later: he was the inventor, his brother the
popularizer of science: one the "Twainish" humorist, the other
the serious professor. Like his older brother, Albert joined the
Scientific Association at Notre Dame; he presented the results
of his pioneering experiments in aeronautics, constructed steam
engines, and developed the first wind tunnel in order to study the
influence of wind currents upon aircraft.[35]

In September, the Zahm brothers, after diligent recruiting,
escorted a large group of new students back to South Bend.
Father Zahm headed the contingent from Denver, Colorado, in a
special railroad car which was identified with the large banner,
"Students for Notre Dame University," while Albert escorted
the group from Chihuahua. The eighty excited passengers,
including some mothers of the Minims and young ladies for
St. Mary's, paraded to the campus in twenty carriages. This
"Western Continent" resulted in the announcement that for
the first time in its history Notre Dame had over four hundred
students during the first month of school. At Christmas time,
Zahm returned again to Chihuahua for two months, and this
time carried a supply of colorful advertising circulars which
pictured the route from Mexico City to Notre Dame and described in Spanish the University's many advantages. The trip
netted ten more students who accompanied him on the "First

---

[35] Albert received his A.B. (1883) and M.S. (1890) at Notre Dame, M.E. at Cornell (1892) and Ph.D. (1898) at Johns Hopkins. He served as Professor of Mathematics
and Mechanics at Notre Dame before attending Cornell; later, he was in charge of
mechanical and aerodynamic research at Catholic University. Following careers as
Chief Research Engineer for Curtiss Aeroplane Co. (1914-1917) and Chief of U.S.
Navy Aerodynamic Laboratory (1917-1929), he became Chief of Aeronautics Division
(Guggenheim Chair), Library of Congress. He died at Notre Dame in 1954.

International Train from Mexico City to Notre Dame." Subsequent summers brought larger western contingents which added to Notre Dame's growing enrollment. A student debate on the topic, "Is Colorado more interesting than any other state in the Union" lasted four hours and one proud son spoke from his prepared manuscript of 122 pages! Zahm also presented travel lectures on Colorado to Notre Dame audiences and his first pamphlet, "Colorado, Its Past, Present and Future," published at Notre Dame in 1883, was a Baedecker-type description of the Centennial State.

During this year, his lectures, which previously had covered science topics and travel descriptions in an expository fashion, became apologetic and Catholic in tone. For example, in a travelogue on "The Great Southwest, Its Attractions, Resources and People" given in 1883, Zahm appealed for a form of cultural Pan-Americanism which would recognize the Catholicity and dignity of South Americans and the Indians in southwestern United States. Critically he wrote:

> Notwithstanding the fact that nearly all the Indians of the Southwest are Catholics, as have been their forefathers for upwards of three hundred years, and in spite of their earnest and repeated protests, they have, In consequence of one of Grant's celebrated Civil Service Reforms (!) been handed over to the care of teachers they know not . . . [36]

Nor love nor trust. Continuing this bitter and accurate criticism, he wrote that these benighted Indians had been denied their Black Robe friends and American friendship. Similarly he complained about the popular newspaper portrayals of the typical Mexican as a "greaser." With some exaggeration, he insisted that the Spanish-Mexicans in Mexico and the United States had been more misrepresented and less understood than any other people. They were not lazy, ignorant, dishonest,

---

[36] John A. Zahm, *The Great Southwest, Its Attractions, Resources, and People* (Notre Dame, 1883), p. 31.

immoral or strangers to a cultured life. Such unjust descriptions resulted, he thought, from the actions of certain criminals who fled from justice in the United States and Europe, and made their homes in Mexico. Even more responsible, however, were the ignorant and bigoted newspaper correspondents and tourists whose experience of the Spanish-Americans was limited to views from baroom stools and hotel lobbies. In conclusion, he said that Mexicans, if not a better people, were certainly no worse than other nationalities.

Zahm first publicly entered the controversy over evolution with a sermon at Denver, Colorado, March 26, 1883, repeated later at Notre Dame and St. Mary's and printed in pamphlet form that same year. Reprinted in the French newspaper *Cosmos: Les Mondes*, this lecture marked the beginning of his international reputation. After restating that there were no real conflicts between Church and scientific truths, Zahm explained he was not speaking as an apologist, for the Church had no need of one. In fact, however, he did speak as one. When discussing the geologists' contention that the world was older than some theologians said, Zahm said the Church had never defined the age of the world ". . . and most probably never will, as the age of the world has nothing whatever to do – at least as far as I can see – with the object of her teaching, viz. : faith and morals."[37] Zahm also explained that Scripture did not state the age: therefore, scientists were permitted all the latitude they required. Although, he said, some commentators said six thousand years, this was not the official teaching of the Church. "If this distinction between opinion and doctrine, between theory and demonstration, were always borne in mind, we should hear less of so-called conflicts between science and religion." Rather, he wrote, it should be called a conflict between

---

[37] John A. Zahm, *The Catholic Church and Modern Science* (Notre Dame, 1883), p. 6.

individuals. Objections raised by scientists to the "days" mentioned in Scripture were declared foolish. The "days" did not necessarily mean twenty-four hours but might be interpreted as indefinite periods of time as St. Augustine, St. Thomas, and St. Albertus Magnus believed.

Zahm warned that evolution was only a hypothesis and it rested upon the assumption of the nebular hypothesis (that the earth and celestial bodies existed in a state of incandescent vapor and after a long period of time condensed in to solid orbs): the assumption of spontaneous generation (necessary, since life could not exist on the globe during the gaseous stage) which even Darwin considered absolutely inconceivable; and the assumption of transmutation of species of either plant or animal into another. This last assumption had no evidence, reported Zahm, and even Professor Huxley admitted this fact. These three assumptions must be proved before the theory of evolution might be considered valid, Zahm specified. Let it be supposed, however, that the necessary postulates for evolution were shown – then what? After stating that Catholics could not accept the theories of the atheistic and agnostic evolutionists, he cautiously suggested, like Mivart before him, that Catholics might accept a theory of theistic evolution.

> I trust you will not consider me as proclaiming a novelty, or as giving expression to a heterodox opinion, when I state it as my belief that there is not [anything contrary to Scripture or the teachings of the Catholic faith]. According to the words of Genesis, God did not create animals and plants in the primary sense of the word, but caused them to be produced from pre-existing material. "Let the earth bring forth, Let the waters bring forth," He says: showing clearly that creation in these instances, was only secondary or derivative.[38]

Thus, the theistic evolutionist merely believed God did *potentially* what many Scriptural interpreters believed He did

---

[38] *Ibid.*, p. 13.

directly and distinctly. Nor did the Church condemn evolution as contrary to faith. As for the Doctors and Fathers of the Church, St. Augustine held that plants and animals were brought into existence by natural causes. The Church Fathers taught that "as the seed contains invisible within itself all that is found in the full-grown tree, so also the world, after its creation by God, contained all the germs of the various forms of life that were afterwards produced."[39] St. Thomas and Suarez, he said, also held this doctrine of derivative creation.

Zahm rejected evolution of the soul. He observed that St. George Mivart defended the theory of the human body's evolution and added: "The hypothesis may be rash, and even dangerous, but I do not think that, considering it simply in its bearing on dogma, anyone could pronounce it as certainly and positively false."[40] Concluding his discussion on evolution, Zahm noted that men would probably never know whether theistic evolution occurred, for it would remain a mystery. He agreed with Mivart who said that certain men in the name of science propagated conflict in order to kill religion. In a final statement Zahm emphasized that there could be no genuine conflict between true science and the Catholic Church since both lead to God. This pamphlet was the first of his writing on a topic which would some years later mark him as the leading Catholic writer and speaker on the relationship between Catholicism and Natural Science. Gradually he assumed the mantle of Catholic apologist after 1883 as he increasingly described the attitude of the Church towards science in the past and the present. For example, in a subsequent lecture series during these early years, entitled, "What the Church Has Done for Science," reprinted in the first three issues of the March 1885, *Scholastic*, he

---

[39] *Ibid.*, p. 14.
[40] *Ibid.*, p. 15.

contended as Count de Maistre had earlier, that the Church through its universities and scholars had historically led the progress of science. To her, the western world owed, therefore, an immeasurable debt. This type of apologetics gave Zahm an influential leadership of national and international proportions. Meanwhile, on the campus at Notre Dame, another Zahm project, begun with his European journey in 1878 and steadfastly continued with fund-raising lectures, pamphlet writing, and student recruiting trips, came to completion. The Science Building, a symbol to his aggressive leadership in education, opened its doors to Notre Dame students at a ceremony led by Father Thomas Walsh on December 14, 1884. Incorporating the latest designs in lecture rooms and laboratories, this two-story Romanesque, yellow-brick building housed the departments of the physical and natural sciences together with the photography laboratory and the mechanical engineering department. The University, proud of this latest sign of progress, featured the building's floor plan in its 1885 *Catalogue.* As the 1884-85 academic year drew to a close, Zahm could look back on a decade of progress in the field of science at the University. His apparently boundless energy in raising funds, popularizing science, and recruiting students, laid the "brick and motor" foundations for Notre Dame's success in the study of science. On the local and national scene, he taught Catholics to view evolution calmly, and with persevering study, to investigate the theory. As a Catholic priest and scientist he gave courage to those who feared the advance of science would destroy the Church; but more than this, he interpreted the theories of evolution in theistic terms.

At the golden jubilee celebration for Sorin in 1888, Zahm declared his belief that Notre Dame held the promise of becoming a truly fine university, equal to the best in Europe.

Unquestionably, too, he agreed with Archbishop John Ireland who spoke out for the man of action. The *Scholastic*, August 25, 1888, reported Ireland's sermon at Notre Dame:

> I despise the many who worship success and who are ever ready to censure failure. Failure, when not the result of culpable imprudence, obtains my sympathy, and the effort that preceded it, my approval. The safe conservatism which never moves lest it fail, I abhor: it is the dry-rot in the Church, and my heart goes out to the man who never tolerated it in his calculations. Safe conservatism would have left the Apostles in Palestine.

Zahm hardly typified the man of "safe conservatism" in his efforts to make Notre Dame a distinctively superior university with an intellectually strong student body. The seven years after 1885 found him enlarging the foundations of a home for scholars and obtaining a national reputation for the University and himself.

Although named to the post of Vice-President of the University in 1885, Zahm continued as the head of his beloved Science school. Likewise, he drove himself and those around him with characteristic vigor as he aimed for the improvement of Notre Dame's enrollment, reputation, and educational facilities. Each September, as over the three previous years, Zahm personally guided a contingent of western students to both Notre Dame and St. Mary's College campuses via specially reserved railroad Pullmans replete with delightfully entertaining service. The Southwestern United States proved to be a fine recruiting ground for these Midwestern schools and Zahm's determination won the hearts of parents and students alike – "With Coloradans Father Zahm is the most popular educator in the country," reported the Denver *News* on January 8, 1887. School newspaper reports such as the one on September 19, 1891, noted that the trip's entertaining manager provided the colleges with students who arrived eager and even happy to begin the long, tedious school year. In 1887, the thirty-six hour journey over

Union Pacific or Burlington lines provided Notre Dame and St. Mary's College with more than fifteen percent of their enrollment.[41]

Early September enrollment increased at the fledgling Notre Dame: the modern Science Hall south of Washington Hall experienced a larger share of the new enrollees as interest in science spread throughout the world and, more especially, as Zahm promoted this study of science. The daily roll call in science subjects was estimated by the *Scholastic* on February 19, 1887, at 200 students – young men whose studies and experimentations ranged from the Departments of Chemistry through microscopy and Physics to practical mechanics. One faculty member exclaimed that Zahm was the University's happiest man because his plans for teaching the sciences, and, as well, for completing the large electric light plant on campus had been achieved. The friendly Buffalo *Union and Times* boastfully stated that Notre Dame rivaled Harvard "and [has] a scientific 'plant' second to none in the country."[42] Famed Dr. Rudolph Koenig judged that Zahm's collection of acoustical apparatus was one of the best in existence.[43] The Providence *Telegram* informed its readers that Notre Dame, while one of the greatest universities in the United States, was certainly the greatest in the West; and judged the science college, "one of the best-equipped institutions of the kind in the world."[44] Closer to home, the South Bend *Tribune* continued to laud the scientific improvements dotting the campus and more especially the completion of the Edison Electric Light

---

[41] *Scholastic*, September 14, 1889. St. Mary's College enrolled twenty-four Colorado students. *Ibid.*, September 14, 1889. The Denver *News*, September 8, 1887, story as reprinted in *ibid.*, September 17, 1887, stated that approximately fifty-one students for Notre Dame and nine for St. Mary's College departed. It is estimated that there would be about seventy-five students after the delegations at Colorado Springs, Pueblo, and La Junta joined the group. Notre Dame's enrollment at this time was about four hundred. *Ibid.*, March 12, 1887.

[42] *Ibid.*, March 29, 1890.

[43] *Ibid.*, May 7, 1892.

[44] Reprinted in *ibid.*, January 4, 1890.

Plant in 1885.[45] In its columns, the New York *Electrical Review* credited Notre Dame with being the first college to be lighted by electricity by explaining that in 1881, the arc light was employed successfully on the campus and the Edison incandescent lamp was introduced in 1885.[46] A gift from the New York Edison Light Company of a complete electric light plant together with a high-speed steam engine from the Providence Armington and Sims Engine Company, both gifts probably engineered by Zahm, helped the college authorities to complete the electrification of all campus buildings.[47] With a burst of local but unsubstantiated pride, the South Bend *Register* on February 10, 1886, claimed that Notre Dame's Science Hall "has no equal in all the educational institutions of the land." Zahm was proud of these reports of his efforts to build a true Catholic university at Notre Dame.

In 1888, Notre Dame began a new era in American Catholic higher education. Increased enrollment in the renovated law school, directed by Colonel William Hoynes, and in the collegiate department, together with the desire to attract older Catholic college students, brought Notre Dame authorities to risk a departure from the practice of housing students in the traditional dormitories. The precise role of Zahm in this radical departure from standard Catholic college practice in the United States is not clear. Albert Zahm, whose memory was remarkably accurate, claimed that his brother formulated a plan for private rooms in a residence hall but Father Thomas E. Walsh, President of Notre Dame, refused to consider it. Albert said Zahm then interested the Superior-General, Father Sorin, in the plan, and the latter sent Walsh to Europe for the 1888 meeting of the International Catholic Scientific Congress. During

---

[45] Reprinted in *ibid.*, November 21, 1885.
[46] Reprinted in *ibid.*, March 26, 1887.
[47] *Ibid.*, January 9, 1886.

those two months Walsh was gone, Zahm had the building designed and the cornerstone laid. As far as written evidence is concerned, only the following facts can be verified. Walsh left for Europe to attend the International Scientific Congress on March 14, 1888, and on April 28, 1888, the *Scholastic* announced that Mr. W.J. Edbrooke was designing a new structure to be named Sorin Hall. Furthermore, it said that Sorin was eager to have the building completed as soon as possible. The cornerstone dedication led by Sorin and Zahm took place on May 27, and Walsh returned from Europe two days later.[48] Thus, Zahm's exact role remains an interesting conjecture; however, Albert's recollection was probably correct as it appears strange that the cornerstone dedication took place two days before the University's president returned!

University authorities became concerned over the parents' reaction to this innovation. The *Forty-fourth Annual Catalogue* cautiously explained the Sorin Hall arrangement to parents of prospective and returning students. It told how for the previous four or five years private rooms had been furnished to advanced students who desired them and assured the readers that the results had been extremely encouraging: neither inferior work nor disciplinary problems resulted. For younger boys, the dormitory and study hall system was pronounced best; however, the lads in their junior and senior years and also law students who were "earnest, industrious, intelligent, and well-disposed young men would find the private rooms more conducive to good study." A year later, even students below the junior year who were exceptionally industrious and studious could obtain space in Sorin Hall in return for a fee of $100 a year. The aristocracy of age continued for older students and they received the privileged rooms at no extra cost. Father James

[48] *Ibid.*, June 2, 1888.

Burns, at Notre Dame at the time, and an authority on Catholic education in the United States, approved the private room system and said it would mark the end of the traditional discipline of the Catholic college because it destroyed the theory and practice of uniform college discipline and life. Also he reported that while conservative faculty members opposed it, students enjoyed the freedom and enrollments increased. With great accuracy, he also stated that intercollegiate athletics was the second factor which changed the Catholic college because the games took the college out into the world and brought the world into the college.[49]

As director of Sorin Hall, Father Andrew Morrissey took charge on January 1, 1889, when qualified students, returning from the holidays, moved into the building which contained sixty resident rooms. Each room was deemed large enough for study, yet small enough to discourage visiting! The left wing had quarters for Hoynes' law department and the right wing contained a chapel. The basement had smoking and reading rooms. Strong though typical optimism colored a *Scholastic* reporter's story on January 2 when he suggested that May 27, 1888, should long be remembered and some commemoration held each year in honor of the Hall's cornerstone dedication on the day "on which Notre Dame entered on a new era that will in time make her the foremost American University." Actually the hall proved so popular that a month after the formal opening, the *Scholastic* on February 16 urged the construction of a similar structure twice the size to accommodate all the applicants. In 1890, Maurice Francis Egan, former editor of the *Freeman's Journal* and then English professor, poet, and critic at Notre Dame, explained the basis for Sorin Hall in an article in the February *Catholic World* entitled, "A New Departure in

---

[49] Reverend James A. Burns, *Catholic Education A Study of Conditions* (New York, 1917), pp. 150-52.

Catholic College Discipline." Actually, he wrote, the common dormitory system in which all sleep "like patients in the wards of a hospital" was intensely disliked by American Catholic students. These young men, hungry for independence, wanted rooms of their own. Catholic colleges which would not provide them, he prophesied, would either suffer decreased enrollments or become mere preparatory schools for junior students. Egan then told of the very real fears experienced in planning and building Sorin Hall at Notre Dame – conservatives feared "that any recognition of modern prejudices against the dormitory system, even for students in senior grades, meant anarchy." However, more than a year of experimentation proved the venture a success. Seventy-five more rooms were scheduled for the new addition to the existing building. The discipline, order, and cleanliness pleased all the originators of the plan. More important, the quiet environment absolutely necessary for the life of a student, resulted from this experiment. The author concluded that Notre Dame had led the way and shown how to bring older students to its university with this important experiment – "The success of Sorin Hall marks an epoch and the beginning of a synthesis between traditions and the demands of the present time."

The work on Sorin Hall was barely finished before Zahm initiated still another project. Finding the Science Hall, constructed a few years earlier, inadequate for the mechanical department, he made plans for a building which would be erected just south of Science Hall. Excited over the project he wrote Albert:

> I want the mechanical dept. of Notre Dame to be equal to any in the U.S. – without exception, & I want you to do here what Thurston has done at Stevens [Institute] & at Cornell – develop the dept. & give it a national reputation. You can write books and thus indulge your library tastes & can show also that Catholic colleges need not be behind sectarian or government

institutions. My ideas may be Utopian but I am thoroughly in earnest & have never been more sanguine of success in anything I have undertaken.[50]

Shortly after ground was broken for the building in February, 1890, Zahm confided in Albert who was studying at Cornell: "Everyone here is perfectly dazed at the new departure. All they can say is 'What next?'"[51] Moreover, delighting in mystery, he said no one at Notre Dame yet knew the size of the building; nevertheless, the project itself is so daring "it has taken the breath away from everyone. I cannot imagine what the average looker-on will say when he gets his second wind." The building, paid for by a friend of Zahm in Chicago, was two stores high in front: this area housed the wood and metal working machines and provided classrooms as well; the rear of the building was reserved for the foundry and blacksmith shops. In conclusion, Zahm wrote, "Our intention is to not simply equal Cornell, but to eclipse it both in buildings and equipment." The students appreciated Zahm's manifold contributions to Notre Dame. On March 20, a *Scholastic* reporter described the annual St. Patrick's Day party in 1886 and the honors bestowed upon Zahm with the statement:

> No one connected with the University is held in higher esteem among the students and alumni of Notre Dame than is Father Zahm. He has been identified with the progress and growth of that institution as an instructor for the past fifteen years. His travels . . . and his labors in the Department of Science of the University have won for him an enviable reputation.

---

[50] Zahm to Albert Zahm, November 8, 1889. Albert Zahm Collection, UNDA.
[51] Zahm to Albert Zahm, February 26, 1890. Albert Zahm Collection, UNDA.

Chapter One

BIBLE, SCIENCE, AND FAITH[52]

ON FRIDAY MORNINGS during Ramadan in Jerusalem, from the Tantur Ecumenical Institute situated at the Bethlehem checkpoint "on the seam" between Israel and Palestine, one can sense the tension between those yearning to pray at the al-Aqsa ["the farthest"] mosque on the Haram al-Sharif [Temple Mount] in Jerusalem, and the Israeli young men and women in uniform instructed not to admit anyone under forty (or fifty, depending on the day). In 2006, Ramadan began on Rosh ha-Shana, initiating the "days of awe" between Jewish New Year and Yom Kippur [Day of Atonement], yet sacred times coinciding always spells tension "on the seam." Tantur Ecumenical Institute is a post-Vatican II initiative of Pope Paul VI to continue the ecumenical thrust of the council. Entrusted to Theodore Hesburgh, C.S.C., who found a "hill between Jerusalem and Bethlehem," with the help of John Leonard, a graduate of the University of Notre Dame then serving as political officer with the United States embassy. So Tantur represents a Catholic opening to ecumenism among the churches, and by extension and its location, to other faiths as well, notably the Abrahamic religions of Judaism and Islam. Notre Dame has faithfully supported this Vatican foundation through the vicissitudes of

---

[52]*Bible, Science and Faith* (Baltimore: John Murphy & Co., 1894).

1

"intifada's" and faltering "peace processes," aware that this location is priceless for its international educational efforts.

John Zahm accompanied the founding president of Notre Dame, Edward Sorin, to the Holy Land in 1887, where his journal records enjoying the hospitality of Franciscan friars. The Dominican who was to found the famed Ecole Biblique, Jean-Marie LaGrange, was not sent to Jerusalem until 1889, but these two intrepid inquirers were both present at the fourth Catholic Scientific Congress in Fribourg in 1897. It does not seem that they met, though each was already blazing trails that would put them both on a collision course with Roman authorities—La-Grange in biblical criticism and Zahm in the bible and evolution.[53] As we shall see, some greater sophistication in biblical criticism might have advanced the case Zahm was to make for evolution, but would doubtless also have complicated already complex relations with Roman authority. Yet what is striking about these two priest-scholars will be their utter devotion to their religious communities, and through those communities, obedience to Roman authority, coupled with an unyielding commitment to their respective intellectual agenda—and both operating in places remote from European centers of academic activity. The support each would receive, in the midst of their controversial inquiries, from their religious communities would vary, according to circumstance. LaGrange was part of a venerable order, whose French provinces would be engaged in recurrent "laicist" struggles, yet with longstanding connections in Rome, where successive Masters of the Dominican order would vary in the quality of their resolve to confront negative complaints, yet prove quite unyielding in their personal support for their intrepid confrere and his work. John Zahm, on the other hand, belonged to a fledgling religious congregation of priests

---

[53]Bernard Montagnes, O.P., *The Story of Father Marie-Joseph Lagrange: founder of modern Catholic biblical study* (NY: Paulist, 2006).

and brothers of Holy Cross (founded in Le Mans in France in 1841), whose presence was only beginning to be felt, largely in North America, where Notre Dame had been founded as a "university" in the frontier state of Indiana in 1842. In the event, it was Zahm himself who had but recently forged relationships in Rome, where he had served as Holy Cross's procurator, representing the congregation's interests in Rome, for two years from 1896-98. As these were the years when controversy over his publications regarding evolution began to emerge, these relationships would prove singularly useful to Zahm himself as well as to the young Congregation of Holy Cross.

As a prelude to his more focused inquiries into evolution, Zahm's zeal for scientific education is displayed in a book-length study of "sound and music," originating as a lecture series at Catholic University of America, and published under that title by McClurg in Chicago in 1892. Replete with diagrams and harkening back to Aristotle's view of sound transmission, the treatment is austerely scientific, by showing clearly how his teaching ambit extended well beyond the Notre Dame campus. He introduced a series of lectures on science and religion at the second meeting of the Catholic Summer School (modeled on Protestant initiatives at Chautauqua) in Plattsburg NY (1893), followed the next year by the inaugural session of the Columbian Summer school in Madison, Wisconsin, and in September 1894, the Third Catholic Scientific Congress in Brussels. Zahm had personally conveyed to that congress the benediction of Pope Leo XIII, who would confer on him an honorary Doctor of Philosophy the following year. In fact, his zeal for promoting scientific education, especially in Catholic colleges and universities—"to arm their graduates for the warfare against agnosticism" (Weber 74)—had so debilitated his nervous system that the medical director of the United States Navy had prescribed (in 1894) "travel, change of scene and change of climate; ... *entire* and *absolute* rest for a period of at least two years," during which time he was counseled "not to go near any religious establishment [and to] try horseback exercise, theaters, the opera" (Weber 72). Like most male members of active religious communities, Zahm egregiously disregarded the medical advice he had prudently sought, yet (in his case) would hearken to it when other doors closed twelve years later.

His early apologetic lectures promoting understanding between religion and science were collected under the title "Bible, Science and Faith," published in Baltimore by John Murphy and Co. in 1894. The theme of these essays is announced forthrightly in the Introduction:

> I have [n]ever been disposed to minimize the force and scope of dogma or sought to explain away certain declarations of the Scripture, for it has never entered my mind to do either the one or the other. No one could be more strenuously opposed to rationalism in matters of religion than I am, and no one could yield more ready and unconditional acquiescence to the teaching of the Church in all matters pertaining to faith and morals. Rationalism in religion, however is quite a different thing from a legitimate use of reasoning discussing questions of science and history and archaeology which may be incidentally mentioned in scripture or are indirectly and remotely connected with some teaching of faith. Herein I claim, as every one may claim—and faith and the Church are the first to grant all the lawful demands of the intellect—perfect freedom of investigation according to the principles of science, prescinding from all the restraints of petty dogmatism, and the questionable authority of systems which are obsolete, or schools which have long survived their period of usefulness (10-11).

Published originally in Catholic academic journals, these essays "cover substantially the same ground as the course of lectures [at] the Catholic Summer School in Plattsburg N.Y." (11). And while the printed version is replete with proper citations, the mode of argument reminds us forcibly of the elevated lecture style at the end of the nineteenth century in America. After the passion and concomitant sense of balance exhibited in his introductory remarks, the overwhelming impression is one of erudition. Zahm's extensive familiarity with patristic and medieval sources on the one hand, and learned scientific literature on the other, largely cited from current journals, is simply prodigious.

"Days" of Creation

Let me offer an example of each. Addressing the "Mosaic Hexaemeron in the light of exegesis and modern science," he lets Origen, Clement of Alexandria, Gregory of Nyssa and Augustine defuse purported "scientific" objections to creation which generate pseudo-conflicts between faith and science by simply juxtaposing current theories of origins to the Genesis narrative. In a thoroughly Catholic way, he reminds his readers that, as the church's book, the bible has enjoyed a rich panoply of commentary over the ages. Following two-edged apologetic practice, he deconstructs *prima facie* conflicts by recalling traditional interpretations of biblical texts, as well as tempers enthusiasm for hypothetical and necessarily provisional theories thought to oppose these texts. From this reconstruction he can respond to typical "La Placian" objections to creation ("we have no need of that hypothesis") by insisting that "creation is not a miraculous interference with the laws of nature, but the very institution of those laws" (83). Here he insists:

> Catholic exegetes have always regarded the Bible as the word of God, but one of the principles of interpretation which they never lose sight of, and which it is important for us to bear in mind, is that we must submit certain questions of Scripture to the examination of both reason and science (85).

Beyond Origen, Gregory, and Augustine, his pantheon can now embrace his friend Leo XIII's encyclical *Providentissimus*

Deus, cautiously encouraging biblical criticism. At this point he floats theories variously trying to reconcile Genesis' "days" with "ages," recalling at the same time that

> Genesis ... was not intended by its author to serve as a treatise on natural or physical science. Moses was neither a geologist nor an astronomer, and the scope of his narrative did not require of him either an exact or a profound knowledge of science. All attempts, therefore, to find in his account of creation an anticipation of the results of modern geology and astronomic discovery, and to exhibit a detailed and exact correspondence between the days of Genesis and the different geological epochs, are as unwarranted as they are sure to prove nugatory (95-96).

The Deluge and its Extent

Zahm considers two more contentious issues in these lectures: the extent of the flood reported in Genesis 7-8, as well as the age of the human race. The second remains a live issue, of course, while the first attests to the manner in which some of Zahm's contemporaries regarded scriptural pronouncements:

> Barring the creation of the world and of man, it may be questioned if any event recorded in the Old Testament has given rise to more commentaries and provoked more discussion than the terrible cataclysm recorded with such minuteness of detail in the seventh chapter of Genesis (119).

A little reflection can tell us why, for this report offers a point of juncture and potential conflict with scientific inquiry. For while the biblical account is cast within "salvation history," broadly speaking, the natural cataclysm recorded should be subject to geological confirmation, or the contrary. Moreover, the interpretative tradition will in this case exacerbate rather than alleviate the situation:

> With scarcely a dissenting voice the Fathers, the Schoolmen, and the exegetes who immediately followed them were at one regarding the universality of the catastrophe of which the sacred text gives such vivid record (119).

So let us follow the way Zahm negotiates the apparently insurmountable difficulties which arise, accepting all the while the *prima facie* veracity of scripture and the Mosaic authorship of the entire Torah [Pentateuch]. He canvasses the fossil records ostensibly attesting to a universal deluge, presenting arguments from geologists *pro* and *con*, followed by a protracted polemical "exchange" with Voltaire, who fastened on this very issue to "discredit the Bible [by] relegating to the domain of fable the Genesis narrative of the Flood," but who weakened his case by employing "arguments that were as ludicrous as they were irrational" against geologists who proffered evidence for its universality (125). Yet notwithstanding Voltaire's scorn for a factual biblical record, Zahm distances himself from purported geological arguments:

> Whether there are now any geological traces of the Noachian Deluge is doubtful. Even granting the Flood covered the whole earth, as some still contend, it is highly improbable that the changes effected on the earth's surface would have been of such a character as to be recognized so many ages after the event (127).

So one of the principal points of contact and potential conflict is neatly removed.

On to the "Fathers and Doctors, theologians and commentators, [who] for the first sixteen centuries of the Church's history almost unanimously believed and taught that the flood was universal" (140). Zahm patiently canvasses biblical uses of 'all' or 'whole [earth]', finding them amazingly variable in extent, and then moves to a favorite theme: the explicit freedoms in interpreting granted to Catholic readers of scripture:

> It must at once be premised that very few of the texts of the Holy Scripture have been explicitly defined by the Church (140). ... Is the narrative of the deluge to be classed among those parts of Scripture to which have been given authoritative interpretation? We can say, unhesitatingly, that in so far as

the Church is concerned, as represented by her supreme ruler, nothing whatever has been decided (141).

Moreover, Thomas Aquinas, whom Zahm would have been instructed by Pope Leo XIII's encyclical *Aeterni Patris* (1880) to regard as the most trustworthy of these worthy "Doctors," reinforces this freedom when he "makes a beautiful distinction between things which are necessarily of faith and things which pertain to faith only incidentally" (143). Given these authoritative assurances from his tradition, which Zahm can regard as liberating rather than constraining, he can conclude:

> And if we are free to explain the Deluge by the action of causes purely physical, we may likewise, *a fortiori*, avail ourselves of the same liberty of interpretation regarding the extent to which the catastrophe prevailed (144-5).

More generally, scientific theories will demand different modes of assessment than philosophical or theological positions. Indeed,

> the solution to [these latter] questions would involve nothing more than simple reflection and ratiocination, … but with questions of physical and natural science, or history and the philosophy of archeology and linguistics, it is quite otherwise. Hence St. Augustine, Origen, and other Doctors felt constrained to leave to time the clearing up of many difficulties which in the state of limited information in their day were insoluble (151).

So happily enough,

> When the results of scientific discovery proclaimed the necessity of revising the interpretations that had been in vogue regarding the total destruction of the race by the deluge, it was found that there was nothing in the Sacred Text that forbade such a revision (159).

Which will allow Zahm to conclude:

> From what has been said, it appears probable, if not certain, that the Deluge was universal neither geographically nor zoologically or ethnographically. What the extent of the flood was cannot be determined, but it seems to be almost certain that it was comparatively limited, both as to the amount of

territory submerged and to the number of the human race destroyed (163).

Throughout, we witness an inquirer utterly devoted to the *truth* of scripture while utilizing strategies practiced within his tradition to effectively isolate those truths which scripture can be said unequivocally to affirm. Using that same razor of Ockham to sift among contending theories—in this case, geological—in support (or otherwise) of the biblical record, he will simultaneously offer a reading of scripture and of current scientific inquiry which minimizes points of contact and hence reduces areas of conflict. With this consistent strategy he can move deftly from one discourse to another, without having to raise those critical issues regarding the text of scripture itself which were to cause trouble for Père LaGrange. It may even be that this myopia served Zahm well, for raising critical exegetical issues would have demanded a versatility whose very virtuosity—even were he able to execute it—would doubtless have further confused his listeners as well as exacerbated Roman authorities quite independently of his subsequent reflections on evolution.

Origins of the Human Race

Zahm will march aggressively into the enduring neuralgic issue of the age of the human race with spiked boots:

> There are, indeed, discrepancies and antagonisms between the protean theories of science and the teachings of faith, but this, from the very nature of the case, is inevitable. The doctrines of the Church are the expression of truth itself, and therefore immutable. The hypotheses and the speculations which certain scientists set such store by are as changeable as the colors of the chameleon and as short-lived as the Mayfly. ... What I wish especially to direct attention to is the *tendency* of modern science to inculcate Utilitarianism in morals, Materialism in philosophy, and rationalism and skepticism in religion. True science and true scientists keep aloof from this tendency, but

there are many students of nature who are unconsciously affected by it, even when they are absolutely free from any pre-
conceived notions in their special lines of research (186).

Zahm finds this *tendency* noxious from his own philosophical
inquiries, which

traced rationalism through its full course and found it to issue
in Atheism and Nihilism. The doubts of Lessing and the skepticism of Kant led to the negations of Strauss, and the Pantheism
of Hegel to the Atheism of Feuerbach and Schopenhauer (184).

Very little hope, it seems, from so negative a pantheon, yet he
remains confident of a reconciling strategy:

I am firmly convinced that a careful and unprejudiced study
of the question of man's antiquity will issue in proving, as has
been so often done heretofore in other matters, that the Bible
and science are at one regarding the question now under discussion, and will eventually render the same testimony (218).

The philosophical complexity of these issues, together with
an anti-religious *Zeitgeist*, will make this inquiry more taxing
and more delicate than the previous two:

however much evolutionists may disagree as to details, they are
unanimous in asserting the animal origin of man. To bridge
over the chasm between brute and organic matter ... they declare that brute matter can of its own motion bridge the chasm
that separates it from sentient and conscious beings (225-6).

Indeed, what is at stake here, in a variety of "scientific" views,
is creation itself:

they assume evolution, in the sense in which they teach it, to
be true and to rest on an impregnable basis of fact. They assume also that matter is eternal, because science, by which
they mean physics, can tell us nothing, because it knows nothing, of creation (228).

And with creation, the creator: "'we must dismiss the creator
without ceremony, and not leave any more the least place for
the action of such a being', says the blasphemous Carl Vogt"
(230). Finally,

scientific Atheists of our day ... fancy they see in the disproof
of the scriptural chronology a condemnation of the traditional

teachings regarding the Adamic origin of the various races of the human family, if not a demonstration of the falsity of the entire Bible as a divinely inspired record (231).

Yet notwithstanding these obstacles, which elicit the controversialist in Zahm, he introduces this inquiry quite soberly: "what, then, does modern science—and by this term we mean conservative, veritable science, and not wild hypothesis and fantastical speculation—teach concerning the age of mankind?" (232). After canvassing "geological and geographical evidences advanced in support of man's great antiquity" (235), he irenically concludes:

> Until geologists and archaeologists shall have produced much stronger evidence than any that has yet been offered regarding the age of man in Europe, we may feel that there is little difficulty in reconciling the age of human remains found in the peat-beds, caverns, and gravel pits with the chronology of the Bible as it is usually given for post-diluvial, not to speak of antediluvian, times (242).

Yet this conclusion is more disingenuous than jejune, for when Zahm finally comes to the scriptural chronology, "after a long and tedious, but nevertheless necessary excursion into the domains of history, astronomy, physical geography, and prehistoric archaeology," he will find that chronology "as vague and as uncertain as the various chronologies which we have been considering, while as regards the church she is committed to no system of chronology and has defined nothing concerning the antiquity of man" (293). In fact, the translator of the Latin Vulgate bible, "St. Jerome, [had] abandoned altogether the task of establishing a system of chronology for the Old Testament" (294). Given conflicting Old Testament accounts and lacunae in New Testament genealogies, Zahm endorses the judgment of "the learned Sulpician, the Abbé de Foville," who remarks (a la Galileo):

> the Bible indicates in measure which suffices for its divine scope the chronological order of the facts it relates. But the

Holy Spirit not having inspired it in order to found or cast light upon the science of chronology, we should not seek in it a detailed and precise chronology (306).

So Zahm will rest content to finesse rather than reconcile these issues, confident in the *apriori* conviction enunciated by Pope Leo XIII's recent encyclical *Providentissimus Deus* (1893), cautiously promoting the scientific study of the scriptures:

If then apparent contradiction be met with, every effort should be made to remove it. Judicious theologians and commentators should be consulted as to what is the true or most probable meaning of the passage in discussion, and the hostile arguments should be carefully weighed. Even if the difficulty is, after all, not cleared up, and the discrepancy seems to remain, the contest must not be abandoned: truth cannot contradict truth, and we may be sure that some mistake has been made, either in the interpretation of the sacred words, or in the polemical discussion itself; and if no such mistake can be detected, we must suspend judgment for the time being (306 n.1).

So we might expect this final lecture on the age of the human race to conclude, as it is "far from being definitively answered either by Scripture or by science, and according to present indications it seems improbable that we shall ever have a certain answer regarding this much-controverted topic" (310). Yet Zahm pushes on further, one suspects, than his inquiries warrant,

because [he avers] I am as firmly convinced as I can be of anything that God is the Lord of science, that science is the handmaid of religion, that the two, speaking of the same Author, although in different tongues, must voice the same testimony. ... Thus far, the conclusions of authentic history and the teaching of Holy Writ respecting the age of the human race are so marvelously concordant that they may be considered as giving testimony which is identical. Aside from certain apparent discrepancies, ... there has never been any serious conflict between the two; there is no conflict now (314).

Perhaps so jejune a conclusion manifests his desire to bring these lectures to an upbeat conclusion, yet withal, faith in scripture has provided him with a quality of conviction able to dispense with certitude on contested matters, while also freeing his scientific inquiry from manifesting the "*zeitgeist* of our generation. For be it known, the *zeitgeist* is a capricious being and more changeable than Proteus" (316). In short, the faith to which he witnesses has enlarged his spirit for unremitting intellectual inquiry, aligning him with those who exhibit what Bernard Lonergan described as the "quest for understanding," contrasted with the "need for certitude."

Chapter Two

EVOLUTION AND DOGMA[54]

JOHN ZAHM'S SUSTAINED inquiry into evolution and its compatibility with Christian faith was published in 1896, just one year later than the lectures on the bible, science and faith. The second part of the work, which addresses directly the topic of the title, evolution and dogma, represents "substantially the same ground" as the lectures he had delivered "before the Madison and Plattsburgh Summer schools and before the winter School of New Orleans." An inveterate teacher and publicist, Zahm would float his ideas orally before engaging in "a more exhaustive treatment of certain topics ... than was possible in the time allotted to them in the lecture hall" (v). In introducing these extended reflections, he once again avows his standing conviction that "in the long run it will always be found, as has so often been the case in the past, that the Bible and faith, like truth, will come forth unharmed and intact from any ordeal, however severe, to which they may be subjected" (xv). Yet the primary example he gives "of the unwisdom of committing one's self to premature notions, or unproved hypotheses, especially before all the evidence in the case is properly weighed, is afforded in the long and animated controversy respecting the authorship of the Pentateuch [Torah]" (xvi), where he presumes that Moses' authorship will be confirmed, yet the very terms of his

---

[54] *Evolution and Dogma* (Chicago: D.H. McBride & Co., 1896).

15

conviction allow for the opposite as well. In short, the confidence he places in faith as a guide leaves ample room for matters once thought to be "of faith" to "develop" (in Newman's sense, which may include ostensible reversal), as he clearly asserts in commending Aquinas' "beautiful distinction between things which are necessarily of faith and things which pertain to faith only incidentally" (*Bible*, 143).

His statement of intent, which will be borne out in our survey and assessment of these reflections, is characteristically both clear and passionate:

> My sole, my ardent desire, has been to show that there is nothing in true science, nothing in any theories duly accredited by science and warranted by the facts of nature, nothing in evolution, when properly understood, which is contrary to Scripture or Catholic teaching; that, on the contrary, when viewed in the light of Christian philosophy and theology, there is much in evolution to admire, much that is ennobling and inspiring, much that illustrates and corroborates the truths of faith, much that may be made ancillary to revelation and religion, much that throws new light on the mysteries of creation, much that unifies and coordinates what were otherwise disconnected and disparate, much that exalts our ideas of creative power and wisdom and love, much, in fine, that makes the whole circle of the sciences tend, as never before, *ad majorem Dei gloriam*.

His enthusiasm is manifest, but there is more than enthusiasm here, as the criteria he advances for conciliation of faith and science display his own training in both discourses: theology is called to be both "ennobling and inspiring," while scientific theories are corroborated by their capacity to "unify and coordinate what was otherwise disconnected and disparate." Even more, when attested theories of evolution encounter duly nuanced assertions of faith, the criteria for assessing both types of discourse coalesce, so that faith and science might mutually illuminate one another. John Zahm is proposing to communicate to others what he had found to be true in his own life.

Evolutionary Theories Assessed

After five initial chapters detailing views on evolution from the Greeks to Darwin, he introduces a distinction that will prove crucial to distinguishing his enthusiasm from his polemics regarding "evolution."

> It may be regarded as a *scientific theory*, devised to explain the origination of the higher from the lower, and more complex and differentiated from the simple and undifferentiated, in inorganic and organic bodies, or it may be viewed as a *philosophical system*, designed to explain the manifold phenomena of matter and life by the operation of secondary causes alone to the exclusion of a personal Creator. In the restricted sense in which we are considering it, it is a scientific hypothesis intended to explain the origin and transmutation of species in the animal and vegetable worlds, by laws and processes disclosed by the study of nature (69).

He readily acknowledges how difficult it can be "to keep the scientific theory separated from the philosophical system, [as] naturalists and philosophers are continually intruding on each other's territories." Indeed, as he avers, "the result is inextricable confusion and errors without number," as contemporary controversies *pro* and *con* continue to exhibit. As a result, much of Zahm's efforts in these extended reflections will be to distinguish among assertions made, to ascertain whether they represent testable theoretic results or philosophical claims reflecting yet other agenda, so offering ample scope to display how a trained philosophical mind makes distinctions.

As Zahm outlines the history of the matter, it began, as we have noted, with the Greeks, yet produced dramatic standoffs only as "the modern theory of Evolution ... suddenly and unexpectedly ... blossomed forth into a working hypothesis of colossal proportions and universal application," to the consternation of most who held a settled belief in "special creations" (72). Zahm describes the standoff as between "two theories, that of creation and that of Evolution, [between which] no compromise, no *via media* is possible. We must needs be either creationists or evolutionists" (75). Notice the deft dialectical move: the "creation" represented here is not the faith assertion which he "ardently desires" to show does not–indeed, cannot–conflict with true science, but rather denotes a way of extending that faith-assertion to insist on species fixed over all of time by way of their original creation by God. So if naturalists can be guilty of inflating the theory of evolution into an ideology, believers can conflate a settled philosophical taxonomy with the bare faith assertion that the universe is freely created by one God. Hence Zahm's reminder that "creationism" is a *theory* is designed to call attention to this unwarranted conflation, thereby denying "creationists" the high ground of faith. That is an astute philosophical move, which recalls (albeit inversely) a similar dialectical ploy on the part of Moses Maimonides, who aligns "the biblical view" of free creation with alternative "theories" in order to examine each on its merits.[55] Zahm is now prepared to "examine the evidences for and against [evolution] as a scientific theory, ... excluding the philosophical theories which have been built on [it], and the religious discussions to which it has given rise" (83). That will be the burden of Part I of this work; while "religious discussions," properly mediated by philosophical distinctions, will dominate Part II.

One issue that needed to be addressed was, of course, that of *species*; Aristotelians would presume them to be fixed, the embodiment of Plato's *forms* which render the changing world intelligible. Zahm had to contend with the distinguished Aristotelian anti-evolutionist, Louis Agassiz, whom he credits with "maintaining that species are entities, real or ideal, which

[55] David Burrell, *Knowing the Unknowable God* (Notre Dame IN: University of Notre Dame Press, 1986).

continue to exist from generation to generation" (101). After canvassing various views on this subject, Zahm is ready to proceed to

> an intelligent appreciation of the arguments commonly adduced in support of the theory of organic Evolution. If species are not the immutable units they have so long been considered; if, far from being permanent and unchangeable, they are, on the contrary, variable and mutable; we have legitimate *a priori* reasons for believing in the possibility of Evolution, if not its probability (105).

Building on the ambiguity endemic to biological inquiry of "branches, classes, orders, families, genera and species" (89), Zahm reminds us of Plato's realistic view of forms, reflected in the early medieval Scotus Eriugena, but neatly avoids a protracted philosophical discussion in favor of attending to the actual practice of working biologists. Yet by exposing the ambiguities inherent in the notions of *species* and *genus*, he can lead us into the new world of scientific classification, where generation will be attended by a more comprehensive environmental context, thereby suggesting a fresh reading of "species" without having to settle the issue, so offering a precious example of what Wittgenstein would call "philosophical therapy" regarding a pervasive notion. So the next step must be an empirical one:

> the actuality, however, of Evolution is a question of evidence; not indeed of evidence based on metaphysical assumptions, but of evidence derived from observation and a trustworthy interpretation of the facts of nature. To the discussion of this evidence ... I shall now direct the reader's attention (105).

The next two chapters canvass evidences for and objections to evolution, respectively. The evidences considered testify to the sophistication of Zahm's research in these matters: tree-like classifications, structure and morphology, rudimentary organs, and embryological testimony, all leading to *recapitulation*: "that every complex organism thus epitomizes the history of its ancestors; that in its embryonic life it exhibits a series of forms characteristic of organisms lower in the series of which it is a member" (121)—ontogeny recapitulates phylogeny. This survey is completed by reporting on geographical distribution of organisms and their geological succession. In summary, Zahm avers:

> as a theory, Evolution certainly reposes on as firm a foundation as do the atomic theory of matter and the undulatory theory of light, or as does Newton's theory of universal gravitation (136). As to Scripture itself, and the teachings of the Fathers and Doctors of the Church, we shall see in the sequel that their testimony is as strongly in favor of derivative creation, evolution under the Providential guidance of nature causes, as it possibly can be in favor of the old and now almost universally discarded theory of special creations (135).

His canvassing of objections to evolution would sound old hat today: misapprehensions of the meaning of *evolution*, paucity of transitional forms, small percentage of fossil forms, imperfection of the geological record, sterility of species when crossed. Once again, the thorny issue of *species* emerges. After extensive comparisons, he concludes (on a note of exasperation):

> it is manifest that whether viewed from the standpoint of morphology, or from that of physiology, species is something extremely vague, and pregnant with difficulties of all kinds (190). [So the only way to move forward is to] be willing to agree that species, as ordinarily understood—that is, something permanently immutable—has, in nature, no real existence (193).

Finally, Zahm acknowledges that "all of the theories of evolution … involve numerous and grave difficulties" (196).

> Yet the lack of [a] perfected theory… does not imply that we have not already an adequate basis for a rational assent to the theory of organic Evolution. [In fact,] the arguments adduced on behalf of evolution in [this] chapter are of sufficient weight to give the theory a degree of probability which permits of little doubt as to its truth (201).

It would be difficult to find a more judicious or more ringing endorsement! Let us now consider the way in which he will assess this theory, such as it is, in the light of philosophical and theological issues germane to Christian faith.

Evolution in the Light of Faith

The second part of the book, as he notes, recapitulates his lectures on the subject, though in a more sustained way. He states his aim clearly, building on his assessment of theories in part one:

> it seems difficult, if not impossible, to ignore the fact that some kind of evolution has obtained in the formation of the material universe, and in the development of the diverse forms of life with which our earth is peopled. The question now is: How are we to envisage this process of evolution, and what limits are we to assign to it? ... And then a far more important question ..., to which all that has hitherto been said is but a preamble: ... how is faith affected by Evolution, or in other words, what is the attitude of Dogma towards Evolution (206)?

Recall that "dogma" is a positive, indeed, a liberating notion for Zahm, for it incorporates the precipitate of a tradition's reflection on revealed matters of faith, so as to offer Catholics a wealth of resources in interpreting the scriptures: patristic and medieval, exegetical and philosophical. It saves us, he contends, from baldly confronting scriptural texts with scientific theories, to which the *sola scriptura* ethos tended to relegate Protestant reflections on these matters. As ever, Catholic tradition incorporated an intellectually mediated approach to interpreting scripture, which Zahm realized could effectively temper *prima facie* conflicts.

This approach is exemplified from the outset, in an elaborate parsing of "two words most frequently misunderstood and misemployed: ... 'creation and 'nature' " (215). Using a telescoped historical analysis to dispense with materialism, dualism, and pantheism (which, he avers, "have infected so many minds in our time" [223]), he reminds us that "creation, in its strictest sense, is the production, by God, of something out of nothing" (219), relying on the consensus statement of these matters in Vatican Council I:

> this one only true God, of His own goodness and Almighty power, not for the increase or acquirement of His own happiness, but to manifest his perfection by the blessings which He bestows on creatures, and with absolute freedom of counsel, created out of nothing, from the very beginning of time, both the spiritual and the corporeal creature, to wit, the angelical and the mundane, and afterward the human nature, as partaking in a sense of both, consisting of spirit and body (222).

He turns next to the term "nature," which has so many and such conflicting meanings that it is "often ambiguous and so easily misapplied, lead[ing] us into grave mistakes, if not dangerous errors" (224); notably exemplified in "the habit scientific writers have, of indiscriminately personifying nature on all occasions; of speaking of it as if it were a single and distinct entity, producing all the various phenomena of the visible universe, [indeed] as a kind of independent deity 'which being full of reasons and powers, orders and presides over all mundane affairs' "(225). He immediately qualifies his distaste, however, by exempting poets—"in their case the figurative use of the term is allowed and expected." As a devotee of Dante, he can hardly be engaging in a positivist dismissal of "the pathetic fallacy," but with pedagogical as well as theological intent, he offers a hermeneutics to discriminate among discourses: "with naturalists, however, and philosophers, who are supposed to employ a more exact terminology, such a figurative use of language cannot fail, with the generality of readers, to be both misleading and mischievous" (226).

The following three chapters seek to probe various connotations of "evolution" which come to it by association with monism (2.2), agnosticism (2.3), and theism (2.4). This triptych will be followed by three quite philosophical analyses of the origin and nature of life (2.5), the Simian origin of human beings (2.6), and reflections on teleology, old and new (2.7). A substantial conclusion is entitled "retrospect, reflections and conclusion" (2.8), as befits such a sustained analysis of evolution in relation to faith tradition.

Three Perspectives on Evolution as a Philosophical System

Now it should be clear that the "evolution" we will now be considering is more the "philosophical system" than the "scientific theory" (69). With *monism* we are plunged directly into a nineteenth-century ploy for eliding both creation and creator, exemplified in Ernst Haeckel, professor of biology in the University of Jena [who] is often called "the German Darwin" (231). Astounded by the way in which this distinguished biologist leverages "evolution" to eliminate longstanding philosophical and cosmological distinctions—material/spiritual, inorganic/organic, even created/uncreated: "the atom, eternal and uncreated, is the sole God of the monist" (236)–Zahm asks himself how anyone could perpetrate so egregious a misreading of a rich tradition. The answer he proposes casts light on Zahm's sense of himself as well as the question at hand:

> the very ardor with which he has cultivated science, and forced everything to corroborate a pet theory, has made him one-sided and circumscribed in his views of the cosmos as a whole, so as practically to incapacitate him for the discussion of general questions of science and philosophy, and much more those of theology. Like all specialists, he suffers from intellectual myopia, and it is almost inevitable that such should be the case (243).

Zahm will excuse the "reading public [who] are, so far as their ability to think and judge for themselves, in a state of chronic catalepsy" (244), but softens so elitist a judgment by offering to a popular, if exceedingly interested, audience tools for recovering from that myopia. Yet he cannot further excuse Haeckel, whose "violent and blasphemous language" reveals "more than simple antipathy [to matters religious, but] downright hatred" (244). But what offends Zahm even more than blasphemy, it seems, is Haeckel's expertise "in verbal jugglery, ... a consummate master in the art of sophistry" (245).

That even a German professor be permitted such liberties, however, Zahm attributes to the *Zeitgeist*:

> Science had become more dogmatic and more imperious than was ever theology. It counts by the thousands [those who] have been taught that modern science is the negation of creation, the negation of the Creator. Accordingly, when a hypothesis, or a discovery, seems to contravene Christian beliefs, it is accepted without further reflection and promulgated with inexplicable confidence. It is in this fact, rather than in its scientific value, what we must seek the *raison d'etre* of *transformism* (253).

Such an impassioned diatribe from an inquirer who can so carefully discriminate among types of discourse offers a rare window into the intellectual milieu in which he swam as a scientist in that epoch, as well as the source of his zeal to clarify such issues by the very best canons of science. Finally, his keen observations into the traps endemic to specialization doubtless helped him to count the blessings of his variegated life as teacher, priest, and even administrator at Notre Dame which he aspired would one day become a full-fledged university: the goal on which his entire heart and soul were focused. Yet one can also imagine him dreaming of better facilities, more time, greater contact with peers—all the manifest downsides of bootstrapping in northern Indiana. Yet that very mixed life also prepared him—as he implicitly avers—to discriminate between evolution as a "philosophical system" from evolution as a "scientific theory," a discrimination clearly demanded by the clarifications to which these chapters are dedicated, as a prelude to engaging the title subject of this work.

Zahm finds the ethos next associated with evolution—"the

new-fangled system, if system it can be called," *agnosticism*–to be "more wide-spread and devastating in its effects" than either "monism or scientific atheism" (254). Epitomized in Thomas Huxley, it emerged palpably in the "Bampton 'Lectures on the Limits of Religious Thought,' delivered in the University of Oxford in 1859 [by] Dean Mansel, one of the most distinguished theologians and metaphysicians of England in the latter half of the nineteenth century" (258). Mansel announced the charter of what would become "agnosticism" in the following manifesto:

> Of the nature and attributes of God in his infinite being, philosophy can tell us nothing; of man's inability to apprehend that nature, and why he is thus unable, she tells us all that we can know, and all that we need to know (258).

Rightly identifying this as "the agnostic creed," Zahm traces its implicit lineage to Kant's strictures on non-empirical knowing, noting that we can "hope there is a God, but we have no warrant for asserting His existence. ... We cannot, by searching, find him out, and our every assertion regarding Him is but a contradiction in terms" (262). Zahm's description of "agnosticism" likens it to a precursor of "logical positivism," which shipwrecked on the logical demand that the position be itself asserted—something which Zahm may have implicitly seen in speaking of "the agnostic creed."

More substantively, however, he identifies "the great and perpetual crux for agnostics, as well as for atheists, [to be] the existence of the world."

> Whence the world and the myriad forms of life which it contains? ... No system of thought is worthy of the name of philosophy, that is not able to give an answer which the intellect will recognize as rational and conclusive (265).[56]

Zahm enlists the unwitting assistance of Herbert Spencer as

---

[56] Aristotle would have to come under this stricture, as Isabelle Moulin has articulated so well in her 2004 Sorbonne doctoral dissertation: "La question Aristotelicienne de Dieu et sa reception chez les commentateurs grecs et medievaux; for a contemporary effort to articulate this point, see *Faith, Reason and the Existence of God* by Denys Turner (Cambridge: Cambridge University Press, 2004) xix + 271 pp.

one "forced to think of a First Cause, infinite, absolute, and unconditioned, ... in spite of his assertion that God is and must be unknowable" (267); as well as Max Muller, "the distinguished philologist and orientalist [who], though not a philosopher by profession, reasons far more philosophically than [even] Herbert Spencer:"

> If any philosopher can persuade himself, that the true and well-ordered *genera* of nature are the results of mechanical causes, whatever names we may give them, he moves in a world altogether different from my own. To Plato, these genera were ideas; to the peripatetics, they were words, or *logoi*; to both, they were manifestations of thought" (269).

Zahm does not hesitate to identify "one of the chief sources of the agnosticism now so rampant ... in the lamentable ignorance of the fundamental principles of true philosophy and theology everywhere manifest" (269), but will then attenuate this accusation by alluding to "the mysteries of nature which everywhere confront us and which baffle all attempts their solution." Yet attending to them reminds him (so he reminds us) that "there is a Christian as well as a skeptical Agnosticism, and all the difficulties suggested by these mysteries of the natural and supernatural orders were long ago realized and taken into account by Christian philosophy and theology" (272-3). Quite different from the "Agnosticism of skepticism" (273), it is, however, no less radical, for "it will be impossible even [for] the blessed in Heaven, ... who shall see God in the clear light of the Beatific Vision, ... [ever] to have an adequate or comprehensive knowledge of God" (274). Yet if "Christian agnosticism" properly insists that "we can know nothing ... of the essence of God," Zahm can call upon the conviction of his faith-community articulated in Vatican Council I to insist:

> From the existence of the world, we can infer the existence of God; for our primary intuitions teach us that there can be no effect without a cause. The evidences of order and design in

the universe, prove the existence of a creator who is intelligent, who has power an will, and who, therefore, is personal, and not the blind fate and impersonal energy and unknowable entity of the agnostic (276).

In one more therapeutic exercise, Zahm neatly separates evolution as a theory from the manner in which it had become so inextricably linked with certain forms of "agnosticism;" indeed, so much so that "a particular phase of Evolution is so intimately connected with Agnosticism, that it cannot [in the popular mind] be disassociated from it" (278). It should be clear by now that he finds "Agnosticism [to be] but Atheism in disguise: ... God, according to the agnostic, is but a creature of the imagination, a figment of theologians, and religion, even in its pure and noblest form, is but a development of fetishism or ghost-worship" (264). For once one insists that "God, if there be a God, is unknowable, and being so, is beyond and above all reach of reason and consciousness" (264), one must fabricate a plausible object for the benighted to talk about. That seems to be the logic of the connections Zahm makes here, and the source of his consternation with this (albeit unstable) "position."

In a more constructive mode, Zahm next asks whether we "Catholics, who accept without reserve all the teachings of the Church, can give our assent to theistic evolution" (279)? To define the hybrid term, he builds on his earlier study, which showed that "the principles of theistic evolution—the evolution ... which admits the existence of a God, and the development, under the action of His Providence, of the universe and all it contains—were accepted and defended by some of the most eminent Doctors of the early Greek and Latin Churches" (279). Gregory of Nyssa is his hero, "who first clearly conceived and formulated the nebular hypothesis [and] found no difficulty in admitting the action of secondary causes, in the formation of the universe from the primal matter which the Almighty had directly created" (280). To clarify the expression "secondary causes," he recounts Thomas Aquinas' dual insistence: (a) that "no creature ... is competent to elicit a single act ... without the cooperation of God" (295); yet at the same time (b) "in order to manifest more clearly his wisdom and power and love, ... the true efficient cause of all things has willed ... to receive the cooperation of his creatures, and to confer on them 'the dignity of causality' " (297). Taken together, these assertions remove any anxiety about the creator "interfering" or "intervening" in the universe, since such crude pictures simply assume the very "zero-sum game" between creator and creatures which Aquinas exposes as anthropomorphism. And as for the specific issue of *species*, by reading the scholastics in context, he can assert: "species were assumed to be fixed and invariable, because the definition of the term, not the facts of nature, demanded it" (318-19).

Three Philosophical Analyses

The chapter on the origin and nature of life exhibits Zahm's usual virtuosity with historical antecedents, only to cut directly to the issue, albeit in a *prima facie* confusing way. The issue is *emergence*, in this case of organic from inorganic materials. He catalogues the ancients' fascination with "spontaneous generation," a notion which he will hardly disdain, given the pervasive creative action of God, yet then firmly asserts:

> but Christian philosophy, contrariwise, teaches that it is impossible for inorganic to produce organic *motu proprio*, or by any natural inherent powers it may possess (321).

At the same time, acknowledging the difficulty of characterizing *life* properly, "the fact remains," he insists, "that at some period in the past history of our planet, the first germ of organic life made its appearance, and that, too, independent of any antecedent terrestrial germ" (325). Such a step is hardly clear, yet he goes on to insist that "should some fortunate investigator detect, in the great laboratory of nature, the transition of inorganic into organic and animated matter, ... such a discovery ... would *not* contravene any revealed truth or militate against the received dogmas of the Church, [given] the views of the fathers and the Schoolmen respecting spontaneous generation" (330-1). Which elicits the forthright conclusion (to be carefully compared with his earlier assertion from "Christian philosophy"):

> Given matter ... and forces competent to transform matter—such forces, as well as the matter they affect, being always under the guidance of the divine administration [conservation]—there is nothing in the theory of the origination of living form non-living matter, that is contrary either to faith or to philosophy (338).

And whether the "spontaneous generation" take place "in the laboratory of nature or in that of the chemist,

> In both cases it is God who is the author of the change, yet God acting not directly, but through the instrumentality of natural agencies; through the "seminal reasons" and the laws of nature which He conferred on matter in the beginning (339).

The gospel image of the householder able to bring from his storehouse treasures old as well as new comes strikingly to mind!

The next chapter, entitled "The Simian Origin of Man," raises issues of "body and soul," which have proven quite intractable in philosophical discourse.[57] Zahm is straightforward about the extent of evolution when it envisages human beings:

> as to the soul of man we can at once emphatically declare, that it is in nowise evolved from the souls of animals, but is, on the contrary, and in the case of each individual, directly and immediately created by God Himself. I do not say that this is a dogma of faith, because the question has never been formally defined by the Church. It is, however, Catholic doctrine, and has been taught almost universally from the time of the apostles (345).

Yet that is not the end of the matter, for human beings are not "pure spirit, but creatures composed to a rational soul and a

---

[57]David Braine, *the Human Person* (Notre Dame IN: University of Notre Dame Press, 1993) offers a sophisticated analysis of this language in a wide context.

corruptible body," so the question naturally arises:

> was the body of the first man, the progenitor of our race,
> created directly and immediately by God, or was it created
> indirectly and through the operation of secondary causes
> (349-50)?

Zahm's way of describing the situation and of posing the question owes a great deal to Aristotle, of course, given the expression "souls of animals," yet was criticized at the time by David Fleming, O.F.M. in the *Dublin Review* for glossing over Aquinas' way of appropriating Aristotle to make the union of soul and body a substantial one (Weber, 84). In other words, there are many ways to use "body/soul" language, and they are not all consistent. In fact, the strategy of neatly dividing body from soul had been that of St. George Mivart, Zahm's British Catholic precursor, to whom Pius IX had given an honorary doctorate in philosophy (Weber, 352-56), which Zahm tries here to reconcile with Thomas Aquinas. Yet he seems acutely aware that this may be patchwork:

> from what precedes, it is evinced that the Evolution of the body
> of man, according to Mivart's view, and the subsequent infu-
> sion into this body, by God, of a rational soul, is not necessarily
> antagonistic to the teachings of St. Thomas. The theory may,
> indeed, encounter certain grave difficulties in the domains of
> metaphysics and Biblical exegesis, but I do not think it can ab-
> solutely be asserted that such difficulties are insuperable (358).

Authorities were deeply divided on this issue, doubtless reflecting the "grave metaphysical and exegetical difficulties" of which Zahm was manifestly aware. Indeed, he presents Mivart's "dualistic" theory about as circumspectly as one can. Yet with regard to exegetical issues, he concludes:

> all that would logically follow from the demonstration of the
> animal origin of man, would be a modification of the tradi-
> tional view regarding the origin of the body of our first ances-
> tor. We should be obliged to revise the interpretation that has
> usually been given to the words of Scripture which refer to the
> formation of Adam's body, and read these words in the sense

in which Evolution demands, a sense which, as we have seen, may be attributed to the words of the inspired record, without either distorting the meaning of terms or in any way doing violence to the text (364-65).

Zahm's language is characteristically precise here: so speak of "the demonstration of the animal origin of man" goes far beyond Zahm's most enthusiastic endorsement of some dimensions of evolutionary theory. It is reminiscent of Moses Maimonides, who insisted that if the universe were to be demonstrated to be everlasting, one could learn to read the opening words of Genesis "in the beginning" as his tradition already taught people to understand the "mighty arm of God."[58] In short, "demonstration" is a decisive term; none of the theories presented can claim to such decisiveness. He concludes his treatment with this exegetical issue, issuing the directives which follow, wisely finessing the metaphysical questions of the implicit dualism in Mivart's thesis—a thesis he only hesitantly recommended, in any case. As we have seen, he seems keenly aware of his limitations as well as his strengths in philosophical analysis.

He signs off in a hortatory mode which clearly discriminates among readers of scripture, warning those who pretend simply to "read off" the text how vulnerable they can be to the vagaries of "their own apprehensions."

> We can never too carefully discriminate between the truth of God's revelation to His creatures, and the truth of our apprehension of His revelation. ... Hence the anthropomorphic and anthropocentric views entertained by the early interpreters of Scripture respecting divers questions pertaining to the Deity, and the creatures which are the work of His omnipotence. Time and reflection and research show what such views are ill-founded, and substitute in their place a nobler conception of the Creator, and one that is, at the same time, more in accordance with the teachings of nature and the spirit of divine revelation (367).

---

[58] *Guide for the Perplexed* 1.1.

Of course, some of the most astute interpreters of Genesis, on whom he relied, were very early (Origen, Augustine), while many of his interlocutors who held natively "anthropomorphic and anthropocentric views" would prove to be contemporaries! Could it be that Zahm is engaging in a rhetorical strategy here, building on the then (as now) current Hegelian predilection for favoring results of more recent "reflection and research," to make a point which might otherwise be too confronting for his more scripturally-bound readers? As we have seen, his attention to such matters seems well-honed, perhaps from extensive lecturing experience.

The final expository chapter in this analytic triptych—"Teleology, Old and New"—exploits the confused and confusing discussions of *teleology* after the emergence of evolutionary theory. For the background of the "new science" of the seventeenth century had it that Aristotelian "final causes" were but a relic of pre-scientific thought, yet the "fit" which evolutionary theory demands will require a robust "teleology," even if selection by random mutations seems to rule out larger purposes at work. Zahm will concentrate on the first to see the theory reaffirming teleology in a new key, whereby nature can once again become a sign of its transcendent origins:

> In spite of all that may be said to the contrary, the unbiased and reverent student must see in nature the evidence of a Power which is originative, directive, immanent; a Power which is intelligent, wise, supreme. ... Evolution, therefore, far from weakening the argument from design, strengthens and ennobles it; and far from banishing teleology from science and theology, illustrates and corroborates it in the most admirable manner (376).

More than a bit too hasty, certainly. Islamic tradition exalts the Qur'an for its power to show "the believers" how to read natural events as "signs" of the creator's presence. (The Arabic word *aya* means both a verse in the Qur'an and a sign.) Yet short of being formed by revelation, it is difficult to read a creator off of nature, however theoretically construed. Does John Zahm really think that this "new teleology," which the theory does indeed demand, can make

> Evolution, when properly understood, [into] a noble witness to a God who, unlike the God of the older Deism, that "simply sets the machine of the universe in motion, and leaves it to work by itself," is, on the contrary One who, in the language of Holy Scripture, is not only "above all, but through all, and in all" (377)?

This concluding crescendo from his lecture series seems singularly out of place in "the more exhaustive treatment" to which we have been submitted. For what can assure that the theory of evolution be (in Zahm's terms) "properly understood" so as to give so transcendent a witness, other than the very revelation with which he wishes to harmonize its results. In short, it looks as though the teleology of Zahm's own project has led him to an utterly premature "conclusion" here, quite at variance with the cautious and discriminating spirit we have seen throughout.

Retrospect, Reflections and Conclusion

The burden of these final reflections mirrors his strategy throughout: to show how *evolution* fits into a larger trajectory, back to Aristotle and his predecessors: "Darwinism ... is not Evolution, neither is Lamarckism" (384). In fact, he conveniently overlooks Aristotle's insistence on fixed species to see his insistence that

> germs, and not animals, should have been first produced; and that from these germs all forms of life, from polyps to man, should have evolved by the operation of natural causes, [thereby anticipating] St. Augustine's teaching, that God in the beginning created all things potentially ... and that these were afterwards developed through the action of secondary causes (381-82).

Moreover, Zahm and his contemporaries, up to and including ourselves, are engaged in this long march, whereby the theory of evolution will itself intentionally evolve, as physics has.

Indeed, he roundly insists: "to say that evolution is agnostic or atheistic in tendency, if not in fact, is to betray a lamentable ignorance of what it actually teaches, and to display a singular incapacity for comprehending the relation of a scientific induction to a philosophical—or more truthfully, an anti-philosophical–system" (389). Recall how judicious is this broadside: it is the *theory* of evolution to which Zahm has been directing us, "what it actually teaches," for he has been able to assess the relations between that theory, as it was developing, and his faith-tradition only by carefully discriminating evolutionary theory from its inflation into a "philosophical system."

Having delineated a theory of evolution, as underdeveloped as it may be, he shows how the universe has always upset "normal science," from Anaxagoras on the composition of heavenly bodies, to Copernicus and Galileo on the order of these bodies in relation to one another:

> for the Ptolemaic system was so closely bound up with the philosophy of Aristotle, and this in turn was so intimately connected with theology, especially since the time of St. Thomas Aquinas, that any attack on the geocentric system was at once regarded as an onslaught on both philosophy and theology (392).

So expect similar objections, however "childish and absurd" (394) to be raised against evolution. Yet as the history of human inquiry shows, conflict can also spur us on to clarifications of the sort this work has been designed to elaborate. For example, that "both evolution and special creation are theories" (418), so we can freely ask: "which of the two . . . is the more probable" (419)? Moreover, if the discussion can continue in that vein, it will prove fruitful. In the meantime, and alongside such discriminating analyses, it can be the case for believers that "Evolution ennobles our conceptions of God and man, so also does it permit us to detect new beauties, and discover new lessons, in a world that, according to the agnostic and monistic views, is so dark and hopeless" (435). These are the final words of a believing scientist, an engaged inquirer, who has also used his philosophical skills of discernment and his rhetorical expertise in teaching to bring us to such an open view of inquiry. And it will be that same consummate trust in intellectual inquiry which he will soon have to call upon to animate and guide his own life in the face of momentous reversals.

A contemporary philosopher and historian of science, Ernan McMullin, has considered Zahm's work in pondering the evolution question. We may conclude this appreciation with his critical appraisal, offered in a personal communication, to place Zahm's contribution in the context in which he was writing:

> At the time he wrote on evolution, the theory itself was meeting strong criticism from many biologists: Darwin did not have an adequate account of inheritance, and Mendelian genetics was still some way off. So Zahm was even more confident about evolution than the science of the day really warranted! But I think his theological/philosophical standpoint was what carried him along, even in the absence of a better account of how natural selection could work. Augustine's *De Genesi ad litteram* was for him a crucial text, and he makes much of the *rationes seminales* ["seminal reasons or causes"]. (He may have picked up this reference from Mivart.) One criticism which he encountered was that he exaggerated the extent to which Augustine and even Aquinas could be said to have supported the evolution theme. Aquinas does consider Augustine's reading of Genesis sympathetically but cannot accept it, as no Aristotelian could possibly accept *transformism* (the transmutation of one species into another). Nor of course could a Platonist: for Augustine, each species has its own seed-principle. So neither of them could fairly be considered evolutionists, so Zahm goes too far then, in that regard, leaving himself open to the violent negative reactions of some of the Roman theologians. Augustine does support a "natural" development of each living kind as opposed to the miraculous origin favored by the literal reading of Genesis ("literal" in our sense, but not in Augustine's), and that was the crucial point for Zahm (letter to author, 18 May 2007).

Chapter Three

ACCOMPLISHMENTS OF A PROVINCIAL AND PRELUDE TO A NEW LIFE

THE PUBLISHED WORK on evolution appeared in 1896, yet represented nearly a decade of lecturing on this and related topics: science as it could be appropriated by people of faith. Yet that very year he was tapped to be procurator for the Congregation of Holy Cross in Rome, a role in which he represented his religious congregation to the curia of the Vatican. Catholic religious congregations enjoy a wide latitude of action, once invited into a diocese by its bishop, so need to keep both informal and formal relations in order, as conflicts of jurisdiction inevitably arise. As Ralph Weber carefully documents, this Ohio farm boy became instantly enamored with Europe, striking friendships with key figures in Rome, notably the minority in support of the novel ways the immigrant American church was adapting to the neutral environment captured in the American slogan: separation of church and state. Needless to say, for a Catholic ecclesial sensibility still reeling from the French Revolution and barely adjusting to the loss of the "Papal States," while inured to complex diplomatic relations with various monarchies, the American experiment sounded radical. Indeed, its parameters of religious liberty were not officially ratified until Vatican II in

1965. Zahm quickly associated himself with a group of American prelates, some of whom were constrained to make frequent visits to Rome, notably Denis O'Connell, rector of the North American College (for training seminarians to priesthood with clerical careers), himself allied with Archbishop John Ireland (St. Paul MN) and John Keane, who with Zahm had addressed the International Catholic Scientific Congress in Brussels in 1894.

Yet ecclesiastical politicking could not thoroughly absorb him, so he completed a paper for the Fourth International Catholic Scientific Congress in Fribourg in 1897 on "Evolution and Teleology," which proved to be such a success to the participants that he was elected president of the American caucus, international vice-president, president of the anthropology section, and a member of the permanent commission on organization (Weber 103). One wonders whether he made the acquaintance at this time of Marie-Joseph LaGrange, O.P., founding director of the Ecole Biblique, whose questioning of the Mosaic authorship of the Pentateuch at the same conference offered a fresh path to Catholic exegetes and sounded a challenge to ecclesiastical authority (Bernard Montagnes, O.P., *Story of Father Marie-Joseph LaGrange* (NY: Paulist, 2006). Zahm's initial visit to Jerusalem with Edward Sorin in 1887 preceded the founding of the Ecole Biblique, so his notes from that pilgrimage include only Franciscans, thanking them for their hospitality. It is fascinating to think of these two intellectual pioneers present at the same conference, in different "scientific" sections, to be sure, to wonder what the synergy of their combined efforts might have accomplished for Catholic scholarship, though given attitudes prevailing in the Vatican at that time, it was probably better for them to blaze their respective trails separately.

On the Roman front, the creative minority into which Zahm had been so warmly welcomed was overshadowed by a phalanx of more cautious American bishops who, while manifestly profiting from the structure of United Sates polity regarding church and state, nonetheless resisted identifying with it, so naturally had a more sympathetic hearing in Rome. Yet the atmosphere in Rome had altered considerably with the naming of Pope Leo XIII, whom history identifies with the "social encyclical" response to Marxism. As Weber relates it, "O'Connell occupied a position of diplomat *par excellence* in Rome; his well-furnished apartment was the setting for many gatherings of American and British visitors. [Moreover, his] friendship with the two cardinals, Serafino and Vincenzo Vannutelli, gave the American liberals influence within the liberal group in the Roman hierarchy" (102). It seems that the young John Zahm, just forty, spontaneously took to this milieu, as he found himself fighting for something he deeply espoused in an environment which could hardly comprehend it. Yet also enamored of things European, and so warmly accepted by prelates of that culture, he nevertheless embodied a culture which he sensed belonged to the future, evidenced in his espousing all that he could of evolutionary science, and working to help his co-religionists do the same. So the trappings of the position of procurator allowed free range to his promotional and teaching propensities, making of him an emissary of things American and Catholic, so endearing him to the core group of United States prelates attempting to do the same. All this was to prove immensely helpful when his published work on evolution met stiff resistance in yet other Roman circles.

A well-meaning friend had pressed for French and Italian translations of *Evolution and Dogma*, which when published precipitated a protracted series of negotiations with the Holy

Office. The editor of *Civilta Catolica*, Salvatore Brandi, S.J., had the book in his sights, and the Sacred Congregation of the Index was to proscribe the work in an official meeting on 10 September 1898, though withholding publication of the decree until "the author will be heard out by his Father General whether he is willing to submit to this decree and reprove his work" (Weber 107). By this time, however, Zahm had been elected Provincial of his community, a post to which he had been appointed by the superior general, Gilbert Français, in early 1898 on the sudden death of the incumbent, William Corby, and to which he was properly elected in the summer of 1898. So he was no longer resident in Rome, though he worked his considerable contacts there to assure that the decree was kept quiet while he acquiesced to the advice of his bishop friend, John Keane, "to submit and show respectful acceptance of the Church's authority [in order to] prevent harm to [himself] and to the Congregation of Holy Cross" (Weber 109). Writing to Français within the month, he stated: "I submit unreservedly to the decree and promise to comply at once with all its injunctions, [for] in writing this book I had in view only the good of souls and the glory of the Church. I gave the theories discussed for what they were worth ..." (Weber 109). Indeed, Zahm's position as provincial demanded that he subordinate any personal considerations to the good of the congregation, which meant assuring that the decree remain unpublished. The ensuing year saw a see-saw battle between Roman forces, resisting Pope Leo XIII's insistence (in response to a direct intervention by Archbishop Ireland) that it not be published. Finally, the contents of Zahm's letter of submission were revealed in the July New York *Daily Tribune* (1899), with the salutary effect of releasing a year's anxiety about the decree's publication, on the part of Zahm as well as his superior general, Gilbert Français.

A recent work, *Negotiating Darwin*, details the arguments mounted against Zahm's work (which are not that different from those offered by McMullin), but the results of the Vatican congregation's deliberations (in August 1898) would be more than academic, even if they tried to consider these matters in proper intellectual fashion.[59] In a report of fifty-three printed pages, Enrico Buonpensiere, O.P., of the Florentine "Dominican House of Santa Maria sopra Minerva, where the abjuration of Galileo had taken place 265 years before" (145), Zahm's work was roundly criticized and condemned, as "a continuous apology of a doctrine contrary to the truth of the Catholic faith: it does not seem to me susceptible of emendation, for it would have to be done over from the beginning. Therefore, it merits proscription" (150). Yet he recommends that the Congregation not publish the condemnation of Zahm's book, but limit itself to warning him and requesting that he withdraw his book from sale and issue a brief retraction. In the end, however, it took a direct plea of the Holy Cross superior general, Gilbert Français, to Leo XIII to secure that the decree condemning the book not be published. Again, John Zahm's personal relations with the Pope doubtless helped in his personally suspending publication of the decree "until Father Zahm, who will soon be coming to Rome from America, can be heard" (158). Yet although Zahm did not in fact go to Rome, the decree was never published. Yet to be properly understood, this entire drama must be located within the larger "Americanist" context.

In January of that same year (1899) Leo XIII had written the apostolic letter *Testem Benevolentiae*, which condemned "certain dangerous opinions which some European opponents termed 'Americanism.' ... Upon receipt of the letter, [those

---

[59] Mariano Artigas, Thomas Glick, Rafael Martinez, eds. *Negotiating Darwin: the Vatican Confronts Evolution, 1877-1902* (Baltimore: Johns Hopkins University Press, 2006), esp., 143-58.

identified as] Americanists without exception also condemned the propositions" in question (Weber 116). Nonetheless, Zahm's personal travail had been caught in the snares of a larger controversy, whose resonances would be felt in the Congregation of Holy Cross. For although Zahm had been elected provincial unanimously in the summer of 1898, his election was still awaiting confirmation from the Vatican congregation responsible for the church in America—an ambiguous situation which perdured until after the visit of Sebastian Martinelli, Vatican delegate to the United States, to Notre Dame in May 1899, when as provincial Zahm proposed a toast lauding papal authority. Only then, it seems, could he wholeheartedly concentrate on the duties of the office to which his confreres had elected him.

Within his religious congregation, he had lobbied hard for a separate house of studies in theology for those preparing for priesthood. His motivation had to do with protecting young seminarians from being exploited for countless tasks at the growing Notre Dame, to allow them to pursue theological studies in a fresh intellectual environment. The American bishops were launching a new Catholic University in Washington D.C. focused on graduate study, and John Zahm's brother Albert, an aeronautical engineer closely linked to the early days of flight, was destined for its faculty. Thanks to the efforts of John Zahm to persuade his young congregation, already looking beyond the foundation in Indiana, to join efforts with the new Catholic University, Holy Cross College (as it came to be called) would enjoy a prime position among other religious houses clustered around the university. It was among the first such satellite houses conceived and executed, for the specific reason of forming seminarians in theology. As early as 1893, when Gilbert Français was selected as superior general after the death of Edward Sorin, founder of Holy Cross endeavors in the United

States, Zahm had urged him to promulgate a definite plan of studies with emphasis on intellectual growth in an atmosphere conducive to study. Français devoted a "circular letter" to this end (1895), appointing Zahm to be Prefect of Studies for the congregation–over the hesitant to negative reactions of many—and even granted "permission to use the money from his books and lectures for the new house of studies" (Weber 96-97). Begun in 1895 and completed during his initial year in office as provincial (1898), yet not without a sustained struggle, this house would also prove to be home for Zahm himself when things went sour at Notre Dame.

The duties of a provincial are manifold, from "temporalities" to attending to the personal vagaries of one's confreres. High in energy and ideas, and ambitious for the young congregation, notably in matters educational, Zahm could hardly be called "a community man," despite his manifest dedication, for he preferred reading Dante to camaraderie. Moreover, he had been suddenly recalled from a life in Rome which had opened spacious dreams for a cultural and intellectual life hardly available in northern Indiana, confessing to his friend O'Connell "that it was best he had not received a letter from him at this time for it would have brought tears and made him unfit for the day's duty" (Weber 106). Harassed interiorly by controversy with Rome over his evolution book, and acting on authority which would have to be ratified in the general chapter of the summer of 1898, he did not hesitate to outline his ideas on education, insisting "on the need for a better intellectual atmosphere within every one of the congregation's schools" (Weber 143). That chapter, held in the Canadian provincial house in Cote-des-Neiges, Quebec, would confirm his appointment by Français, and authorize him to execute plans for the house of studies in Washington, which would be completed within a year, prompting Français to remark "that he had not seen such initiative and so smooth administration for a long time" (Weber 145).

But vision and initiative are not always appreciated, especially from one whose temperament had, it seemed become more fitted to Europe than to northern Indiana, so as Zahm began to implement energetic plans at Notre Dame, more cautious confreres became alarmed, already by the summer of 1900. Yet not to be thwarted, he set out to raise endowment for scholarships, and then inspired others to accept the bishop of Portland's proposal that Holy Cross assume responsibility for his struggling Columbia University, taken over from the Methodists in 1901 and soon re-named "University of Portland." He was also conspiring with his friends from his sojourn in Rome, Archbishop John Keane and Bishop Denis O'Connell, to devote Holy Cross resources to begin an undergraduate college at the Catholic University of America, hitherto dedicated solely to graduate study. This scheme did not fly, either with the Catholic University faculty or with the Provincial Council at Notre Dame, but the publicity regarding it certainly helped to solidify the impression of Zahm as a "high-flyer."

Before long, this whirlwind image was bound to raise doubts about fiscal responsibility, to which Zahm was constrained to reply when he received a letter from his longtime supporter, Father Français, which, as Zahm expressed in his reply: "evinced suspicion, distrust, curtness, unkindness—something which I had not before experienced in you and something for which I could imagine no reason" (13 Jan 06–PA). A contemporaneous note from Brother Albeus, provincial treasurer, assured Français "that the net debt of Notre Dame, at present, is about thirty-five thousand dollars ($35,000.00), bearing interest at the rate of three per cent per annum" (13 Jan 06–PA). For those aware of the expanding economy of those years, this should have allayed any fears; Zahm's financial dealings, while often unconventional, had hardly been unduly risky. Yet fears, once set in motion, are difficult to quell, and a growing dissatisfaction among the teaching Brothers of Holy Cross began to gain momentum as well. Feeling left out of the rapid expansion of Notre Dame facilities under Zahm's direction, they claimed discrimination and insisted upon a forum to air grievances. Zahm's own intellectual propensities doubtless fueled his single-minded administrative focus on higher education, while his direct manner of dealing with issues ill-prepared him to meet the psychic gap felt by those who were teaching in grade schools, and slowly finding themselves underbid by a growing phalanx of teaching sisters willing to live and work for less.

At its inception in 1841, the founder of the Congregation of Holy Cross, Basil Anthony Moreau, had attempted to integrate a band of diocesan priests with a group of teaching Brothers founded by an older priest, James Dujarie, who had entrusted their direction to Moreau when he passed on. In the enthusiasm of restoring Catholic ethos to France in the aftermath of the revolution, together with a strong missionary impulse towards Africa, Asia and the Americas, this hybrid arrangement, enhanced by the presence of sisters as well, tried to give flesh to Moreau's vision of a microcosm of church: male and female, lay and clerical. Rome did not permit a common canonical structure including both men and women, but did approve his co-equal association of priests and brothers. So brothers and priests collaborated in the early foundations in the New World, and often enough sisters accompanied them as well, for such had been the original vision of the founder, despite Rome's canonical scruples. Yet even religious communities cannot be free of hierarchical modes of ranking, so clericalism was bound to infect Moreau's vision, if not subvert it. Philip Armstrong, C.S.C. has resumed this history in his portrait of Brother Ephrem O'Dwyer, C.S.C., the dynamic leader and spokesman for Brothers who spearheaded a strategic division of brothers from priests in Holy Cross, to be effected in 1946 (*A More Perfect Legacy: a Portrait of Brother Ephrem O'Dwyer, C.S.C.* (1888-1978) (Notre Dame IN: University of Notre Dame Press, 1995). By this time, however, the mushrooming of Catholic high schools, plus a more rigorous intellectual training for teaching Brothers, had given their vocation a place in the sun. During Zahm's tenure at the outset of the century, the outlook was bleak, so the situation must have looked quite intractable.

It seems incontestable that the "co-equal" status of lay brothers with clerical members was regularly undermined by an endemic clericalism. Conscious or not, it was often acutely felt by the brothers, who were not ordained. This dynamic has been delicately and forthrightly traced by James Tunstead Burtchaell, C.S.C., in a booklet published by the Holy Cross Historical Association in 2003: "One Congregation, Two Societies: How Much Fellowship?" It turns out that John Zahm became a lightning rod for the antagonism which developed between the two groups, notably for displaying an attitude of disdain for the life and work of the Brothers. In his life of Brother Ephrem O'Dwyer, Brother Philip Armstrong, C.S.C., treats of Zahm in connection with this issue, noting that

> down through the years, [he had] been considered by some as opposed to the advancement of the brothers, or at best apathetic toward their welfare. Whatever its justification perhaps this accusation is harsher than he deserves. Admittedly, during his tenure as provincial of the United States Province of Priests and Brothers much of his attention was centered on the needs of the priests' society (e.g., building Holy Cross theologate in Washington, D.C.) and to the University of Notre Dame as such (44-45).

Burtchaell's account enters into a great deal of detail, quoting from letters of grievance composed by Brothers in regard to a pervasive attitude of disdain towards them on the part of their brother priests, often on account of a lack of professional training, to which many Brothers felt they were denied access, so the cycle spiraled downwards. Burtchaell's account offers an illuminating comparison of John Zahm with Ephrem Dwyer, one of the most articulate Brothers, who represented their case valiantly for half a century:

> In Fr. John Zahm and Br. Ephrem O'Dwyer, one can see a complex contrast. Both were bright, accomplished, articulate, and of discriminating judgment. One was respected and loved by the brothers; the other notoriously disliked. Yet Ephrem O'Dywer directly insulted and angrily abuses far more Holy Cross brothers than John Zahm even spoke to. Though he was not very consistent in making his apologies, Ephrem, the red-haired Irishman, was almost always forgiven, for they knew he realized what he had done. In Zahm's case, they (which may include a significant portion of the priests as well) saw little fellowship behind his authority, and felt that he rarely realized what he had done. As a result they not only did not forgive; they may have held grudges against him beyond what he had fairly earned. That kind of oblivion generated that kind of obsession. This comparison, if not typical of Holy Cross, is at least suggestive of our class problem (38-9).

Ralph Weber notes that "the Brothers' objections began long before Zahm's term as Provincial. While it is true that some of the problems were accentuated during his administration, it is equally important to emphasize that this was largely because of conditions over which he had no control. This same problem continued after his Provincialship and was solved finally by the development of new high schools" (156). For as Brothers had been systematically replaced in elementary schools by teaching sisters, who would work for less and so be less expense to the sponsoring parish or diocese, the expanding high school niche offered an honorable work and life, as well as demanding a commensurate level of training.

I have already suggested that the role of Provincial seemed to have worked against the grain for John Zahm, who had accepted it in the "spirit of obedience." In that respect, as Burtchaell suggests, his rapport with his fellow priests may not have been a great deal better than his with the Brothers. If we reflect on the dynamics of community life at the time, where leisure time was regulated into periods of "recreation," usually following evening meals, it is not unimaginable that Zahm's penchant for study or for turning to Dante as "recreational reading" may have entailed minimal participation in such fraternal gatherings. In this sense of the word, he would not have been regarded as "a community man," which usually means one content to find his enjoyment within the ambit of the community itself. That could hardly describe John Zahm, which might suggest why he was ill-prepared and endowed for negotiating community conflicts; so it could well have been that the vote to replace him as Provincial by Andrew Morrissey, whatever its temporary effects on the University, was both a wise one on the part of his confreres as well as a blessing for Zahm himself.

So as one reflects on this period of John Zahm's life of service, it is doubtless impasses of this sort—utterly human and unimaginably convoluted—which brought on the nervous exhaustion of which he so candidly—if utterly confidentially—speaks to Français a few months before the fateful chapter at which his community thanked him for his service by replacing him with the one who had systematically blocked his vision for higher education, both for seminarians in the community and for Notre Dame itself: Andrew Morrissey. Weber's biography traces the plots engineered by those fearful of Zahm's leadership to make sure the chapter would not re-elect him. Yet a letter to Français in the wake of the events of that chapter describes graphically how his body has been telling him that re-election could have been fatal; that the way he had been serving his community had not been the best way for him to do so: "for more than a year I have not had a single night's refreshing sleep. . . . Owing to this lack of rest and the nervous exhaustion that it entailed I have not been able to read a single book for more than a twelve month. Study that previously had been so great a part of my life has become an impossibility. But that is not all. During the last year and more I have not been able to say my Breviary a dozen times, and to-day it is impossible for me to read even a single page of a magazine without the greatest effort" (25 August 1906–PA). For one so characteristically endowed with boundless energy, this was perplexing enough to seek expert advice. An enclosed letter from a Dr. Harold Moyer, whom Zahm notes "is recognized as one of the leading specialists in Chicago on nervous troubles of all kinds," insists that "he should be relieved from all worry and responsibility. ... It seems to me that a prolonged vacation is absolutely necessary, and I have strongly urged him to go abroad and take a complete rest for a period of at least two years. If he does not get this rest and change, I am quite confident that an early breakdown will result" (7 August 1906–PA). Zahm's age was 55.

In confiding in his superior, Zahm offers a way to implement this professional advice: "What I would now suggest is that I be permitted to begin anew what I was prevented from accomplishing eight years ago [when he was abruptly recalled from Rome to take up the duties of provincial], that is, to go to Bengal and secure material for a series of illustrated articles on our Missions, to be written as soon as my health shall warrant, and published in the manner that shall be productive of the best results" ... I have already spoken to Monsignor [Hurth (vicar for East Bengal)] about the matter, and he gives it his cordial endorsement. Before undertaking such a journey, however, I should need a rest of six months or more abroad, preferably among my literary and scientific friends who for years have been inviting me to visit them" (25 August 1906– PA). Some period of renewal he could normally expect, the stark warning of the medical specialist made it imperative. What Zahm himself realizes is the intellectual nourishment his psyche needs—"among my literary and scientific friends," though his larger plan continues his pattern of service to the community: "I am sure, with God's help, that I can by this means secure for Monsignor Hurth far more than the expenses of my trip to Bengal, and at the same time, make known his work and the necessities of his Missions in such a manner as to guarantee for him, in this country, for years to come, a source of revenue that he would never have otherwise." His manner of obeying the doctor's orders for a "prolonged vacation [and] a complete rest" displays a keen awareness of his own needs and temperament, enhanced by conversations with his doctors: "I must, the doctors tell me, have constantly before me something that will excite my interest and make me forget myself, something that will keep the mind occupied without the semblance of work. To idle away my time in the United States or Canada, unable as I am either to read or study, would, for me, be little better than solitary confinement." And, we could add, to let the prescribed "vacation and rest" be of service to the Bengal missions would be therapy in itself. How to put his considerable talents to work without harnessing them; that is the trick: to "keep the mind occupied without the semblance of work."

Towards a New Life

If attention to his body could not but warn John Zahm to prepare for a new mode of life, a brief retrospect of his trajectory in Holy Cross should help us comprehend the community's decision at the 1906 chapter. Ordained to the priesthood in 1875 (at the age of 24), coincident with being appointed professor of chemistry and physics, co-chair of the science department, and director of library and curator of the museum, as well as a member of the board of trustees, Zahm was chosen by the founder of the university, Edward Sorin, C.S.C., to be "vice-president" of Notre Dame in 1885 (at 34), only to become his traveling companion as they visited the Holy Land in 1887. In 1896 he was sent to Rome as procurator in a surprise move which effectively altered his life by expanding his perspectives on nearly everything, yet just as suddenly recalled two years later to assume the office of Provincial vacated by the death of the incumbent. Confirmed in that role by his community for six more years, he would spend himself (as we have seen) to the brink of a breakdown in 1906, culminating thirty years of unstinting service to Holy Cross and to the Notre Dame which he loved, complemented by intellectual outreach to a young Catholic community in the United States through recurrent lecture series, together with publications that would gain international attention and, thanks to the Vatican, even notoriety. Now recall how he would spend his spare time, reading Dante or Homer in the original, rather than playing cards, and then ask how so meteoric a trajectory would strike his Holy Cross confreres in northern Indiana?

Add the requisite touch of sibling rivalry endemic to male communities of any kind, and one could have read the outcome of the chapter of 1906 in advance: to his friends, better that he not continue in office and enjoy a merciful reprieve; and to his competitors, a needed come-down. But how must it have felt to Zahm himself? The letter to Français, in which he opened his heart and soul, closes with a plea: "let me beg you to consider this communication as strictly confidential." For he hardly needed more community gossip about himself and his future, but rather what he explicitly asked for: time "among my literary and scientific friends who for years have been inviting me to visit them." And if this request was a personal one, it is no less imperative in the context of his religious commitment, which also requires a special degree of confidentiality in the midst of the community which he had so loyally served: "no one knows anything about all this, and I do not wish it to be known. There is no reason why anyone, except yourself, should know it, and I shall depend on you to keep this communication as sacredly confidential. If I can get abroad the rest the doctors so strongly insist on, I still feel that I shall recover my former health and strength. If, however, this be denied me, I am convinced that my days of usefulness in the community are at an end, and that I shall be a confirmed invalid for the rest of my days, a burden to myself and to others as well. Knowing my condition as I do, I feel that even with the best of good will it will be physically irresponsible for me to attempt any serious work of any kind during the next two years at least." Yet he also knows enough not to rest on a self-assessment: "I hope I am mistaken, and I hope, too, that the doctors are mistaken, for I dread the idea of physical and mental inactivity for so long a period. But, as I now see it, nothing is to be done save follow the doctors' prescription to the letter. Any further delay will, l feel certain, be fatal."

Here we see a person inured to serving others being forced to confront himself in his own body, and being brought to the brink of collapse at 55, made aware of alternatives more stark than any he had ever faced before. Indeed, without knowing what it will be, a new life is demanded of him, and he must face that, together with the community within which his life to date had so thoroughly unfolded. Weber tells us that he "left Notre Dame for the east coast in August, 1906, after failing to obtain the Superior-General's permission for European travels. ... Probably, he went to Holy Cross College in Washington, D.C., which was under the rectorship of [his friend and protégé, James] Burns" (180). Burns had already prophesied that "Father Zahm will never be understood, nor his work appreciated by this generation. He is too far in advance of the men among whom he is living. He is a man of the 20th century, and we are still I believe, living in the 19th" (Weber 153). He could not help but feel this lack of appreciation, yet in the company of friends like Burns, and others whom we shall meet as well as others whose names we do not know, he would find within himself, despite his debilitation, the resources to "travel to new and foreign lands and write of their citizens, history and culture" (Weber 180). The result of this unexpected yet thoroughly welcome freedom turned out to be seven books during the fifteen years remaining to him—his adaptation to the prescribed "vacation and rest." He maintained a policy of strict isolation the initial twelve months, with Weber conjecturing that his brother Albert and his superior Français being "the only ones who knew his tentative travel schedule" (181). While denied permission to deepen his acquaintance with Europe, Zahm understood there to be two Americas, so undertook an exploration of South America during this sabbatical year, which resulted in two volumes we shall examine, as well as an enduring friendship with Theodore Roosevelt, who praised his historical and ethnographic work as the best of its kind on South America.

For the rest of his life Zahm would make his home in the house he had fought to establish and whose construction had been his initial act as provincial: Holy Cross College in Washington. Given the fact that Holy Cross seminarians would all spend four years at Holy Cross College studying theology, his presence there was bound to have influenced several "generations" of future priests in Holy Cross. While he was not a formal part of the teaching staff, his presence in the house had to have been palpable, given the daily prayer and common table which constitute religious houses. Moreover, the fact that he had become "controversial" could only enhance his effect on the more adventuresome. And while he could not have been foresighted enough to anticipate how Holy Cross College would give him a home and an audience in his later years, it was precisely that initiative which allowed his influence to take root and to bear fruit well beyond the confines of his own lifespan. Such is one of the fringe benefits of a religious community; and indeed, of the same community that James Burns noted would be unable to appreciate him during that lifetime. And that Notre Dame would before long assume the trajectory for which his heart had yearned belongs also to the dynamics of the religious community whose members would carry the vision in their hearts—a vision which his life with them in Washington had doubtless implanted.

Chapter Four

[J.H. MOZANS]
Following the Conquistadores
a trilogy on South America (1910-16)[60]

WHILE HOLY CROSS COLLEGE was to become his home, John
Zahm was neither disposed to sit still nor to immerse himself in
the local life of a community which he had served so selflessly
for more than six years, for we have seen the toll that such unstinting service took. He was, after all, under doctor's orders to
"seek absolute relief from all responsibility, and devote yourself
to rest and distraction by foreign travel for the next two years at
least." Moreover, fearing that Zahm's devotion to his community, together with his innate zeal, would render even insistent
advice nugatory, his doctor concluded with a solemn warning,
in the event that Zahm failed to heed him: "your further usefulness to your community will be lost. Paresis certainly awaits
you. I have taken this method to express my opinion. I have
talked to you and advised you without avail. ... Pardon my insistence. You have been a good friend to me, and I cannot better
express my appreciation of that friendship than by telling you
the truth" (letter from J.B. Perteling, 2 May 1906). It seems that

---

[60] *Following the Conquistadores: Up the Orinoco and Down the Magdalena*
(New York: D. Appleton, 1910), *Following the Conquistadores: Along the Andes and
Down the Amazon* (New York: D. Appleton, 1911), *Following the Conquistadores:
Through South America's Southland* (New York: D. Appleton, 1916).

Zahm finally listened. Could that have been part of his adopting the anagrammatic pseudonym "H. J. Mozans" as well as establishing a mail drop at the Cosmos Club? He had been persuaded, apparently, that he must distance himself from all that would portend responsibility, after having assumed everything that responsibility entails in serving as provincial. But what to do? And where? For one so accustomed to putting his life and talents at the service of others within the context of a community dedicated to service, those could be unsettling questions. So he opens the introductory pages of the first of what will be two books on South America—*Up the Orinoco and Down the Magdalena*, to appear from Appleton & Co. in 1910—with a lyrical description of discernment at work, incorporating the doctor's advice in the way that he was finally to hear it.

> On a dark, cold day toward the close of January, 1907, the writer stood at a window in New York, observing some score of a mittened army removing the avalanche of snow that cumbered the streets after a half week of continuous storm. He was pondering a long vacation, musing where rest and recreation might be found, at once wholesome and instructive, amid scenes quite different from any afforded by his previous journeys. He was familiar with every place of interest in North America, from Canada to the Gulf, from Alaska to Yucatan. He had spent many years in Europe, had visited Asia, Africa, and the far-off isles of the Pacific. He cared not to revisit these, much less to go where he must entertain or be entertained. He sought rest, absolute rest and freedom, untrammeled by conventional life. For the present he would shun the society of his fellows for the serene solitude of the wilderness, or the companionship of mighty mountains and rivers. Not that he was a misanthrope or that he wished to become an anchoret. Far from it. Still less did he wish to spend his time in idleness. This for him would have been tantamount to solitary confinement. He dreamed of a land where he could spend most of the time in the open air close to Nature and in communion with her—where both mind and body would always be active and yet always free—free as the bird that comes and goes as it lists (1).

It was a bare six months after the reversals of the provincial chapter had sent John Zahm into virtual exile from the place which had defined his life and mission, Notre Dame, into a liminal state which he can now welcome. The key phrases, which betoken a fund of self-knowledge with due acceptance of the ways of providence, are to "always be active yet always free," with the mutually reinforcing images of dreaming and of birds. In the light of his characteristic mode of total dedication to the duties before him, this fresh start will demand that he "shun the society of his fellows for the serene solitude of the wilderness, or the companionship of mighty mountains and rivers." While he cannot renounce companionship, distance from his community would prove imperative. He has a keen sense (at 55) that a new life opens before him; he can count on the formation he has received to receive that new life as well, yet for the nonce must let the past be past. But such sudden freedom can be dismaying as well as liberating; how to know where to set his sights? The passage continues in a similar vein, revealing that side of Zahm which had already drawn him to Dante, the dimension which reading and travel over the next fifteen years of life will bring to unimaginable fruition:

> Whilst thus absorbed in thought, and casting an occasional glance at the laborers in the street battling against the Frost-King, whose work continued without intermission, the writer was awakened from his reverie by the dulcet tones evoked from a Steinway grand and the sweet, sympathetic voice of one who had just intoned the opening words of Goethe's matchless song as set to music by Liszt:
>
>> Know'st thou the land where the pale citron grows,
>> And the gold orange through dark foliage glows?
>> A soft wind flutters through the deep blue sky,
>> The myrtle blooms, and towers the laurel high,
>> Know'st thou it well?
>> O there with thee!

O that might, my own beloved one, flee.
It was La Niña—the pet name of the young musician—that came as a special providence to clear up a question that seemed to be growing more difficult the longer it was pondered. The effect was magical, and all doubt and hesitation disappeared forthwith. La Niña, as if inspired, had, without in the least suspecting it, indicated the land of the heart's desire. Yes, the writer would leave, and leave at once, the region of cloud and frost and chilling blast, and seek the land of flowers and sunshine, the land of "soft wind" and "blue sky," "the land where the pale citron grows," where "the gold orange glows" (2).

Continuing in his lyrical mode, he related how, "a few days afterwards the writer, with a few friends, had taken his place in a through Pullman car bound for the Land of Easter—the land of Ponce de Leon"—less lyrically, Florida—whence the journey would begin to South America.

But let us engage in a bit of speculation over the composition and place of this final paragraph of discernment. The composition recalls the key episode in Augustine's *Confessions*: a voice emerging to break a spell. Augustine was in a friend's garden; Zahm most probably in the apartment of friends in Manhattan—the Schwab's, perhaps, who would finance his voyages and with whom he was traveling when he was taken sick and died in Munich in the influenza epidemic following "the great war" in 1921. He would dedicate his ground-breaking volume, *Women in Science* (1913), to Eurana Schwab, whose letter of gratitude reminds him that "Charlie and I will always think of you as a very dear friend" (21 September 1913). Following this train of thought, the young musician, La Niña, could be their guest, spontaneously directing Zahm into the second half of his life, with a bow to Dante's own everyman journey inspired by Beatrice. Scant evidence, no doubt, yet enough to know he was not alone in a hotel at this prescient moment!

In fact, like the Augustine we meet in his "Testimony" (Gary Wills' inspired translation of *Confessions*), Zahm will seldom be alone in "the serene solitude of the wilderness." He will relish, no doubt, "the companionship of mighty mountains and rivers," yet will seldom lack human companions as well, even when ostensibly traveling alone. That fact offers a clue to a person otherwise quite private, yet may be further illuminated by the fact that he never went anywhere unprepared. The breadth of his reading is truly astounding, and it would have alerted him to persons or institutions critical to contact on arrival. Unlike his final work, all of which was composed *before* setting out for the Levant, it appears that these works were composed afterwards, following the lead of daily diary entries. Yet their veracity as travelogues were still challenged by a lawyer for the Columbian legation in New York, who had heard, "from persons whose judgment is worth heeding, that the book ... is, to use a slang phrase, a 'fake'; that not merely is the name H. J. Mozans a pseudonym but that no such journey as that described in the work was ever actually made by the author, but that the book is merely an extremely clever compilation" [letter from Phanor Eder to "Messrs. D. Appleton & Co.," 18 February 1911]. Eder appears to have been satisfied by the official Appleton "assurances" that "we are acquainted with the author ...; we know him to be a man of reputation and a scholar of distinction, and we have every reason to believe that the experiences which he relates in this book are based on actual fact" [24 February 1911], promising to "repeat them to everybody with whom I have discussed the matter." Yet he still regrets "that Mr. 'Mozans' apparently does not care to disclose his name," and urges his publishers to "persuade him to do so, in view of the adverse criticisms that may have been made" [25 February 1911]. In fact, however, we are no better informed than Eder, whose charge was never directly addressed by Appleton, yet the course of events in Zahm's own life at this point would corroborate that this book and the next provide actual accounts of the journeys related, yet carefully composed afterwards in his Holy Cross College study, in the period between completing these twin voyages (1907) and their publication in 1910-11.

In the spirit of our retrospective appreciation of his life and person, however, let us move to the context of the work, which Zahm outlines in the Foreword as well as announces in the series title given to both works: "Following the Conquistadores":

The following pages contain the record of a journey made to islands and lands that border the Caribbean and to the less frequented parts of Venezuela and Columbia. ... When we recollect that the lands in question were not only the first discovered but that they were also witnesses of the marvelous achievements of some of the most renowned of the conquistadores, our surprise becomes doubly great that our information respecting them is so meager and confined almost exclusively to those who make a special study of things South American. Never, perhaps, in the story of our race was the spirit of adventure so generally diffused as it was at the dawn of the sixteenth century—just after the epoch-making discoveries of Columbus and his hardy followers. It was like the spirit that animated the Crusaders when they started on their long march to recover the Holy Sepulcher from the possession of the Moslem. It was, indeed, in many of its aspects a revival of the age of chivalry. That ocean of legend and mystery with its enchanted islands inhabited by witches and gnomes and griffins had been explored.... A new world was revealed the astonished Spaniard. Every animal, tree, and plant seemed new to them often entirely different from anything the Old World shows. There was, too, a new race of men, with strange manners and customs. ... Those who came to the New World acted as if they were in a land of enchantment and were prepared to believe any tale, however, preposterous, that appealed to their lust for gold or love of adventure. No enterprise was too difficult for them, no hardship too great. ... The feats of individual prowess were as brilliant as the success of Spanish arms was pronounced and far-reaching. It was an age of epics, of poetry in action (x).

No irony in the use of "discover" here; though the book itself will make explicit how the prowess which led to such

achievements was in fact a brutal conquest. For among his interlocutors will be Bartolomeo de las Casas, corresponding to
the concluding paragraphs of his outline: "In the following pages the author has endeavored to give not only his own impressions of the lands he has visited but also, when the narrative
permitted or required it, the impressions of others—conquistadores, missionaries, and men of science. ... In the words of
Pliny, ... it has been the aim of the author 'to give newness to
old things, authority to new things, beauty to things out of use,
fame to the obscure, favor to the hateful, credit to the doubtful,
nature to all and all to nature' "–which he acknowledges to be
"a difficult task truly" (xiii). Yet the difficulties are as concep-
tual as they are logistical, for notwithstanding the rigors of the
anticipated journey—a seasoned traveler had admonished him:
"you are attempting the impossible" (4)—his enthusiasm for the
exploits of the conquistadores, Zahm will soon encounter heartfelt anguish of a fellow priest for the "new race of men, with
strange manners and customs," whom the Spaniards so quickly
enslaved. He cites the last will and testament of the Dominican
friar, later bishop of Chiapa, Bartolomeo de las Casas:

> By all the thefts, all the deaths, and all the confiscation of es-
> tates and other inalienable riches, by the dethroning of rulers
> with unspeakable cruelty, the perfect and immaculate law of
> Jesus Christ and the natural law itself have been broken, the
> name of our Lord and His holy religion have been outraged, the
> spreading of the faith has been retarded, and irreparable harm
> done to these innocent people (28).

Nor is Zahm slow to appropriate the prophetic message for himself, as a north American:

> Let us not forget, in contemplating the humiliation and punish-
> ment of Spain, that we too have sinned as Spain sinned. And
> let us pray that the blood of millions of Indians that have been
> exterminated in our own land may not call down the vengeance
> of Heaven on our children and our children's children. Nations,
> like individuals, are punished when they have sinned (29).

As their journey unfolds, visiting Cuba, Haiti, Santa Domingo, and Puerto Rico, they cross the rest of the Caribbean to Curacao, to land at the Venezuelan port of La Guayra, a distance of six miles from the capital, Caracas, though twenty-three by train to climb the massif. Spending a delightful month in Caracas, which Zahm compares favorably with Taormina (Sicily), the group was nevertheless frustrated:

> We could elicit no information that would warrant us in starting on so long a journey as that to the Orinoco, and one that might involve many hardships and dangers without adequate compensation. Yet, notwithstanding our ill success so far, we did not for a moment think of abandoning our contemplated trip to the valley of the Orinoco. Far from it. The more we thought of it the more fascinating the project became...–the grassy plains and vast forests of the Orinoco basin (44).

So they set out for Trinidad, "skirting along the Pearl coast, [extending for five hundred miles to the mouth of the Orinoco,] celebrated in legend and story—darkened by deeds of barbarous cruelty and resplendent in records of heroic achievement" (46). These islands had supplied Europe with magnificent pearls, including one of "two hundred and fifty carats, of the size and shape of a pigeon's egg, ... obtained by Philip II" (50). Yet Zahm fastens on Las Casas, who came here after he found, by sad experience, that his efforts in behalf of the Indians in Cuba, Española and Puerto Rico were frustrated by influences he was unable to control. It was here, aided by Franciscans and Dominicans, who had preceded him by only a few years, that he purposed laying the corner stone of that vast Indian commonwealth, for which he had secured letters patent from Charles V. For this great experiment in colonization, the greatest the world had ever known, he had received a grant of land extending from ... the Caribbean Sea to Peru. In his colossal undertaking he planned ... to establish for [the Indians'] benefit an ideal Christian state such as a century and a half later was realized in the fertile basins of the Paraná and Paraguay (48).

His plans were thwarted by "the rich and powerful," blinded by lust of gold and pleasure, [who] left nothing undone to insure the failure of his project, and in the end succeeded (48). Yet while this dream vanished,

> Until the day of his death at the advanced age of ninety-two, whether as a simple monk or as the bishop of Chiapa, his voice was always raised in behalf of the children of the forest, and against their enslavement by cruel, soulless seekers after fortune (48-49).

So it is not difficult to ascertain where Zahm's own soul rests, as they proceed from Trinidad on their daunting journey into the delta of the Orinoco, after a delightful respite on the fabled island, where, "thanks to the kind and considerate hospitality of its people, we had enjoyed all the comforts of home and the same freedom of movement as if we had been given the keys of the city" (64).

Up the Orinoco and Down the Magdalena (1910)

Indeed, the channel between Trinidad and Venezuela was the very one through which "Columbus passed ... and from which he got his first view of the mainland of the New World. But he did not realize at first the magnitude of his discovery" (65). It was that magnitude and grandeur which Zahm proposed to enter and try to appropriate, with his small group of friends; most notably C., "the loyal and generous young cavalier" to whom the work is dedicated, and whose presence Zahm celebrates on the final page: "if he had not been of superior mold, would more than once have lost his heart during the course of our long journey" (426). As his careful composition reveals, such a voyage proved to be, for Zahm himself, exactly "what the doctor ordered." The enthusiasm elicited by spectacular vistas, lush flora and exotic people, is illuminated throughout with comprehensive historical background, punctuated by spontaneous literary allusions, and larded with comments on potential for development as well as scientific data designed to bolster those speculations. Here is a thoroughly instructional travelogue, guided by a master teacher who is the readier to learn from each new opportunity as he has already prepared himself to see what might easily pass others by.

Liberated as he was from teaching responsibilities, he could never suppress the inherent need to instruct others, notably his North American compatriots, regarding the spacious beauty of the continent south of them, together with the dignity of its peoples, however penurious their circumstances may be. Unsurprisingly, as Zahm began to "devote [himself] to rest and distraction by foreign travel, [anticipating] the next two years at least," this imposed therapy began to do its work by opening him to spontaneous and potentially lasting friendships, while these written accounts elicit the splendid teacher he had always proven to be. Without attempting to monitor the entire river voyage, a few judicious selections can show how this is displayed in the text. Finally entering the river itself, after the enticing visits enroute we have detailed, he exclaims:

> We shall never forget our first view of the Orinoco and of the impressions we then received. Was it that we were at last sailing in the placid waters of the one river of all the world that we had from our youth most yearned to behold, or was it that we had been dreaming of the site and beauties of the Terrestrial Paradise, as fancied by Columbus to exist in these parts, or was it because of both these elements combined? We know not, but one thing is certain, that is that our first view of the Orinoco and its forest-shaded banks, festooned with views and flowers, revealed at once those musical words of Dante,
>
>> Sweet hue of eastern saffire, that was spread
>> O'er the serene aspect of the pure air,
>> High up as the first circle, to mine eyes
>> Unwanted joy renewed (*Purgatorio* 1:13-16)

> And brought vividly back to memory his inimitable descrip-
> tion of his entrance into the Garden of Eden, where he was to
> meet again his long-lost Beatrice (72).

No ordinary travelogue, this; we are being invited into the advent of John Zahm's new life in his mid-fifties, in synch with
Dante's opening *nel medio di nostra vita.* Continuing up the
river,

> While passing up this majestic river and admiring the ever-
> varying panorama of rarest floral beauty, we recalled a couple
> of paragraphs in Darwin's *Journal of Researches*, in which he
> refers to the futility of attempting to describe, for one who has
> never visited the tropics, the wonders of the scenery there and
> above all the marvels of the vegetable world (83).

The following two pages, from Darwin's journal, lyrically
evoke the effect of tropical vegetation on one viewing it, closing
with the way:

> the form of the orange tree, the cocoanut, the palm, the mango,
> the tree-fern, the banana will remain clear and separate; but
> the thousand beauties which unite these into one perfect scene
> must fade away; yet they will leave, like a tale heard in child-
> hood, a picture full of indistinct, utmost beautiful figures (85).

Zahm's penchant for historical context illuminates "a place
of more than passing interest between Barrancas and Ciudad
Bolivar [their destination by river steamer]. ... It was here, in
1618, that young Walter Raleigh, the son of the Admiral, lost
his life in an encounter with the Spaniards who had possession
of this stronghold. It was here, also, that Bolivar, at a critical
hour during [Columbia's] War of Independence, saved his life
by hiding in a swamp near the village" (89). Then the departure
of "our mining party ... for their long journey of one hundred
and fifty miles on mule back to Callao" (90) incites him to take
up "Raleigh's ill-fated search for El Dorado" (91). He quickly
returns to the present for a fulsome description of "the native
population, ... represented chiefly by the Waraus, Arnacs, and
Caribs" (94). The Arnacs are

one of the oldest of the great South American tribes. They were the first Indians with whom the Spaniards come in contact and are today, as they were in the time of Columbus, a friendly, good-natured, peace-loving people, in spite of the harsh treatment their forefathers received from their cruel conquerors (95). ... The Caribs [on the other hand] belong to that dread race of whom Columbus heard such blood-curdling stories from the peaceful inhabitants of Cuba and Española. ... They were the terror of all the tribes with whom they came in contact. They enslaved the women and celebrated their victories by devouring the men. ... Indeed, the word "cannibal" is but a corruption of the word "Carib." [Yet] thanks to the tireless efforts of the Spanish Franciscans, the Caribs who inhabit the eastern part of Venezuela were eventually civilized and Christianized, and converted from wild nomads into peaceful and useful citizens, ... chiefly engaged in the breeding of cattle and in agriculture. [Indeed,] a century ago there were in the territory bounded by the Caroni, the Cuyuni and Orinoco no fewer than thirty-eight missions with sixteen thousand civilized Indians. But by decrees promulgated by the Republic of Columbia in the years 1819 and 1821 these missions were suppressed and today one sees scarcely a vestige of their former existence. The Indians are not only much less numerous than formerly, but most of them have returned to the mode of life they led before the advent of the missionary (96-98).

Early missionaries distinguished three dialects among the Caribs: one for men "which everyone speaks," with another "so proper to the women, that, although the men understand it, they would consider themselves dishonored if they spoke it," and a third "known only to the men who have been in war [which] they use in important assemblies of which they desire to keep the resolutions secret" (99).

Soon Ciudad Bolivar appeared, "situated on an eminence, on the right bank of the river [where] the cathedral, and the government buildings around the plaza in the higher part of the town, loom up with splendid effect" (102-03). Yet for all its former beauty, "everything was in a state of abandonment that was sad to behold. … Oppressive taxes, … intolerable monopolies, controlled by the leading government officials or their favorites, had reduced the majority of the population to a condition bordering on despair" (105). Although this had been their original destination, a small steamer appeared

> from Orocué, a small town in Columbia, on the river Meta, [which suddenly gave us the] opportunity of seeing more of the great Orinoco, and of sailing on the waters of its great tributary, the historic Meta. Dreams of the past began at once to flit before us as possible realities in the near future. If we once got to Orocué, what was to prevent us from going further up the river–as far as its waters were navigable? Then by crossing the *llanos* of eastern Columbia, and the Cordilleras of the Andes we would be in far-famed Bogota, the Athens of South America (109-10).

He had obviously thought of such a voyage or he would not have been able so quickly to project it, yet it had been at best "a remote possibility. And now, in a few moments … the journey was decided on, and nothing remained but to make the necessary preparations" (110). Yet since the boat would not be ready for two weeks, they made a hasty return trip to Port-of-Spain, where "we found, what above all was needed at this juncture—a good, brave, enthusiastic companion for the long and arduous trip before us. Our *compangon de voyage*, who would fondly affect the ways and dress of a dapper young *caballero*, and whom, therefore, we shall call C.—*caballero*—was a professor of languages; … like ourselves, fond of adventure, and was not averse to its being accompanied by an element of danger" (110-11). So inspired, the group made sure that "we were fully equipped with everything necessary for our long trip across the continent" (111).

On return, they watched

> for several days the swarthy stevedores of Ciudad Bolivar … busy transferring to our little steamer the freight that had been accumulating for her during the previous six months, [while]

our friends and acquaintances [were] endeavoring to dissuade us from what one and all presumed a rash and dangerous undertaking. All meant well, but all were prophets of ill. No one, we were assured, had ever gone to Bogotá by the route we purposed taking (112). The group had already come to be skeptical of dangers so vividly described, from swarms of mosquitoes (*la plaga*) to unbearable heat, so descriptions of hordes of savage Guahibos, the terror of stern Columbia (118),

to be found along the banks of the Meta, did not deter them either. They rather took it as a "favorable omen [that] the usual time of the opening of navigation to the Upper Meta was anticipated by more than a month" (119). Their most tangible fear—that the military would commandeer their boat to quell a rebellion in the area—came to naught as an army officer whom they encountered midway finally permitted them to proceed. Yet that "we should be obliged to remain in Urbana for an indefinite period, and perhaps—the thought was almost maddening—be forced to abandon entirely an enterprise on which we had set our hearts" (124-25) constituted, in retrospect, the most taxing moment in an often harrowing journey, offering a glimpse of the passion for adventure which beset Zahm and his companions.

They were fascinated with "the *llanos*—unlimited pampas, with their rich, succulent grasses, ten to twelve feet high, capable of supporting millions of cattle (128)–extend[ing] southward from the mountain range bordering the Caribbean to the Orinoco and its great tributary, the Meta, [with] an area more than four times as great as the state of New York" (126). Yet even more fascinating were the Llaneros themselves, who "have often been called the Cossacks of South America" (129), "who during the war with Spain contributed so much towards achieving the independence of both Venezuela and New Granada [Columbia]" (130). As they come to the confluence

with the Meta, Zahm reflects ruefully on the fortunes of young
Venezuela:

> It would be difficult to name another country, except possi-
> bly Haiti, where, in proportion to the population, war has
> wrought greater ravages and counter more victims. A country
> that should be a land of peace and plenty has for generations
> been an armed camp of contending factions. ... Like northern
> Italy, after the death of Frederick II, Venezuela, in the words of
> Dante, has been for nearly a century
>> Full of tyrants, and the veriest peasant lad
>> Becomes Marcellus in the strife of parties
>> (*Purgatorio* 6:124-6)
> Such has been the fate of Venezuela since the time of Bolivar,
> whom its people hail as the Liberator (136).

Once again, one can better wrangle with nature than human
venality.

As the steamer started up the Meta, Zahm confesses that

> I personally felt a pang of regret on leaving the Orinoco. Noth-
> ing would have pleased me more than to have continued on the
> waters of this great river until we should have reached the won-
> derful Cassiquiare, which connects the Orinoco with the great
> Rio Negro and with the still greater Amazon. ... This had long
> been a fond dream of mine. Will it ever be realized? In the
> language of one of my Spanish companions, *Dios verá*—God
> will see—for it is not impossible (142).

An answer is presaged in the concluding words of this narrative: "I was ready to undertake a longer and more difficult
journey ... to follow the conquistadores along the Andes and
down the Amazon" (427), and will be recounted in the companion volume. Yet though they had been assured that they were
undertaking an itinerary by which "no one had ever gone to
Bogotá," Zahm relates how "the journey–from the Orinoco to
the Amazon–has often been made and is frequently made every
year by traders, missionaries, and others" (142). Recalling the
explorations of Alexander von Humboldt in the early nineteenth

century, Zahm again bemoans the demise of the extensive missionary network which had facilitated Humboldt's crossing the interior of this continent in the way Zahm is already dreaming of undertaking next. He celebrates "the zealous and scholarly Padre Juan Rivero, who spent sixteen years as a missionary in this part of the New World," and whose writing "must always be consulted by one who desires accurate knowledge regarding the condition, character, rivalries and wars of the diverse savage tribes to whom he preached the gospel of peace and brotherly love" (148). Indeed, his work was finally "published by the Columbian government ... in 1883, after lying in the dust in manuscript for nearly a hundred and fifty years" (149), for they needed his expert advice to quell Indian rebellion in this remote region.

Then reflection on missionaries takes us to Zahm's encounter with the people of the Meta, on whom they were dependent for provisions. "We always found them very hospitable and very entertaining. They always gave us a cordial welcome to their humble home, and rarely allowed us to depart without giving us something from their simple store. ... Here we were among people who lived a simple life and appeared all the happier for it. We saw no evidence of suffering anywhere. The only thing that seemed to concern them was the instability of the government" (160). More amply:

> How often, when partaking of the simple fare of our kindly hosts in tropical America, were we forced to compare their never-failing hospitality with that of the Greeks of Homeric times! They thought nothing was too good for the honored guest, for he might be a god in disguise, or, if not a god, he was at least a friend of the gods. Like the early Christians, who treated their guests as if they might be angels who had come upon them unawares, our Meta hosts always gave us the best at their disposition, and expressed their regret at being unable to do more. Their home was ours as long as we chose to remain,

and their every act showed that they were pleased to be honored—as they expressed it—by the strangers' visit (188).

One evening, "while silently sitting on the prow of our
launch admiring the countless, ever-changing beauties of that
marvelous moonlight night—our last on the Meta, giving free
rein to our fancy, and shifting our course as the meandering
river demanded, behold! Suddenly like a vision, the Andes
stood before us in all their majesty and glory, looming up to
the very heavens" (191). His reflections on the poverty of their
response could speak for the entire journey:

> We saw things wonderful and unspeakable, but all our super-
> latives were inarticulate and feeble, matched with the scene
> before us. ... [They] were little more than the Indian's grunt,
> and less devotional than the Moslem's phrase, "Allah is great!"
> Coming from the cold and tame nature of the North to that
> of the glorious and marvelous equator, we were like Plato's
> men, bred in cavern twilight, and then suddenly exposed to the
> bright effulgence of the noonday sun (191).

They soon had to leave the river to cross the cordilleras of the
Andes on foot, having made arrangements for mules to be
brought to the tiny port of Barrington, whose "entire population ... –a negro woman, her three daughters and a young
man, likewise a negro" (194) had met them at the dock. Neither
mules nor muleteers were in sight, but then "the telegraph line
to Orocué had only recently been put up, ... and had never been
in satisfactory working order" (196). What saved them again
was the gentility of the people; this time it was "our captain,
God bless him! observing our distress, [who] came to us, and
with a kindness and courtesy we can never forget, said, "Do not
worry, gentlemen, the launch will remain here until the arrival
of your animals" (198). By noon on the second day there appeared "about thirty mules and horses, and more than a dozen
men. We had telegraphed for mules only, as we did not think
we should be able to get horses, but to our delight we found that

we were to have two good saddle horses for our personal use, besides the mules destined for our baggage" (200).

Traversing the Columbian *llanas* would prove taxing in the rainy season, yet the presence of the "happy and independent … Columbian Llanero" (210), with their *bayeton*, "double ponchos, made by sewing together two blankets, one red, the other blue" would keep them both warm and dry. Indeed, "provided with a poncho, a hammock, and a many-pocketed saddle, … the Llanero is always at home" (214). Yet it was an encounter with a mother and daughter, after six hours of hard riding in heavy rain with no water left to drink, that offered a personal introduction to the Llanero:

> she waded out almost to the middle of the stream [by her small bamboo hut] and in a few moments returned with a new supply of water fresh from the Andes. As we prepared to leave, mother and child—the father was sick abed with malaria—both expressed their regret that we could not remain longer. … For hours afterwards her touching accents seemed like music in our ears, and the image of her lovely child, her darling *niñita*, nestling by her side, with her hands waving a fond adieu, was before our eyes long after we had left the llanos far behind us (218).

Their climb through the cordillera of the Andes began at Villavicencio, whence the mules and horses had come, as they climbed 1140 feet above the town to Buena Vista, whence "far below us, and extending away—north, east, south—towards the dim and distant horizon, were the llanos, every feature of which was brought out in bright relief by the brilliant noonday sun" (235). Yet again, it was the people who attracted Zahm's attention even more:

> They are ever willing to assist one another, and we were often surprised to see how ready they were to share their limited store with others, whether in want or not. A more friendly people we never met than the good people who dwell on the eastern slopes of the Columbian Cordilleras. They always have a kindly greeting for every one they meet (240).

They were amazed to notice flocks of familiar birds flying overhead, eliciting from Zahm a lengthy reflection on the intricacy and extent of the migratory path of birds. They are now ready to undertake the arduous climb over the cordilleras to Bogota.

Yet however taxing or arduous the climb, it proved to be exactly the therapy which this exhausted servant of Notre Dame and the Holy Cross community needed:

> We enjoyed a sense of freedom–the freedom of the child of the forest—we had never known before. We were beginning to see how easy it was to dispense with many of the things that are so often regarded as essentials to pleasure and comfort. ... The *wanderlust* and *abenteuergeist*–the love of travel and adventure–grows on one, it seems, in the wilds of South America more than elsewhere (262). ... We could not help comparing the splendid panoramas around us with the noted showplaces of Switzerland. [Yet] in the Andes it was the forest primeval, or the humble cot, or the picturesque village of the unspoiled and simple people of eastern Columbia, where a foreigner is rarely seen, but where he is always sure of a cordial welcome. ... [So] we never, for a single moment experienced anything even approaching a feeling of loneliness or remoteness from the world (263).

Continuing in a voice peculiarly his own, Zahm's quality of recollection is redolent of Jung:

> To be frank, we were not sorry to get away from the atmosphere of science, and find a land where the legends and traditions of the people were akin to those that were the delight of our childhood. For, much as we love science, we have never been willing to renounce the pleasure of indulging the imagination, as we did in years long gone by, when the fairy tale and myth so captivated our youthful mind. We confess it freely, we were glad to be among the simple, primitive people of the Andes, and were deeply interested in their peculiar folklore. It afforded us, in another form, the pleasure we derived from our first acquaintance with the creations of Homer, Hesiod, and Ovid; and with such productions as the Niebelungen Lied, Sakuntala, the Knights of the Round Table and Cid Campeador. All the science in the world could not diminish the pleasure we still find in these creations of fancy. We cherish them as much,

if not more, today as we did when they first became part of our
intellectual life. For this reason, if for no other, the reader will
conceive our unalloyed delight in being beyond the reach of reports of physical and psychological laboratories, wherein nothing is admitted that has not the imprimatur of Baconian science
or Comptian philosophy, both of which lay an absolute interdict
on all the most charming creations of poetry and romance (268).

An incredible testimony to the classical education he had received at a Notre Dame "with a faculty of 39 and a student body
of 442" (Weber 4) in the 1860s—a formation which had trained
his agile intellect to profit from what he saw and met, and at
this time in his life, allowed that mind, heart, and imagination
to entice him into unforeseen arenas. Travel as therapy, indeed,
yet especially for one whose natural endowment and cultural
background so richly informed his response to beauty.

Their climb from the valley of the Meta on horseback to
Bogotá (at 8616 feet above sea level) would soon be complemented by a descent to the Magdalena, giving a fair idea how
isolated was the capital of Columbia at that time. Founded in
1538 by the intrepid "Gonzalo Jimenez de Quesada ... and his
followers, after one of the most remarkable campaigns ever
conducted in the New World" (285), "Santa Fé, also known as
Santa Fé de Bogotá, was for a long period the capital of the
Viceroyalty of New Granada. After the War of Independence
the name was changed to Bogotá—from Bacatá—the name of
the old Chibca capital, where the *zipa*, the most powerful of the
Indian *caciques*, at the arrival of the Spaniards, had his official
residence" (286). Zahm was especially taken with two edifices: "The old Colegio del Rosario--now known as the School
of Philosophy and Letters—[was] founded in 1553, nearly a
hundred years before ... Harvard; [along with] the astronomical observatory ... erected in 1803" (289). But it was not the
buildings but the pervasive literary and scientific culture which
earned Bogotá the name "Athens of South America," beginning

with its founder, Quesada, who initiated a literary tradition replete with names which Zahm recalls at length, concluding with the observation that "in Columbia there seem to be as many 'doctors,' that is, men who have the degree of Doctor of Laws, as there are generals in Venezuela" (299-303). Zahm's historical sense prompts him to recall the chance "meeting of three distinguished conquistadores, Gonzalo Jimenez de Quesada, Nicholas Federmann and Sebastian de Balalcazar, ... the famous lieutenant of Francisco Pizarro, ... coming from so great distances, from three different points of the compass—one of the most interesting episodes in the history of the conquest." Zahm quotes a contemporary account to show how "critical a moment it was for the Europeans. If they had failed to agree [and rather turned] their arms against one another, those who would have escaped alive would have been at the mercy of the Indians. ... But fortunately wise councils prevailed and a clash was averted" (294-97).

After recounting Columbia's recent political history, with the formidable presence of Bolivar, Zahm finds himself "loath to depart" from Bogotá: "we had visited many places in which we would have desired to tarry longer, had it been possible, but so far no place had so completely captivated us as Columbia's famous metropolis" (313). The Muisca trail, descending from the end of the railway line to the Magdalena, brought them to the "summit of El Sargento: ... the most superb spectacle I had ever contemplated. C. and I instinctively stood still in silent rapture" (340). With the precision of a scientific observer, he tells us:

> It was not merely the physical features ... that produced the admirable picture that held us spellbound. It was the marvelous combination of light and shade, the position of the sun in the heavens, and the strange optical illusion caused by the bright and fleecy clouds that constantly swept over the landscape. ...
> It seemed as if the genius of the Andes wished to give us, as we were leaving his domain, a series of dissolving views on a

stupendous scale. View succeeded view with kaleidoscopic rapidity, all distinguished by color schemes of supreme delicacy and splendor (341).

Calling upon his own travel and culture to try to convey this experience, Zahm continues:

> Never before had mountain scenery occasioned keener delight. Only once before had it been my privilege to contemplate a vista at all approaching the one that unfolded itself before us in the picturesque valley of the Magdalena. That was long years ago, as I stood on the summit of Mt. Parnassus. It was a balmy morning in summer. "Rosy-fingered dawn" was just making her appearance beyond the plain where Troy once stood, and was hastening to gladden by her smile the islands of the Aegean and the one-time famous land of Hellas. ... But beautiful, sublime, glorious as it undoubtedly was, it has since yielded the palm to the unrivaled vista that greeted us from the summit of El Sargento" (342).

Before long, "our long, yet delightful ride across the oriental Andes was at an end. Crossing a steel suspension bridge, the noblest structure of its kind in the republic—which spans Columbia's great waterway—we were in Honda, the head of navigation for the lower Magdalena" (345).

A relatively tranquil journey by boat to Barranquilla, the chief port of entry to Columbia, affords Zahm the leisure to reflect on the exploits of Quesada, "one of the bravest and most humane of the conquistadores, [who] successfully performed a task before which a less valorous commander would have given up in despair" (362), as well as to ponder how well Columbia could develop "by connecting Bogotá with Europe by means of the Meta and Orinoco. It will not be a difficult feat of engineering to build a railroad from the capital to a suitable point on the Meta" (356). Finally, inspired by a grove "composed of palms of unusual height and beauty," (372) he reflects on the "countless uses made of palms, especially by the inhabitants of the tropics" (373). Suffering a debilitating encounter with a hidden log, which rendered their rear paddlewheel inoperative, they could only rejoice that they were in sight of "the entrance to the canal that leads to the docks of Barranquilla" (375), inspiring Zahm to cite Dante:

> Let not the people be too swift to judge,
>
> ....
>
> For I have seen
> A bark, that all her way across the sea
> Ran straight and speedy, perish at the last
> E'en in the haven's mouth (*Paradiso* 13: 130, 136-38)

The journey "up the Orinoco and down the Magdalena" is now complete, but contingencies will allow the party to experience two places they had not anticipated. Instead of the direct passage to Colon, in Panama, which they had booked, they were diverted there via Puerto Limon, in Costa Rica, stopping enroute in Cartagena, Columbia:

> a city that, in some respects, possessed greater interest for us than any we had hitherto visited. ... The picture of Cartegena, as it first presented itself to our view, was one of rarest loveliness, ... not unlike Venice as seen from Il Lido or ... Alexandria, as viewed from the Mediterranean. ... One of the most important places in the New World, its fortifications and massive walls ... are still in a marvelous state of preservation and evoke the admiration of all who see them, ... notwithstanding four long sieges. ... The architecture of many of the buildings ... is Moorish in character and carried us back to many happy days spent in fair Andalusia in its once noble capitals, Granada and Seville (380-83).

It was from Cartagena that stupendous sums of gold were transported to Spain, which made it especially vulnerable to buccaneers. As they leave the fabled city, Zahm is forcibly reminded that they "were sailing in waters that had been rendered famous by the achievements of some of the most remarkable men named in the annals of early American discovery and conquest" (386). Yet after naming them all, he confesses that "the best and noblest of them all was the gentle and indefatigable Las Casas, the protector of the aborigines and the Apostle of the Indies, whose memory is still held in benediction in all Latin America:

> His voluminous writing, making more than ten thousand pages octavo, much of which is devoted to the defense of the Indians, constitute a monument which will endure as long as men shall love truth and justice. But his greatest monument—one that is absolutely unique in the history of civilization—is his former diocese of Chiapa. ... When he went to take possession of it, it was occupied by savage warriors who had successfully resisted all attempts made by Spaniards to subdue them. ... But Las Casas, armed only with the image of the Crucified and the gospel of peace, soon had these wild children of the forest prostrate at his feet, begging him to remain with them as their father and friend (387).

Zahm will never cease to be moved by exploits of the conquistadores, yet his heart remains with Las Casas. Indeed, as he goes on to recount, in their lust for gold, the conquistadores spawned their mirror image in ruthless buccaneers, who held nothing sacred in their quest for spoils, and were often surreptitiously sustained by major powers in a surrogate war against Spanish supremacy.

The final chapter recounts their utter charm at "the astonishing variety and richness of the flora of Costa Rica, [which Zahm surmises] is due to the fact that it is the connecting link between the floras of the two great continents of the North and the South" (409). After being overwhelmed by the luxuriance of the fruits of the coastal cordillera visible on their climb by narrow gauge railway, "we were quite charmed with San José and its hospitable and cultured people. In many respects, we thought it the most delightful city we had seen in Latin America, especially for a protracted sojourn" (414). In the city market,

> one beholds in lavish abundance citrous fruits of every species, bananas of untold varieties, and scores of other fruits equally

common here but scarcely known ... in our northern latitudes:
... guavas, mameys and mangoes; zapotes, avocados and chiri-
moyas; papayas, pomegranates and sapodillas; anonas, bread-
fruit, mangosteens, and others too numerous to mention (416).

Yet again, it is the people (and especially the women) whom
Zahm remarks above all, "a majority evidently mestizos":

> The number of beautiful, Madonna-like types one meets with
> is surprising. This impression is probably enhanced in some
> degree by the beautifully embroidered *pañolones*–large Chi-
> nese silk shawls—which they know so well how to display to
> the best advantage. When to the tasteful costume and deli-
> cate features one adds the culture and refinement that often
> distinguish the Josefina, one can easily realize that she best
> continues the best traditions for beauty and grace of mind and
> heart that have so long distinguished her sisters in the land of
> Isabella of Castile (421-22).

Zahm concludes his voyage of appreciating beauty with the inevitable sadness of parting: "the pang of leaving places that
have especially appealed to one and of saying farewell to newly-
formed friends almost as soon as one has learned to know their
goodness of heart and nobility of character. To me, I confess,
this has always been the greatest drawback of traveling and is
something I have never been able to outgrow" (422). He confesses to especially missing C., whose companionship "I would
fain have enjoyed ... longer while following the conquistadores
in lands farther south; but it was not to be" (426). Leaving the
group behind, Zahm confesses to feeling

> not unlike Dante when he suddenly found himself deprived
> of the companionship of Virgil, who had been his friend and
> guide during his arduous journey down through the fearsome
> pits of Hell and up the precipitous ledges of the mountain of
> Purgatory. But this impression, strong though it was, could
> not long remain dominant. ... The moment, then, that I stepped
> from the gangplank that connected our steamer with Panama-
> nian soil, the Rubicon was crossed, and I had resolved, *coute
> que coute*—alone, if necessary—to realize the long-cherished

dream of my youth, to visit the famed land of the Incas and explore the fertile valleys under the equator. If my experience in the llanos and among the Cordilleras had not made me "fit to mount up to the stars," as Dante was when he left the terrestrial Paradise, it had at least renewed me "even as new trees with new foliage," and I was ready to undertake a longer and more difficult journey (426-27).

His immediate reference is to the voyage recounted in the companion volume "following the conquistadores," yet one cannot help but read it as a metaphor for Zahm's own new life, as he had framed this journey on Dante's interior pilgrimage. However arduous the "rest and distraction" had been, in the undertaking and in its composition, the doctor's aim was clearly attained: Zahm has become a new person!

Along the Andes and Down the Amazon (1911)

It seems that he lost little time in preparing and executing the "longer and more difficult journey," as the account of it—*Along the Andes and Down the Amazon*—would appear a year later (1911), with a dedication to "my friend of many years, Charles M. Schwab," and an Introduction by Theodore Roosevelt, signed "Sagamore Hill, April 20, 1911,"

Doctor Mozans [who] has every qualification for making just such a journey as he made, and then for writing about it. He is an extraordinarily hardy man, this gentle, quiet traveler; ... he loves rivers and forests, mountains and plains, and broad highways and dim wood trails; and he has a wide and intimate acquaintance with science, with history, and above all, with literature. This volume supplements his previous volume. ... We are fortunate in having a man like Doctor Mozans traveling in the lands to the south of us. He speaks with just admiration of the great work done by Secretary Root, when, in an American warship, he circles the Southern continent, representing our country as an ambassador whose work was of the highest moment. But Doctor Mozans himself acted as such ambassador; and his sympathy with, and appreciation of, the people whom he met ... earned for him thoughtful and unwearied kindness

in return, and admirably fitted him, while on his journey, to interpret our nation to those among whom he traveled, and now
admirably fit him to interpret them in return to us (x).

With Charles Schwab, chairman of United States Steel, and
former president Roosevelt as patrons, and the experience of
northern South America to sustain him, this second journey
would not only carry him to the fabulous land of the Incas, but
(as we shall see) do so in quite regal style. A 1911 letter from
Franklin Adams at the Pan-American Union, to "My Dear Dr.
Zahm," reveals a longstanding relationship with that body, as
he felt free to ask Zahm's second for nomination to the Cosmos
Club. So we should not be surprised when Theodore Roosevelt
begins his Introduction by recalling

> Shortly after returning from his trip along the Orinoco and the
> Magdalena, Doctor Mozans called upon me, and we soon grew
> to be great friends. He is a devoted student of Dante, and I
> am one of the innumerable laymen who greatly admire Dante
> within having the slightest pretensions to having studied him.
> I think that the intimacy of Doctor Mozans and myself was
> largely due to his finding out the interest I had taken in trans-
> lating, so to speak, Dante's political terminology into that of
> the present day (ix).

He continues to comment on Dante's "lack of self-conscious-
ness [whereby] he illustrated the fundamental vices and virtues by placing in hell and purgatory the local Italian political
leaders of the thirteenth century side by side with the mightiest
figures of the elder world … of Greece and Rome at their ze-
nith" (ix). Concluding in a similar vein, he praises Zahm for
his "evident entire truthfulness … to what he sets forth as our
accomplishments … and to his allusions to our shortcomings,
as shown by our ignorance and lack of appreciation of the great
continent south of us, and our failure to try to bring it and its
people into closer relations with us" (xii). In Zahm, Roosevelt
found a kindred spirit with whom to struggle against the northern European Protestant prejudice regarding all things Latin, so

endemic to the intellectual and political culture of the United
States at the time, a spirit embodied in the thirteenth-century
Italian poet, Dante Alighieri!

Zahm himself will turn the contrast between North and
South into a fruitful comparison by employing Secretary Root's
image of " 'the laboratory of life, where English, German, Italian, French, and Spanish and American were all being welded
together into a new type', [where] we can see the same process
at work that for the last century has been operating with such
splendid results in the United States" (xiv)—indeed, at his beloved Notre Dame. "In the following pages, as in my [previ-
ous] work, … I have endeavored not only to give a picture of
the country and the people as I saw them, but also to summa-
rize their hopes, aspirations and prospects" (xv). His final list
of benefactors "who contributed so materially towards making
my journey to the southern continent so enjoyable and so prof-
itable" includes the President of Peru and his brother, "prefects
and governors, who gave me such generous hospitality," and
"Mr. E. G. Townsend, general superintendent of the Railways
of the South of Peru" (xvi), who put private trains at his dispos-
al. Zahm begins the narrative portion in Panama, in the midst
of herculean American efforts to construct the canal, only possible in the wake of Colonel Gorgas' stunning eradication of
yellow fever. The party will depart from Panama via steamer to Guayaquil, climb by rail to Quito, and then proceed by
steamer to Callao, the port for Lima, and thence to La Paz, Lake
Titicaca, and Cuzco to steep themselves in Inca civilization and the Quichua people. After a visit to Lima, Zahm
will cross the Andes "in the footsteps of Pizarro and Orsua,"
tasting the "heart of the Andes" with the "grand canyon of the
Marañon," the headwaters of the Amazon, before sailing down that
majestic river to join ocean steamers at Iquitos, midway to the
Atlantic, and thence to New York.

Zahm waxes eloquently about their Caribbean journey, recalling Bilbao's Quixotic appropriation "these seas and lands
and coasts and ports and islands of the South" in the name of
the Spanish monarchs (34): "Never before was I so impressed
by the solemnities of sea and sky, as in the equatorial Pacific;
… Here Nature seems to revel in the unveiled magnificence
of her ever-varying moods" (40). Debarking at Guayaquil for a
river steamer on the Guayas to begin the journey to Quito, the
"coastal mountains loomed ahead, overpowering in their magnitude and majesty. Never before in any part of the world, had
I beheld so imposing an exhibition of mountain grandeur" (47).
Which meant, of course, that the climb would be a harrowing
one, two miles above sea level and traversed by rail but "a few
years before my arrival in the country" (55); while "the first
train entered Quito June 28, 1908, two generations after it had
been first projected, and thirty-seven years after it had been begun, [at] an average cost of seventy-three thousand dollars a
mile" (57). So Zahm completed the journey by "French mo-
tor-car [over a road that] was by far the best we had yet seen
anywhere in South America" (93), only to discover "one of the
world's most favored cities. It was what Damascus and Baghdad in their halcyon days were to the Arabs, what Cordova and
Granada were to the Moors" (102), and "its literary and scientific luminaries at times shone as brightly as those of" Bogota
(103). What impressed him most was the observatory, from
which—given its equatorial location, "we could, from a single
point, gaze upon stars and constellations of both hemispheres—
something that is possible in no other observatory in the world"
(104-5). Never one for understatement, it seems that Zahm fell
instantly in love with "Quito bonito" (102).

As they continued by sea from Guayaquil to "Payta, which
has one of the best harbors of the republic" (116) of Peru, Zahm
skipped from tracing Pizarro's landing here to found "the first

city ... in the empire of the Incas" (115), Piura, to projecting a
rail link between this port and "San Borja, a port on the left
bank of the Upper Amazon" (116), listing the manifold advantages such a trans-continental passage could bring to Peru and
all of South America. He takes note of the startling difference in rainfall and vegetation between Ecuador and Columbia, and Peru and Chile, attributing it to the ocean temperatures
generated by the Humboldt current, such that "the desert begins where the current first strikes the coast near Coquimbo in
Chile, and ends where the current veers towards the west ... in
northern Peru" (122). Along the coastal voyage to Callao, the
port for Lima, "we never wearied gazing at the Andes, which
at a distance looked like a regular bastion" (123). The purpose
of this initial visit to Lima was to traverse "the famous Oroya
railroad—the most remarkable piece of railway engineering in
the world" (127), and do so, with a party of four Americans,
"thanks to the courtesy of the manager of the Peruvian Corpo-
ration, ... in a special train, [allowing them] to inspect at our
leisure the chief points of interest along the road, and to enjoy
the unrivalled scenery in a way that would otherwise have been
impossible" (127-28):

> I am familiar with all the engineering feats exhibited by the
> railroads of the United States and Europe, but I know of noth-
> ing that is comparable with the stupendous achievements that
> constantly startle the traveler as the train winds its way over
> the swinging bridges that span the awful chasms which are met
> at every turn of the Oroya railroad (130).

And what seemed to charm him even more was that the young
American bride, enroute with her mining engineer husband to
a small town in the Cordillera, was a graduate of Bryn Mawr
in language and literature—"alert, self-reliant, courageous and
cultured" (128) had but to mention Dante, and "with such a bond
between us, we became friends from that hour (131).

After such a stimulating interlude, the coastal steamer took them from Callao to Mollendo, through the islands whose treasure of *guano* had already been cultivated by the Incas, and which "for more than half a century have supplied the world with its richest and most prized fertilizer" (135). Another railroad, from Mollendo to Arequipa, captured Zahm's engineering sense, as he rode in "a richly-upholstered Pullman car [as] the guest of the *Ferro Carriles de Sur del Peru*" (139), to arrive, after six hours of spectacular grades and mountain switchbacks, in Arequipa, which he found to be "if not the most beautiful place in South America, as its admirers claim, ... certainly the most restful. ... I can truthfully say that I never found people anywhere whose generous hospitality and noble qualities of heart and mind made a deeper impression on me" (143). Listening one evening to "words sung from one of those sentimental *yaravies* of Mariano Melgar, a native of Arequipa, [I was reminded that] Arequipa has long been famous in Peru for its schools and scholars, for soldiers and statesmen" (144). In addition to the *yaravies*, whose "chief merit consists in the perfect accord of the music with the words" (146), Zahm was deeply impressed (in different ways) with the "astronomical observatory—a branch of the one at Harvard University—and the celebrated volcano of Misti, whose snow-covered summit [of 18,500 feet] is barely ten miles from the city's central plaza" (146).

Twelve hours by train took them to Lake Titicaca and a steamer to Guaqui, Bolivia, where Zahm sensed himself to be in "the famed cradle of the Inca race" before a vista which "impressed me, in some respects, more deeply than anything I had before seen in any part of the world: in one single view we had before us the Alpine marvels of Switzerland and Alaska, the broad glaciers and snow fields, sources of countless rivers, and massive, rocky pinnacles that seemed to touch the empyrean" (152-53). Yet these beauties of sight fulfilled a personal quest:

> I was now in the Thibet of the New World, and on the roof of the South American continent. I had attained another of the goals I had, at the outset of my journey, so eagerly desired to reach, and had, at the same time, realized another one of the fond dreams of my youth—a visit to the land of the Incas and the Aymaras (152).

Better still, given the role these travels were playing in Zahm's own life, "visit" is too trivial a word; what is coming together is his life's dedication to praising God by tracing the contours of wonder. And part of that intellectual quest for Zahm involves speculating on the results of more advanced "pisci-culture: ... if our Fish Commission [presumably, US] were to take the matter in hand, there is every reason to believe that Lake Titicaca would ... soon be made an invaluable source of food-supply for all the inhabitants of the tableland from La Paz to Cuzco" (155)!

Following "the legends and traditions connected with the origin and development of the great Inca empire" (155), as recorded "from the lips of a venerable Inca in Cuzco [by] Garcilaso de la Vega, the historian of the conquest of Peru" (156), Zahm wonders, as so many have, how "these two children of the Sun—Manco Capac and Mama Ocllo, his sister and subsequently his spouse and queen," would "be able, within a few short years, to regenerate a people that had fallen into the lowest depths of savagery and degradation" (156), and "lay the foundations of that vast empire which, under the Inca Yupanqui extended its conquests to the Maule in Chile, and under Huayna Capac, planted its victorious banners ... in the extended territory of Quito" (157). These reflections emanate from the journey across Lake Titicaca, where "thanks to the unwonted splendor of the moon and stars which permitted us to distinguish all the salient features of lake and Cordillera with the greatest ease, the nights I spent on Lake Titicaca were glorious beyond words to express" (164). Yet again, it was the people who captured his heart. Before boarding the train for La Paz, he was taken with "two or threescore of Aymara Indians [transferring] from the steamer to the wharf several hundred boxes of specie [bank notes] that were destined for the national treasury of Bolivia, [yet] the agent who was responsible for its safe delivery to La Paz did not exhibit the slightest apprehension regarding the security of the vast fortune entrusted to his care. ... I recalled the *True confession and protestation in the hour of death* made to Philip II by Marcio Serra de Legusiano, the last of the conquistadores: 'The Incas governed in such wise that in all the land neither a thief nor a vicious man, nor a bad, dishonest woman was known. [So] when they saw we had thieves amongst us, they despised us' " (166-67).

A stop at the island of Titicaca, once the site of a fabled temple to the sun, allowed a visit to the Marian shrine of Copacabana, where "during the time of pilgrimage [one could hear] the sacred canticles chanted in the Aymara language by a confused multitude of Indians and Spaniards from different and distant lands" (161), followed by a visit to "the small town of Juli, ... possessed of a printing press several years before the first one was introduced into the United States, [where] in 1612, the zealous and learned old missionary, Padre Ludovico Bertonio, published the great dictionary, of more than nine hundred pages, of the Aymara language" (162). Zahm's penchant for reconciling both indigenous and colonial perspectives in a stereoscopic vision leads him to recall some legendary connections between the two: in stories from Uruguay, where "the Indians of that country were acquainted with certain Christian tenets which they said they had, long ages before, received from Paz Tumé, the name they gave to St. Thomas, the Apostle, who had, they claimed evangelized their country," while a similar tradition in Paraguay, "declares one of the missionaries, 'caused the Indians to receive us with such demonstrations of joy and affection' " (170).

What stunned him next was the sudden view of La Paz, which seemed to be located at the bottom of the crater of an immense volcano. It was as if the traveler, standing on Inspiration Point, were unexpectedly to find a large and flourishing city in the valley of the Yosemite:

> Athens, as viewed from the Acropolis, Jerusalem as seen from the Mount of Olives, with its extraordinary setting of multicolored rocks, rivaling the bright hues of those that tinge the famous canon of the Yellowstone, will always remain among the cities of the world as absolutely *sui generis* (172-73).

Yet again, on arrival, it was the people, "of whom one-half are Indians, mostly Aymaras ... [who] seemed to be the most gentle and pacific people I ever met" (174). And the women's dress fascinated him, especially "the collection of skirts which every *chola* [half-breed] displays, particularly on feast days. In Bethlehem the young girls carry their dowry on their person in the form of silver and gold coins used as ornaments. In La Paz the chola's fortune is in her skirts, all of which she takes pride in wearing at the same time" (174). He then commented on the ubiquity of the coca leaf, from which cocaine is extracted, yet "whose wonderful physiological effects have been known by the Indians from time immemorial" (177). "The Spaniards ... discovered that the Indians' capacity for work was greatly influenced by the use of coca; that the leaf was not only a stimulant but a nutritious refreshment to them" (179). Indeed, "the amount of work done by an Indian in Bolivia or Peru is in proportion to the amount of coca he consumes" (180).

"Although La Paz is quite isolated from the rest of the world," Zahm found the elite with whom he was invited to dine, "not only refined and cultured, but highly educated and fully abreast with the intellectual movement of the world. Their sympathies were broad and they displayed an intelligent interest in literature and science, that would have done credit to the polished habitués of a Paris salon" (185). He is then invited by President Montes to make his way to the Amazon by one of the Bolivian rivers, and is sorely tempted to do so, but decided in the end to "adhere to my original plan and follow, as closely as possible, in the footsteps of the conquistadores" (188). But the president's invitation elicits yet another dream, already "conceived at the mouth of the Meta," as noted in his preceding volume, "through the heart of South America from Caracas to Buenos Aires," which now became a "fixed purpose to be, *Deo volente*, sooner or later realized" (188), and narrated in his *Through South America's Southland*.

After a guided tour, via special train, of the pre-Incan ruins of Tiahuanaco, replete with "megaliths rivaling anything found in Italy, Greece, or Asia Minor" (190), and presumably contemporaneous with the Egyptian pyramids, yet "everything about [them] is, as yet, veiled in impenetrable mystery, ... like the Mound Builders of our own country, or the rude sculptors of the colossal statues found on Easter Island" (196). Returning to Peru across Lake Titicaca, Zahm was again greeted with the offer of a private train to Cuzco, inviting two Yale University travelers to join him. At fourteen thousand feet above sea level the train crossed the "watershed between the closed basin of Lake Titicaca and the incomparably greater basin of the Amazon, [which is also] the dividing line between the Aymaras and the Quichuas" (202). At the then-terminus of the line, he and his party were invited to share the table of the person responsible for extending the railroad to Cuzco, who anticipated soon having three thousand Indians on his payroll, as "all able-bodied Indians in this part of the country are obliged by the government to work on the road from fifteen to thirty days" (205). But Zahm was brooding on the fact that he was on the scene where

> The ill-fated Tupac Amaru—the heroic Inca chief—in 1781 made his last effort to redress the grievances of his people, and it was near this place that he was betrayed into the hands of the Spaniards, who put him and his family and sympathizers to a cruel and ignominious death. The Inca's execution sounded the death knell of the hopes and aspirations of his countrymen, but his death was not in vain. ... New laws were enacted looking to the relief of the Indians, who had in many places been treated as serfs. ... But the iniquitous deed was committed and Tupac Amaru's betrayal and execution will forever remain a foul blot on the annals of the colonial government of Peru (208).

Yet Zahm and his company were enjoying superb hospitality arranged by telegraph by his Peruvian railways' host, enroute to Cuzco, as they journeyed by train, and then "in a comfortable surrey from Cincinnati" (209), to the "Rome of South America."

As the capital of the Incas was the goal of Pizarro, so it was for Zahm. Cuzco captured his acute historical sense as well as his fascination with feats of engineering. If Pizarro was captivated by its fabulous wealth—"a law was made that neither gold nor silver, that once entered Cuzco, should ever leave it again" (221), Zahm tried to reconstruct its Inca grandeur, only to integrate that into the subsequent Spanish hegemony. The sites of former palaces of the Incas have been transformed into cathedrals as well as into religious institutions to serve the people. If Spain carted away the treasure the Inca had amassed, the legacy of their presence will last in these works, and the faith of a people who, while their leaders had been toppled, were never themselves conquered, but injected an indelible local strain

into a resulting mestizo people. Zahm will leave a full description of the citadel of Sacsahuaman to others, who note its architectural perfection as a fortress, "a monument that, as an exhibition of engineering skill and daring, can rank with the pyramids
of Gaza" (227). From the southern flank of this massive fortress,
"at the foot of the sheer, precipitous mountain side as Cuzco, a
city that was once to the subjects of the Incas what Mecca is to
every true Mohammedan" (236). And if the "stately edifices of
the Incas are no more, there are, in their stead, some of the most
ornate and imposing structures of the New World, ... testifying
to the faith and the zeal of people who profess another faith and
owe allegiance to another ruler" (238). Indeed, "the largest and
most imposing structure of modern Cuzco is the Cathedral of
the Assumption. Ninety years in building, ... it occupies the
site of the palace of Viracocha, the eighth Inca" (218).

> Nowhere else, to my thinking, is there a city that presents
> a picture so charming and at the same time so imposing as
> Cuzco, seen from the heights of its ruined citadel. Not Sparta,
> as seen from a crumbling watchtower of long deserted Mis-
> tra; not Athens, as viewed from the beauteous temple of the
> Parthenon; not Rome, as it meets the view of the spectator
> on the summit of the Janiculum. ... Situated at the head of a
> salubrious and productive ... valley, and surrounded on all
> sides ... by the mighty barriers of the Cordilleras, it is a picture
> that for beauty of location and artistic setting cannot be dupli-
> cated, much less surpassed" (238).

Yet once again, the people are of greater import for Zahm,
especially "the language and literature of the Quichuas," a study
of whose language, he surmises, would "contribute much towards the solution of the long-discussed question regarding the
origin of the ancient Peruvians" (234). (Indeed, the recent work
of Sabine MacCormack has borne him out.) He will have far
more sobering reflections of the degree of "civilization" which
can properly be attributed to the Incas, and do so in the context
of yet another horrendous Spanish betrayal, but takes his leave

of Cuzco, the "City of the Sun," for Lima, the "city of the vice-roys." Planned by Pizarro to be the capital of a territory embracing "nearly all of South America, except Brazil, the viceroy of Peru was the ruler of a territory more extensive than any monarch in Europe" (243). Pizarro himself laid the plans for an extensive city, locating it "but two leagues from the ocean, where there was one of the best harbors of the coast. ... And as the city had to be 'in God and for God and in His name' [in Pizarro's own words], work was first begun on the church" (244-45). The current cathedral—"the most remarkable and imposing building in the city, ... occupies the site of the church built by Pizarro" and contains his remains in a side chapel. But why, Zahm inquires, is there no other monument to Pizarro in his city? His interlocutor attributes it to his "low birth: ... an ignorant swineherd, born out of wedlock, a soldier of fortune unable to write his own name, did not appeal to [the viceroys and grandees of Spain] as one worthy of special distinction" (249). Zahm wants to leave him more space, however: "notwithstanding all of his limitations, the fact remains that Francisco Pizarro was one of Spain's most distinguished sons, and one of Peru's greatest benefactors" (251).

However Zahm will assess his hand in "the judicial murder of Atahualpa" (249), which we shall soon consider, he clearly regards the colonial presence, with its transformation of the continent, on balance, as a benefaction, for he himself represents a product of the complementary colonization of the northern continent. A clear reason for Zahm's assessment is, of course, the evangelization of its peoples, for he counts as benefactions Santa Rosa, a Dominican sister of whom "the people of Lima never tire of sounding the praises" (252), and Santo Toribio, the second archbishop of Peru:

> Remarkable for his labors in behalf of the Indians, among
> whom his name is still held in benediction in all parts of Peru,

... [for] he left nothing undone to secure them in the rights that were theirs as children of a common Father ..., and much of the legislation that had its origin in the various councils and synods convened during his administration, had in view the welfare of these longsuffering victims of injustice and oppression (253).

Another clear benefaction lies in Lima's "schools and scholars, [among which] is found the oldest university of the New World, that of San Marcos, established in 1551. ... For generations, Lima was the center of learning and culture in South America, ... [so] that it was for a long time regarded as the Athens of South America. [Only after] Peru separated from Spain and wars and civil dissensions multiplied [was that title] claimed by the capital of Columbia," Bogota (254). He reminds his readers that the "terrible invasion from the south euphemistically called the War of the Pacific ... , unprovoked by Peru, but signalized on the part of the invader [Chile] by acts of barbaric atrocity," (258) laid waste to much of Lima's cultural heritage in 1881, yet with the help of other nations, "public-spirited Peruvians [managed] to recover enough books and manuscripts—about eight thousand all told–... to form the nucleus of a new library. ... It and the museum constitute two of the richest storehouses of books and specimens in the whole of South America" (259-60).

At this point Zahm recalls the over-riding motivation directing his writing to compatriots:

Nothing, indeed, impressed me more while looking over the rare books and manuscripts of Lima than the splendid opportunity here offered the man of letters and the historian, of working among materials that are practically unknown and yet of the greatest value. ... Who are more competent than the directors of the library and museum ... to annotate and edit these works? ... Who are so familiar with the manners and customs of the Quichua and Ayamara Indians, and so familiar with their language ... (260-61)?

He makes a host of specific recommendations, closing with a stirring call to American business to invest in this already enterprising world, which had so quickly recovered from "the horrors of the disastrous Chilean occupation but a few decades ago" (264), while confessing that "I have dwelt somewhat at length on the library and scientific features of Lima because they appealed to me more than any other" (262). Ever inquirer and teacher, Zahm intends to illuminate his own world, so much of which was content with what they had accomplished, never dreaming of larger vistas.

"The time had at last arrived for starting on my long journey across the Andes and down the Amazon" (265). Zahm is again presented with alternatives, as he had been in Bolivia by President Montes; this time by President Pardo, who offered to put at his disposition one of two new launches for the river journey, projecting a route across the Cordilleras which would require but "a few days travel on horseback between Oroya, the terminus of the railroad [which Zahm had already traversed], and Puerto Bermudes, the head of navigation on the Pichis river [and thence] to Iquitos on the Amazon" (265). Zahm was forced to reconsider, yet "the fact that the journey by way of Cajamarca would be much longer and more arduous, far from deterring me from undertaking it, was rather an additional incentive … I had come to study the people of the country rather than dark and uninhabited forests" (266). And his resolve was confirmed by "the former prefect of Chachapoyas: 'if one wishes to get off the beaten track, and see the Peru of colonial times, where the manners and customs of the people are still as they were in the time of the viceroys, one should by all means visit the country between Cajamarca and Moyobamba'" (266-67)—no contest for Zahm! So the journey was set: from the port of Lima on the Pacific to Trujillo, upriver and thence over the Cordilleras—the ancient conquistador route. Moreover, on his last day in Lima, he encountered one of his newfound friends on the street, who announced that "his Excellency, the President, … has given instructions that you be furnished with a military escort from Trujillo to Iquitos, ... not because of any danger ..., but that you may be able to enjoy your trip free from all unnecessary cares and labor" (268)! The environs of Trujillo brought him to the ruins of "the largest and most populous pre-Columbian city in the New World—*el garn Chimu*, ... comparable to Memphis in extent and to the ruins of Nineveh and Babylon in the number and magnitude of its temples and palaces. The last rule of this rich and powerful race ... was named Chimu Canchu—the great Chimu, [and] his dominions extended a distance of nearly six hundred miles [before] he himself was forced to become a vassal of the victorious Inca Pachacutes, 'the Reformer of the World.' ... What most excites the wonder of the visitor is the beauty and delicacy of the arabesque and stucco-work; ... they remind one of similar decorations in the Alhambra and in the Alcazar of Seville" (272-73). The spontaneous query: "Who were the mysterious people who left behind them such imposing ruins and such evidence of material and industrial progress" (287)? elicits eight pages of speculation on the origins of the indigenous people in the western hemisphere, with no obvious resolution.

The next step "in the footsteps of Pizarro and Orsua" to Cajamarca was "away from steamer and railroads" (296) yet in the company of "a gallant young lieutenant and a private" (295) supplied by the prefect of Trujillo. "After traveling about four hours, we found ourselves on an elevated projection from the Cordillera, when, lo! there suddenly appeared before us one of the most perfect and brilliant rainbows I have ever witnessed" (297), which Zahm follows with ethnographic reflections of the ambivalent meanings of rainbows to the Aymras, the Quichua, and the Incas. Then, turning

> towards the west to take a last view of the Pacific, ... never shall
> I forget the gorgeous picture that burst upon my ravished vision

at that moment. If "heaven's ethereal bow," spanning with its
bright arch the glittering peaks of the Cordilleras had before
been a source of ineffable delight, the glory of the setting sun,
now slowly sinking beneath the ocean wave, that trembled as
it glowed, was like a vision of the enraptured Dante as he journeyed through Paradise (298).

At a certain point, when Zahm had outdistanced his escort, to
the latter's amazement, he reflects on what his "previous experience in the Cordillera had taught" him: "that the race is
not always to the physically strong, nor to the possessors of
health and youth." He attributes his greater endurance, despite
the fact he "was nearly old enough to be the young officer's
grandfather," to the fact that "I ate less food than my companions and ate only what I was able to digest" (310). If one reflects how famished they all must have been, this remark offers
acute testimony to Zahm's inherent discipline. He recalls that
"Pizarro [as Xeres recounts] 'arrived at this town of Cajamarca
on Friday, the 15th of November, 1532, at the hour of Vespers.'
With his arrival was sounded the death knell of the great Inca
empire, and the day following Atahualpa was his prisoner. With
a handful of men—less than two hundred—the dauntless conquistador had, in a few hours, overcome and dispersed an army
of from thirty to fifty thousand trained Inca veterans, and the
untutored swineherd of Estremadura was the uncrowned King
of Peru. It was just three hundred and seventy years later, to the
very hour, that, following in the footsteps of the conquistadores,
I entered the city so famous in the story of the Children of the
Sun" (313).

The ugly events which ensued will severely temper "the
splendors of valley and mountain which make of this old Inca
metropolis one of the most charming pictures to be seen anywhere in the entire region of the Cordilleras" (313). Yet the
prospect of Cajamarca elicits a favorable comparison with

Cuzco, "walled in by snowcapped mountains [in a] splendid valley ... about a hundred square miles in extent, partitioned off into well-kept gardens teeming with fruit trees." Characteristically, Zahm adds: "But attractive as is the city itself, its inhabitants, I hasten to say, are more attractive. And what shall I say of their hospitality" (314-15)? He then proceeds to critically deconstruct early fascination with the road-building skills of the Incas, which he avers (after eight pages comparing records with his experience) that "descriptions of the Inca roads must ... be classified among those exaggerations which so often characterize the accounts of battles between the Incas and the conquistadores in which the chronicler is made to exalt the glories of Spanish valor by recording events that did not and could not have occurred" (325). His party then visits the Franciscan friars and the Daughters of Charity of Vincent de Paul, where all are astounded at the intrepid missionary zeal of each of these groups. Then "adjoining the convent of the Sisters of Charity [is] what is represented to be the building in which was collected the famous ransom of Atahualpa" (334). Captured by the far smaller Spanish force, he was first required to fill the building concerned with gold and silver, a ransom calculated to be "more than $17,000,000 our money [in 1907]" (335), and then summarily "garroted under conditions which leave a stain on the memory of all who were in any wise responsible for his execution–... characterized by Las Casas as ... 'a long and lamentable and dismal story and pitiful to relate' " (335). But Zahm cannot leave it there; he assesses (for five pages) whether, given the context of war and the extreme circumstances of the Spanish force, it was as dastardly a deed as often imagined. Which then leads him into a closer scrutiny of "the social and political status of the Incas, [to meet] the oft-repeated objection of those who have impugned the Spanish right of conquest in Peru" (338).

The context is an anonymous "objector" who contrasts the legitimacy of Spanish (for both objector and Zahm, one might read "Catholic") conquest negatively with European conquest to the north, by insisting that "the Children of the Sun were a civilized people and as such should have been left in undisturbed possession of their lands and liberty" (339). Which forces Zahm "to define the much-abused words 'barbarous' and 'civilized'" (340)—a thicket so far deftly avoided, and one which will force him to diverge from his hero, Las Casas, whose *Apologetica Historia* had contended that "the Indians were inferior to none of the peoples of the Old World, and superior to many of them" (339). He then offers some diverse criteria for being civilized, such as a phonetic alphabet, and "a knowledge of smelting iron ore," concluding from the absence of these, that "the cultural status of the Incas was that of the middle period of barbarism," somewhere "between that of a Moqui pueblo and that of ancient Troy" (341). The import of this judgment that "the Incas were not civilized in the proper acceptation of the term, was that here could be no progress, because the development of the personal will of the subject was impossible. ... [T]his is evidenced by the fact that the empire collapsed as soon as Atahualpa fell into the hands of the Spaniards, and without the bloodshed or carnage that usually attends the conquest of a nation as extensive as that of the Children of the Sun" (342). In the end, it was the utter bondage of the subject to the will of the sovereign which would determine, for Zahm, that "their government ... was radically defective, and social and economic progress, as we understand it, was impossible," leading him to conclude that the conquest of the Incas was justified, if ever conquest was justified" (243-44). He then dismisses tales of indiscriminate Spanish slaughter as so much *macho bravadaccio*, but also insists that the conquerors had

> brought the aborigines what the old Romans, in the words of
> Virgil, called *moeresqaue viris et moenia*—religious culture

and material civilization. They made Christians of idolaters, freemen of slaves, and converted savage and warlike tribes into the most peaceful people in the world (344).

The rest of the journey may appear somewhat anti-climactic to us, yet represents for Zahm the realization of his aspiration to utilize the massive Amazon river system to cross the entire South American continent. Once again, his experience of the indigenous peoples belies the sober warnings he had received from the Lima elite, though it must be said that he often met the native people in the context of "the governor's house, where we were expected and where we were accorded the most courteous reception and the most generous hospitality" (349). Yet the climb could be as daunting as the sudden view of the Marañon—"the name give to the upper Amazon"– was overwhelming and "in many respects, more imposing [than] the Grand Cañon of the Colorado" (357-58)—an asseveration which manifestly shocked Theodore Roosevelt: "It does not seem to me that anything on this earth can be grander than the Grand Canyon" (xii)! Their descent into it was so precipitous that "our feelings were, then, I think akin to Dante's while groping his way down the treacherous and dismal slopes of Malbolge" (359). The arduous riding—"twenty hours in the saddle"—required to follow the Marañon through its valley brought the party to "surroundings [that] were romantic in the extreme and kindled the imagination as would entrance into the penetralia of fairyland," so imagine their fascination upon hearing the *puena*, "the flute of the Quichua Indian [that] is rarely heard, except in the sierras" (363). Indeed, "the ever-changing landscapes were such as would have delighted the artistic souls of Titian, and Correggio and Tintoret, while the marvelous effects of light and shade, and the interminable play of sunshine, were of a kind to enrapture a Cuyp, a Rubens, a Claude" (366). Yet the harrowing descent of La Ventana displayed, once again, how "only experienced mountain mules would attempt to make such a rough precipitous descent" (379), though, once negotiated, Zahm found himself in "a Peruvian paradise" where, at each stage in their journey, they were entertained by the respective prefects of the place, and Zahm himself notes (from his diary) that "the farther one gets into the heart of Peru, the kinder and more courteous the people become" (392).

The remainder of the land journey passed through nearly impenetrable forests, where they "were all obliged to journey afoot" (402), and required fording rivers where "sometimes the water rose to the arm-pits of my valiant *cargueros*," that is, those "who were to carry me in a portable chair in case of necessity or fatigue" (403). Drenched one night in a downpour as he lay beneath "an opening in the thatched roof [of a lean-to]," suddenly the "sky cleared and the stars appeared with unwonted splendor" (405): an experience which called to Zahm's mind Dante's letter to a Florentine friend, accepting exile over dishonor to remark: "May I not gaze on the mirror of sun and stars wherever I may be" (406)? Denigrating common descriptions of the dangers lurking in such a forest, he remarks: "what has been asserted of the variety of flowers in tropical forests may likewise be affirmed of the scarcity of larger forms of animal life" (410):

> What most impresses the traveler, when he enters for the first time the primeval forests of the equatorial regions, is the immensity, the gloom, the silence and the solitude of his environment (414).

Reflecting on the complex synergy of such an environment, Zahm reveals the roots of his scientific vocation:

> This knowledge, this exceedingly great reward, Nature reserves for those only who visit her in chosen penetralia, and who know how to hold communion with her while she unfolds the mysteries which render her to all but her votaries so enigmatic—so inscrutable (421).

As they reached Balsapuerto, and the river became navigable, so "our baggage was transferred without delay to the gov-

ernor's canoe—a large but graceful *piragua* made from a single
log of cedar" (423). Along the way, they experienced the kindness and hospitality of Indian villages, to the point where "the
days I spent on the Paranapura are among the most cherished
recollections of the tropics" (433). On arrival at Yurimagua,
they were feted by the sub-prefect, whose party toasted President Roosevelt, and ended expressing "the hope that we would
all meet at Panama in 1915 for the opening of the great canal"
(437). Yet Zahm, it seems, was as at home in Indian villages as
in such semi-official banquets. Yet most impressive of all, to
Zahm's acute sense of history, culture, and religious sensibility, was the "story of the evangelization of the Indian along the
Huallage and the Amazon," as the distance from Quito

> involved an arduous journey of two months afoot and by ca-
> noe, through trackless forests and often the territory of inhos-
> pitable and hostile tribes. And when the evangelists arrived at
> their destination, there was the almost insuperable difficulty
> of learning the languages of the wild men of the woods. ...
> [E]very tribe, however small, had its own language, which, we
> are assured, was as different from that of the adjoining tribe as
> German is from Hebrew. This meant that every missionary, if
> his field of labor was at all extensive, had to be a polyglot (440-
> 41).... And what is more, in teaching the Indians craftsmanship
> and husbandry and stock raising, they prepared him not only to
> live as a civilized being, but also to earn his own living without
> any further assistance from the white man. The result was that
> Spanish America was but little vexed with that terrible Indian
> problem which, in our northern continent, led not to one but
> three centuries of dishonor. In a few decades the followers of
> the Poverello of Assisi, of Dominic and Ignatius Loyola, were
> able to effect what our great statesman, Henry Clay, declared
> to be impossible—the civilization of the red man (445).

Zahm locates the difference in "recommendations from ...
bishop, sovereign and Pope, [that]

> recognized them as children of a common father and acted to-
> wards them with a consideration that was in marked contrast
> with the relentless cruelty and injustice which ever character-

ized our dealings with them in our land of boasted freedom and equality (445-46).

Ever the Catholic apologist as well as critical inquirer, Zahm's experience reinforces his faith to supply the perspective from which to criticize the country he loves and represents. Yet he must also sadly admit that the laicizing governments of South America had conspired to so undermine these flourishing endeavors that

> everywhere along the Paranapura, the Huallage and the Amazon, there exists the same evidences of ruin and abandonment as I had observed along the great waterways of Venezuela and Colombia. ... Say what we will against the Spaniards, the Indian of the montaña fared better under Spain than he has ever fared under any of the South American republics (452-53).

The rest of the journey affords ever more fascinating vistas as the Amazon grows to the sea, and he departs Para for New York. On the voyage home, he testifies to the personal import of these extended journeys:

> As the hazy coastline of Amazonia receded from view, ... I experienced a sense of longing I had never known before. Longing, however, does not wholly express the feeling that then took possession of me, for it was more than longing. It was what the Portuguese call *saudade*, what the Germans denominate *Sehnsucht*, words that have no equivalent in English, and which signify not only intense yearning and regret, but also sweet remembrance.

One may speculate that however far Zahm had wandered before this, there was a pull "back home," whereas he now came to realize that "home" would have to be where he found himself: "the *Wanderlust*, which was strong when I left New York nearly a twelvemonth before, far from being abated, was stronger and more insistent than ever" (514). This desire will find expression in a third voyage, this final one being with Theodore Roosevelt and narrated in *Through South America's Southland (New York: Appleton, 1916), yet the import of the *Sehnsucht* which he identifies seems to envisage further intellectual journeys as well. He takes pains to remind his readers how his endurance belied the insistent fears of his pusillanimous friends, who had tried to discourage such a venture well beforehand. Yet the personal returns are ever greater:

> I left New York an invalid, and presumably requiring the convenience and comforts of home. But no sooner did I begin to rough it in the wilds of the equatorial regions than health and strength returned apace, and it was not long before every vestige of illness had entirely disappeared (516).

He would no longer need a physician to tell him what shape his life must take: intellectual and imaginative engagement without collateral duties, which, we shall see, will creatively occupy the rest of his life.[61]

The final pages of the narrative exhort Americans to follow this path to South America, especially to take advantage of the opportunities for investment then monopolized by Europeans, with the singular exception of W. R. Grace & Co. Catching "the first glimpse of the Statue of Liberty in New York harbor," he reflects that "it was a year, almost to the hour, from the time I left home" (526). He then sums up the results of this pilgrimage for himself as well as for others, voicing amazement at what had been accomplished in him:

> I had visited all the land, and more, which I purposed seeing on setting out on my long journey through the untraveled and little known regions bordering the equator. And without haste and without difficulty, I had been able to make it in the time I had allowed myself before departure. I left home as an invalid seeking health and recreation. I found both, and returned to my own with health restored and with a greater capacity for work than I had known for years. Naturally I was gratified, … But gratified also that I had thereby proved that one may

---

[61]As Weber notes (182-3), Zahm is not entirely candid here; he had confided to his brother Albert "that he had suffered pleurisy for four months and a slight lung hemorrhage which seemed serious at first." He sought rest and a homeopathic cure in New Jersey before returning to Washington to work on the narratives of these two journeys.

traverse even the wildest and least populated parts of South America with comparative ease and comfort (526).

Yet despite the *Sehnsucht*, "I was never so delighted to return to the land of my birth as on this occasion, ...[which] made me realize, as never before how pleasurable is the recurrent change of seasons in our northern latitudes as compared with the uniformity of climate in the tropics. ... The leafless trees and snow-covered ground possessed for me unwonted beauty. ... And as I stood forward on the upper deck, while we were steaming into the great city's harbor, where loving hearts were awaiting me, I was reminded of Petrarch's return home, after a long absence, and of his noble apostrophe to his country:

> Hail land beloved of God, O holiest, hail!
> To good men safe, a menace to the proud; ...
> To thee at last I yearningly return,
> Still, thy citizen. ...
> Thee, fatherland, I own and greet with joy,
> Hail, beauteous Mother, pride of nations, hail! (526-27).

Through South America's Southland (1916)

The third installment of a trilogy which Zahm "had in contemplation when, nearly a decade ago, I began the first volume of the series bearing the general title "Following the Conquistadores" (vii), consummates his enforced recuperation in grand style, with "a large company of nearly two score persons and which has since become known as "The Roosevelt Scientific Expedition in South America" (vii-viii). With characteristic attention to detail as well as to personal context, Zahm outlines the sinuous route to executing his dream of "enlist[ing] Colonel Roosevelt's interest in the wilds of South America" (vii) for a proper scientific expedition which "I felt [would also harness Roosevelt's] boundless energy and prestige [to] do a certain much-needed missionary work there: that he could do more than all the diplomats of a century to dissipate the prejudices our southern neighbors have long entertained respecting the United States, and all the unfounded fears which have caused them so long to regard our ends and aims in the southern hemisphere with unfriendliness and distrust" (5). The "I felt" in this brief positioning statement takes us back "nearly a decade" to his poignant discernment in the New York hotel which opened the initial volume where his exhilaration at the new life opening before him was laced with trepidation. He needed the *divertissement*, which his body-psyche craved and doctors ordered, in the wake of the sudden derailment of a trajectory so intimately linked with the fledgling university to which he had given his life, within the religious congregation which had nurtured those dreams and ambitions. The two journeys just canvassed had accomplished that beautifully, but hardly quenched his thirst for travel, as he confesses here: "I had scarcely crossed the threshold of my home in the United States when I felt a longing to return to the land where I had spent the most delightful period of my life" (2). Yet that inner imperative had now been transformed into an ongoing project, with two books completed, yet Zahm's travels had already attracted the attention of president Roosevelt, so he had felt free to "call on him at the White House ... and propose to him that, when free from presidential cares, he and I should go up the Paraguay into the interior South America" (4).

As it turned out, a prior African trip rendered it "not possible ... for Colonel Roosevelt and myself to go to South America at the time indicated, [but] the project was never abandoned. It was merely deferred" (7). Not to be daunted, Zahm had already resolved on a joint venture, and tells us why:

> During my first visit to South America, I was, for the greater part of the time, virtually alone, having no companions but my escort, or such travelers as I happened to fall in with during the course of my journey. This was a great drawback, for it is

impossible fully to enjoy the magnificent scenery of the tropics, or avail oneself of the rare opportunities for studying Nature in her most glorious manifestations, unless one has with
him one or more congenial companions, who have an intelligent interest in the fauna and flora, a well as in the people with
whom one is brought into daily contact. I resolved, therefore,
if I should ever go to the interior of South America again, that I
should not be without at least one companion who had not only
an interest in the fascinating animal and plant life of the regions to be visited, but who had also made nature study a pre-
dominant part of his life-work (3-4).

Zahm's experience confirmed Aristotle on friendship: without others we cannot fully enjoy what we undertake. So, "as
the possibility of Colonel Roosevelt's going to South America
appeared to become daily more and more remote, I resolved
to delay no longer an undertaking on which my heart had so
long been set, [so] I began to cast about for someone—preferably a naturalist—to accompany me." (8). He sought advice
from "Frank Chapman, the distinguished bird-curator of the
New York Museum of Natural History," only to be folded into a
luncheon the following day (1913) with "quite a number of men
of science," anticipating the presence of Roosevelt, who greeted
Zahm effusively, informing him that he was "at last, ... able
to take that long-talked-of trip to South America" (9). In the
event, "instead of ... devoting most of our time to a study of
the geographic features of the various countries which we purposed visiting, the Colonel's sphere of action was, in a quite
unexpected manner, immensely enlarged, and he was given
an opportunity of meeting and becoming acquainted with the
leading representatives of all the countries through which he
passed, from Patagonia to the Equator" (10)—as Zahm and others would be as well. For scientist though he was, enlarging the
original perspectives proved to befit Zahm's desire as well, for
(as he reminds us) "my interests have been rather in the history,

the poetry, and the romance of the places visited; [so] I have had little to say of the material, political, or economic conditions of the countries through which we journeyed" (viii). Yet it was he who assembled the coterie of explorers to make up the expedition, being sure to attend as much to personal qualities as to diversity in expertise, as his careful description of the members of the group reveals.

And as a final testimony of his heart's investment, he dedicates this work (in Latin) "as a testimony of friendship, in Holy Cross, to a noble pair of brothers: the reverend and beloved James Aloysius Burns and John William Cavanaugh," who had imbibed his vision for Notre Dame while studying in Washington during those crucial years following the reversals of 1906, and who would become, respectively, briefly president of Notre Dame, followed by Provincial of the Indiana Province of Holy Cross; and President of the University. Intensive explorations and engagement with stimulating scientific partners had hardly obscured his attachment to the religious community and the university which remained his touchstone and nourishment. Yet he flourished as well in the midst of inquiring minds and hearts like those whom he had assembled for this journey, which began in October 1913. Indeed, he remarks, "They had scarcely been located in their staterooms when they were to be seen engrossed with their books and scientific apparatus preparatory to the more active work they were to do on their arrival at the scene of their future labors." Moreover, "nothing was more remarkable than the character and variety of the volumes which an examination of our book kits disclosed. There was something for every taste, from the latest Spanish or Portuguese novel to the "Chanson de Roland," and the "Nibelungenlied," from the "Divina Commedia," and the "Os Lusiados" of Camoens to the "Autobiography of St. Teresa" and the

"'Soliloquia' of St. Augustine" (16). Zahm was especially taken with Roosevelt's "taste for literature [which he found to be] absolutely omnivorous." Moreover, "when we came to communicate the results of our reading or to exchange views on any particular subject of general interest to the members of the expedition, Colonel Roosevelt always took a prominent part in the discussion which followed. It was then that we were often amazed by his broad and exact knowledge not only of the fauna of the countries we were about to visit, but also of the political and social histories of their peoples as well" (19). He was in his element as a natural inquirer, yet attuned as well to the fact that his presence with the former president, as a Catholic priest, had far-reaching implications in South America, as will become evident in one venue after another, whether official or more informal.

Yet unless I am misled, the ensuing narrative lacks the verve of discovery attending his earlier voyages. Again, if my impressions are correct, that would be a natural consequence of the fact that this expedition was less for him a "voyage of discovery" than the completion of an ardent and longstanding desire, as well as a personal ambition, to become accepted in an eminent circle of inquirers in a way that a far less eminent circle of confreres had failed to accept him. He could keep his nascent vision for Notre Dame alive by participating in such groups, where it would also be vindicated by distinguished public figures like Teddy Roosevelt, only to share that satisfaction with younger colleagues who might be able to carry out what he had not been able to accomplish in Indiana. Not that this need to have been all that conscious, but there is a tone of *déjà vu* in this narrative which may betoken other things at work in the narrator. That having been said, his descriptions of the marvels of nature are no less stirring, nor are his reflections on the ecclesial history any less poignant—especially when it comes to the

Jesuit "Reductiones" and their untimely demise in a collusion of ecclesiastical with royal politics in suppressing the Society of Jesus. But first a taste of his descriptive powers, this time in crossing the Cordillera from Argentina to Chile. From his perch "on the front of the locomotive, during the greater part of the passage across the Andes" (269), he tells his readers how to experience what he did:

> While standing the summit of Santa Lucia ... near the hour of sunset, ... the view of the vast mountain range is incomparable. Then the scintillating snow-clad peaks rise heavenwards like pinnacles of burnished gold. But soon the gold shades into ruby and topaz, chrysoprase and sapphire. At the same time the foothills, with their bare masses of gray granite, black basalt and reddish-brown porphyry, with all the sculpuresque beauty and sublimity of mountain structures, have cast over them, by an unseen hand, delicate veils of gauze and gossamer with ever-changing tints of mauve and lilac, emerald-green and Tyrian purple. The tutelary genii of Mercedario, Aconcagua and Tupungato seemed bent on making me forget all past mountain glories from those of Misti and Sorsata, Cotopaxi and Chimborazo to those of the cloud-piercing peaks of arctic Alaska and of the coral-girt islands of the Southern Sea (286).

Returning to less glorious human affairs, Zahm contextualizes his extended treatment of the Jesuit "Reductiones" in a way reminiscent of one of his goals in these travels: to enlighten North Americans about the Catholic Church's attempts to avoid utter complicity in Spanish and Portuguese colonialism:

> The outcome of the desire of the missionaries, whose efforts were cordially seconded by Philip III, to liberate the Indians from the cruelties of the *mita* and *encomienda* systems; to protect them from the iniquities of slave-hunting Mamelukes, and thus to prepare them for a cheerful and intelligent reception of the truths of the Gospel. They were translations into action of the bull of Pope Paul III, who declared that the Indians were human beings with immortal souls and that they should be treated as such (394).

He then lists official Spanish documents as well as various religious communities, detailing attempts to mitigate colonial exploitation of the indigenous peoples, with an extended encomium to the work of the Salesians, who were busy realizing

> the dream of their founder Don Bosco, [and who] by infinite patience, tact, labor and devotion, had achieved what anthropologists and men of science had positively asserted to be impossible—the civilizing and Christianizing of the Fuegians— savages who, as Darwin declared, it was hard to believe were "fellow-creatures and inhabitants of the same world" with ourselves. … For generations, no Indians in Brazil had committed greater depredations, or inspired more terror among the neighboring whites than the Coroados and Bororos of Matto Grosso. [Yet] in a short time the people of Matto Grosso were astonished to learn that the dread savages had been converted into useful and law-abiding members of the community (432-33).

Again focusing on human ecology, he has trenchant comments comparing the social milieus of Chile and Argentina:

> In theory they are democracies; in reality they are oligarchies. A few hundred families descended from the Conquistadores and from the heroes of foreign birth who achieved distinction in the war of independence are the rulers of the republic as well as the owners of the greater part of the land. The great world of employees, functionaries and small tradespeople are little more than dependents, or clients in the old roman sense of the word. As to the poor *rotos*, who live in miserable *conventillos*, they are no higher in the social scale than the Mexican peon and have no more than Mexico's peasant class to say in the administration of the affairs of government. The absence of a third estate is a great drawback (298).

While these remarks reflect a conventional North American optic, they are also prescient in the way many of his observations have been, setting the stage for the movement of liberation theology of the era succeeding Vatican II. Otherwise, Zahm is quite bullish about development, and especially about the United States' proper share in what was nearly monopolized by Europe at that time.

The narrative ends rather abruptly: "It was in Utiarity [where he had made intimate contact with some Indian families during their extended stay], which will ever remain associated with some of the pleasantest memories of the wilderness, that my journeying into the jungle had its northern terminus" (501). He had already "navigated the Amazon from the Andes to the Atlantic," as related in the second volume, and reminds us that his "chief interest was only in traversing those regions which had, in the long ago, felt the footsteps of the Conquistadores." But since the others were "all eager to contemplate the glories of the historic waterway which so long bore the name of its illustrious discoverer, Francisco de Orellana. ... [So] accompanied by Sigg—my *Fidus Achates*—who was always ready for everything and did everything well, I returned to Tapirapuhan, ... thence we proceeded, by the Paraguay and the Parana, through the fertile plains of La Plato to Montevideo." Whence Sigg departed for "Asuncion to cast in his lot with some friends of the struggling Republic of Paraguay" (502), while Zahm "boarded a steamer for Cape Verde and the Canary Islands—still following the commanding figures of the conquest—whence I sailed to Spain, a country which I had frequently visited with ever-increasing interest–... the motherland of those illustrious men in whose footsteps I had been treading for more than a third of a century." There is a quality of finality to this ending: having traced the footsteps of the conquistadores, and intently oriented North Americans to the rich culture of southern Europe, as transplanted in South America, he needs to return to their origins as well.

An Independent Postlude to this Final Journey
Two books have recently appeared which cast light on Zahm's participation in this final journey, and make his bland

comments about returning to Tapirapuhan less than candid: since "the others were 'all eager to contemplate the glories of the historic waterway'" which he had already seen. They are Joseph Ornig's *My Last Chance to be a Boy: Theodore Roosevelt's South American Expedition of 1913-1914* (Baton Rouge: Louisiana State University Press, 1994), and Candice Millard's *River of Doubt: Theodore Roosevelt's Darkest Journey* (New York: Doubleday, 2005). Ornig is identified as a Chicago businessman who spent twenty years researching the life of Roosevelt; Candice Millard is a former writer and editor for *National Geographic*. The first work is replete with references to the research carried out; the second begins with five pages of acknowledgments, yet never mentions Ornig's book, though it must be indebted to his work. The central fact is that Zahm's leaving the journey was not his choice but rather a group decision which Roosevelt had to execute, doing so with the explicit corroboration of the others in a signed memo which Millard reproduces: "Every member of the expedition has told me that in his opinion it is essential to the success and well being of the expedition that Father Zahm should at once leave it and return to the settled country" (Millard 107; Ornig 112 [KRP 58 = Kermit Roosevelt Papers, Library of Congress]). Candice Millard interprets this action by a letter from Teddy's son, Kermit Roosevelt, to his wife Belle Millard: "Father Zahm is being sent back from here. He showed him[self] so completely incompetent & selfish that he got on everyone's nerves, and then he did a couple of things that made it easy to send him back ...

fortunately father has managed it without any real bad feeling" (Ornig, 112 [KRP 55]). The "couple of things" Kermit referred to are identified by Millard as Zahm's request that he be carried "in a divan chair on the shoulders of four strong Indians," which leads Millard to aver: "Roosevelt and Rondon must have been rendered speechless by the image of Father Zahm riding across the highlands like Montezuma on the bent backs of his subjects" (105). Yet given the fact that leaving the expedition was not Zahm's choice, can we ascertain why it was unanimously decided that he must depart?

If we rely on Ornig, as we shall see, that will be difficult to answer; whereas Millard makes it easy. He was to be judged as Kermit Roosevelt had "from the moment he met him in Bahia: ... unfit for this type of expedition," though Kermit would concede that "Zahm had no real harm in him; ... he's just a very commonplace little fool" (103). Kermit's summary judgment would doubtless sound jejune, to put it mildly, to one who knew Zahm's prodigious capacity for work and scholarship, yet Millard accepts it without demurral. Why? There are repeated clues that she finds Zahm so enigmatic as to defy measured judgment. Her initial portrait (26-29) begins: "a slight, balding man with heavily lidded blue eyes and cup-handle ears, Father Zahm was a strange pastiche of seemingly incongruent interests and passions, which had placed him at the crossroads of religion, science, and politics" (26). Millard can only find his courageous border-crossing to be incongruous, so one might well expect that she will find it "paradoxical" that he "was also a proponent of evolution." Why so? Because Darwin's theory was "derided by most Catholics as, in the words of one journalist, 'the philosophy of mud and the gospel of dirt' " (26). So Zahm's discriminating and astute defense of the theory becomes, in her breathless assessment, one of "Father Zahm's contradictions." Another was that he was "hardly an ascetic [but] had a deep appreciation and affinity for the good things in life," which she cannot square with his admittedly being "a devoted priest and a serious scholar." Proof: "he had become a member of the exclusive Cosmos Club, a luxurious club that the American writer Wallace Stegner would call 'the closest thing to a social headquarters for Washington's intellectual elite.' " But if he had become an integral part of "Washington's intellectual elite," would it not be quite natural that he belong to the Cosmos Club? But Millard will not entertain such a benign reading: "he was also a skilled self-promoter, ... revel[ing] in his friendship with Roosevelt" (27). With what, exactly, is this lifestyle incongruous? And with what is his astute defense of evolution in contradiction? Nothing more than Millard's stereotype of a Catholic priest, it seems, for there is little of Zahm himself in these tendentious descriptions. Finally, is "self-promotion" always unseemly?

For a bevy of reasons of which she may be quite unconscious, the author cannot abide Zahm nor, it seems, like Kermit Roosevelt, Zahm's very presence: "Kermit certainly would not miss the elderly priest," she writes, yet everything about Zahm's stamina belies the easy descriptor "elderly." The imposing presence of an intrepid Indio explorer, Colonel Candido Rondon, offers the author a way of epitomizing the conflict between Zahm the priest and Rondon, the "positivist." She finds the Brazilian's determination and assertiveness attractive, despite the documented loss of life among those accompanying him in earlier "infamous ... Rondon Commission's expeditions into the Brazilian interior. At best, they were long, exhausting, lonely treks through unfamiliar territory. At worst, they were terrifying forced marches that subjected the soldiers to disease, starvation, and relentless Indian attacks" (77). Yet she notes a deep affinity between Rondon and Roosevelt, for "Rondon represented the kind of man he had championed and admired throughout his life, a disciplined officer who thrived on physical challenges and hardship, and accomplished great feats through force of will" (80). In this respect, Rondon provides a ready foil for John Zahm, as she notes how "any prospect that Father Zahm might have had for reviving his hopes of glory with his new itinerary was ... undone by his worsening relations with the rest of the men, and his concern for his own comfort" (104). So according to Candice Millard, Rondon is the hero of the expedition, becoming Teddy Roosevelt's "boon companion," while Zahm finishes disgraced in everyone's eyes, including his patron, the one who had been so happy to see him at the Museum of Natural History, and entrusted the planning to him. Yet as Ornig notes, "Rondon's arrival brought an end to Father Zahm's influence on the course of the expedition. Roosevelt now looked to his Brazilian fellow colonel to manage the day-to-day operation" (79). So a sharp sibling rivalry could easily have ensued, with rather predictable results, without requiring a scapegoat to account for what would result. So it should be clear that I prefer Ornig's account to Millard's, and that on ground of sober historical rather than personal preference.

Chapter Five

WOMEN IN SCIENCE

[J.H. Mozans] (1913) and *Great Inspirers* (1917)[62]

PERHAPS AS A COUNTERPOINT to his endemic *wanderlust*, at the time of the expedition "through South America's southland," Zahm had already become involved in composing another sort of book, an encomium to women which took the form of cataloguing their accomplishments in science from the earliest centuries of recorded history; and soon after, a companion volume which celebrates two signal instances of feminine contributions to the creativity of men: to wit, Saint Jerome and Dante. The first study, *Women in Science* (1913), appears under the pseudonym of J.H. Mozans, as did the travelogues through South America, while the author of *Great Inspirers* (1917) is listed as "The Reverend J.A. Zahm, C.S.C., Ph.D.," with a facing page identifying other books by "J. A. Zahm (H. J. Mozans)," so unveiling the pseudonym, perhaps as no longer needed or fitting. Each of these works displays Zahm, the masterful publicist, with his enthusiasm for the subject suffusing every page, yet ever careful to document whatever claims he makes.

---

[62]*Women in Science* (New York: D. Appleton, 1913), reprinted Boston: MIT Press, 1974; University of Notre Dame Press, 1991; *Great Inspirers* (New York: D. Appleton, 1917).

Women in Science

Women in Science "proved to be a popular seller," with over five thousand copies sold in the five years following its publication (Weber 194), and has been twice re-issued, first in 1974 by MIT Press, and again in 1991 by University of Notre Dame Press, as if to show how what was startling at the time of its publication, when suffragettes in America were valiantly lobbying for the vote for women, continues to be timely in a decidedly feminist era. In her Preface to the 1991 edition (whose pagination we shall employ), Cynthia Russett, Yale professor of history, notes how forward-looking was this initiative which Zahm shared with John Stuart Mill: to restore the "intellectual birthright [of which] women have been deprived" (xvi). For as she reminds us, "Mozans was writing at a time when the intellectual ability of women, above all their aptitude for science and mathematics, was still widely disparaged, [with] turn-of-the-century scientists themselves among the most enthusiastic disparagers" (xv). Devoting twenty-some pages to countering "the dreary tale [first of classical, and then] of scientific attempts to certify women's intellectual inferiority through anatomy and physiology and the careful measurements of craniometry" (xv), Zahm easily discredits such pseudo-scientific endeavors as proceeding "with minds warped by long ages of imperious instincts, ignorant preconceptions and social bias" (111). But that deconstruction (Chapter 2) interrupts an extended narrative inspired by a fresco adorning the portal of the University of Athens to celebrate Aspasia, the wife of Pericles, "surrounded by the greatest and wisest men of Greece" (xxi). For the entire monograph is introduced as "the outcome of studies begun many years ago in Greece and Italy [where] I saw on every side tangible evidence of that marvelous race of men and women whose matchless achievements have been the delight and inspiration of the world for nearly three thousand years" (xix). Such an extended canvas, again evidencing Zahm's broad humanist education at a fledgling "University of Notre Dame," is matched by an equally ample list of topics: women in mathematics, astronomy, physics, chemistry, natural sciences, medicine and surgery, archaeology, then as inventors, followed by women as inspirers and collaborators in science (two of whom will be singled out in the later volume), crowned by his prognosis of the future of women in science.

In the final chapter, his enthusiasm waxes for the imminent victory of the cumulative assessments of women's worth which his thorough study offers. "Assuredly Zahm's vision was overly optimistic," Cynthia Russett avers, but "will anyone say it was unworthy" (xviii)? Some samples will give us the flavor:

> Considering woman's past achievements in science, as well as in other departments of knowledge; considering her present opportunities for developing her long-hampered faculties, and considering especially, the many new social and economic adjustments which have been made within the last half century, in consequence of the greatly changed conditions of modern life, it requires no prophetic vision to forecast [a] share in the future advancement of science ... far greater than it had been hitherto (400).

Moreover, these changes will not only be felt in the professional realm but within the family itself: "from what has been said, it is clear that man's ideal of the woman of the future will be quite different from what it was but a little more than a century ago" (410), especially as all women

> realize also that if they are to attain the highest measure of success as wives and mothers, a broad and thorough education—a knowledge of science as well as familiarity with art and literature and the teachings of religion—is essential to them for their children's sake (415).

Here Zahm's inherent pastoral sense inspires him to detail the effect of this revolution in women's self-understanding for a family project which must equally involve men:

> It is only when the mothers of this, the women's century, shall
> dispute with men the primacy of erudition ... that their grown-
> up sons will have the same confidence in their intelligences
> as they now have in their hearts. Then only will mothers be
> properly equipped for developing the character of their chil-
> dren; for inspiring them with a love of the true, the beautiful
> and the good; for stimulating their talents and aiding them to
> attain to all the sublimities of knowledge; for assisting them
> in doubt and despondency and firing them with an ambition to
> strive for supreme excellence in all that makes for the nobility
> of manhood and the glory of womanhood; for making them, as
> Beatrice made Dante after he was renewed and purified in the
> waters of Eunoe, "fit to mount up to the stars" (415-16).

No better advertisement could be imagined for the universal
education of women, as anyone's experience of the children fortunate enough to be reared in such families abundantly testifies.
So however it may be argued, Zahm sees clearly how auspicious
the future opening to women will be for all of us.

But the way was long and the struggle exacting, as the
100-page initial chapter, entitled "Women's Long Struggle for
Things of the Mind," testifies. Beginning with ancient Greece
and Rome, it proceeds through the Middle Ages to the renaissance, and then covers the period up to the twentieth century. Replete with examples in their proper context, this chapter exhibits Zahm's keen sense for organizing a presentation,
since the figures to be treated in their respective intellectual domains are here introduced in such a way as to whet our appetite.
Moreover, against the grain of his time, the Middle Ages are
not written off as the "Dark Ages," but rather yield Hroswitha,
Hildegard, Herrad, Gertrude, and two Matildas, whose writings
offer "the best evidence of the studious character of the nuns of
medieval times, and of their devotion to the cause of education"
(50). Indeed, he contrasts this period starkly with early modern France and Germany, when "men began ... to revive the

anti-feminist crusade which had so retarded the literary movement among the women of ancient Greece and Rome" (74). The Reformation augmented the ban, for "in the estimation of Luther, the intellectual aspirations of women were not only an absurdity, but were also a positive peril: 'Take them ... from their housewifery and they are good for nothing.' " As a result, "the masses of women, especially after the suppression of the convent schools in England and Germany, were, in many parts of Europe, ... in worse conditions than they were during the Dark Ages"—in evidence of which he cites "the noted English divine, Thomas Fuller, chaplain to Charles II" (75).

Ever the Catholic apologist, he underscores the fact that "women professors achieved distinction in the Italian universities even as early as the closing centuries of the Middle Ages. The same was true during the Renaissance, and it has been equally true during the period which has elapsed since the *cinquecento*. ... Yes, what a contrast, indeed, between the Universities of Bologna and Padua, with their long and honored list of women graduates and professors, and the Universities of Cambridge and Oxford from which women have always been and are still [1913] excluded, both as students and professors" (78-80). Contrasting the

> honors shown to women as students and professors of medicine in Salerno, in the thirteenth century, with the riots excited among the chivalrous male students of the University of Edinburgh, when, less than a half century ago, seven young women applied for the privilege of attending the courses of lectures on medicine and surgery, [and] the almost brutal opposition which women in our own country encountered when, but a few decades ago, they applied for admittance to the medical schools of New York and Philadelphia,

Zahm concludes: "the difference between the Italian and the Anglo-Saxon attitude toward women in the all-important matters in question requires no comment" (80). His mind- and heart-opening sojourn in Rome had turned Zahm into a dedicated Italophile!

Mathematics proved an especially fertile field for Italian women, five of whom Zahm names before expounding on Maria Gaetana Agnesi, "who was born in Milan in 1718 and died there at the age of eighty-one."

> At the age of five she spoke French with ease and correctness, while only six years later she was able to translate Greek into Latin at sight and to speak the former as fluently as her own Italian. At the early age of nine she startled the learned men and women of her native city by discoursing for an hour in Latin on the rights of women to the study of science. ... But it was in higher mathematics that Maria Gaetana was to win her chief title to fame in the world of learning: ... she was, at the early age of twenty, able to enter upon her monumental work—*Le Instituzione Analitiche*—a treatise in two large quarto volumes on the differential and integral calculus, to [which] she devoted ten years of arduous and uninterrupted labor. {Moreover, when it] was completed and given to the public, it would be impossible to describe the sensation it produced in the learned world (143-45).

Zahm cannot resist linking her with "a Sappho, an Aspasi, a Hraswitha, a Dacier, [and] an Isabella Rosales who, in the sixteenth century, successfully defended the most difficult theological theses in the presence of Paul III and the entire college of cardinals," for

> she had demonstrated once and for all ... that women could attain to the highest eminence in mathematics as well as in literature, that supreme excellence in any department of knowledge was not a question of sex but ... of education and opportunity, and that in the things of the mind there was essentially no difference between the male and the female intellect (145).

He cites a letter to Maria Gaetana from a member of the French Academy of Science assigned to report on her work: "I do not know of any work of this kind which is clearer, more methodic or more comprehensive than your *Analytical Investigations*," but it was "against their constitutions to admit a woman to membership" (146). Nonetheless, Pope Benedict XIV "recognized at once the exceptional merit of Maria Gaetana's work and showed his appreciation ... by having her *motu proprio* appointed ... as professor of higher mathematics in the University of Bologna" (148). But the next step she took moves him even more:

> she disappeared completely from those literary and scientific reunions where she had so long been the most conspicuous figure, and was thenceforth known only as the ministering angel of the suffering and the abandoned. For half a century hers was a life of the most heroic charity and self-abnegation (150).

Pressed to compare and contrast this mid-life change with the fact that her work was to be translated into both French and English, as well as speculating on how she would be ranked had she "devoted her life to science instead of abandoning it just when she was prepared to do her best work," he is nonetheless constrained to acknowledge that "by consecrating herself to charity she probably accomplished far more for humanity and for the well-being of her sex than if she had elected to continue her work in the higher mathematics" (150-51). The strategic 'probably' in this assessment indicates Zahm's own appreciation of the intractability of any comparison among quite incommensurable goods.

Zahm follows this vignette with that of "the distinguished French mathematician, the Marquise Emilie du Châtelet, described as a 'thinker and scientist, precieuse and pedant, but not less a coquette—in short, a woman of contradictions, ... best known by reason of her liaison with Voltaire, [yet] a highly gifted woman who, besides having a thorough knowledge of several languages, including Latin, possessed a special talent for mathematics, [her] most noted achievement ... was her translation of Newton's *Principia* ... into French, [so] it was necessary that, in order to make it intelligible to others, [she] have a thorough understanding of it herself" (151). She is followed by a fellow French woman, Sophie Germain, who overcame the usual obstacles to win the Academy of Science "prize for the one who would 'give the mathematical theory of the vibration of elastic surfaces'—[a problem] Lagrange had declared insoluble without a new system of analysis." Yet when "the savants of Europe ... learned that the winner of the *grand prix* of the Academy was a woman, she became at once the recipient of congratulations from the most noted mathematicians of the world. ... It was in 1816, after eight years of work on the problem, that her last memoir on vibrating surfaces was crowned in a public séance of the *Institute de France*" (155). She is followed by "the daughter of a [British] naval officer, Sir William Fairfax, [who] is best known as Mary Somerville. ... Like Sophie Germain, ... her success was achieved only after long labor and suffering and in spite of the persistent opposition of family and friends" (157). Finally, with the help of "her uncle the Rev. Dr. Somerville, afterward her father-in-law, she was able to become proficient in both Latin and Greek, and [become], at thirty-three years of age ... the happy possessor of a small library of mathematical works" (157). Confessing that "'I was considered eccentric and foolish, and my conduct was highly disapproved of by many, especially by some members of my own family,' in March, 1827 [she] received a letter from Lord Brougham ... begging her to prepare for English readers a popular exposition of Laplace's great work—*Mécanique Céleste*" (159). When her work appeared, in less than a year *The Mechanism of the Heavens* proved to be "far more than a translation and epitome; it contained the independent opinions of the translator with respect to the propositions of the illustrious French savant. No sooner was the work published than ... she was elected an honorary member of the Royal Astronomical Society," and on the recommendation of "Dr. Whewell, the great master of Trinity," the book itself was "introduced as a textbook in the University of Cambridge and prescribed as 'an essential work to those students who aspired to the highest places in examinations' " (160).

Zahm last describes Sónya Kovalévsky, born in Moscow in 1850, as an eminent mathematician as well as a " 'representative of' the highest intellectual accomplishments to which women have attained; ... although her career was brief it was one of meteoric splendor" (161-62). She migrated to Germany at eighteen, first "matriculating in the University of Heidelberg, where she spent two years in studying mathematics under its most eminent professors," then was refused entrance to Berlin "but was fortunate enough to prevail on the illustrious Professor Weierstrass, regarded by many as the father of mathematical analysis, to give her private lessons" (162). After three years of work with him,

> she was able to present to the University of Gottingen three theses which she had written under the direction of her professor [so] that she was exempted from an oral examination and was enabled, by a very special privilege, to receive her doctorate without appearing in person. ... Not long after receiving her doctor's degree—one of the first to be granted a woman by a German university—she was offered the chair of higher mathematics in the University of Stockholm. She was the first woman in Europe, outside of Italy, to be thus honored. But her appointment had to be made in the face of great opposition. ... The fame which came to Sónya through her achievements in the German and Swedish universities was immensely enhanced when, on Christmas eve, 1888, "at a solemn procession of the French Academy of Sciences, she received in person the *Prix Borden*—the greatest scientific honor which any woman has ever gained; one of the greatest honors, indeed, to which any one can aspire" (162-63).

Moreover, Zahm takes care to inform us how

> she could with the greatest ease turn from a lecture on *Abel's
> Functions* or a research on Saturn's rings to the writing of verse
> in French or of a novel in Russian or to collaborating with her
> friend, the Duchess of Cajanello, on a drama in Swedish, or to
> making a lace collar for her little daughter, Fouzi, to whom she
> was most tenderly attached (165).

Her own reflections on this versatility are revealing: "it is impossible to be a mathematician without being a poet in soul. ... All my life I have been unable to decide for which I had greater inclination, mathematics or literature ... ; nevertheless, I cannot give up either of them completely" (165-66, n. 1).

The penultimate chapter, "women as collaborators and inspirers in science," presages his next volume, *Great Inspirers*, yet mentions many more than the two examples elaborated there: Petrarch and Laura de Noves, St. Francis and "Chiara Schiffl, better known as St. Clara" (358), Michelangelo and Vitoria Colonna. More recently, a bevy of composers: Mozart, Mendelssohn, Schubert, Beethoven, Weber, Schumann and others; as well as "Francois Viéte, the learned French mathematician, who dedicated his "work on mathematical analysis entitled *In Artem Aanlyticam Isagoge*, to his longtime pupil become friend and benefactor, Princess de Rohan:

> It is to you especially, august daughter of Melusine, that I am
> indebted for my proficiency in mathematics, to attain which
> I was encouraged by your love for this science, as well as
> your great knowledge of it, and by your mastery of all other
> sciences, which one cannot too much admire in a person of
> your noble lineage (363).

Moreover, whoever has become acquainted with the person of Galileo through recent reconsiderations of his trial will be fascinated with Zahm's account of his relations with "Sister Maria Celeste, a Franciscan nun in the convent of St. Matthew, in Arcetri, the great astronomer's eldest and favorite daughter" (363).

Her letters to her father were published in full only in 1891, and Zahm's analysis of them reveals his own personal affinity with Galileo himself, as well as his sensitivity to the need for support others can give to us when our plans are frustrated. The letters

> show how he made her his confidante in all his undertakings, and how she was his amanuensis, his counselor, his inspirer; how her love was an incentive to the work that won for him undying fame; how she was his support and comfort when suffering from the jealousy of rivals or the enmity of those who were opposed to his teachings (364).

He imagines their converse as Galileo responds to Maria Celeste's invitation "to spend an afternoon with her and her sister Arcangela," also a nun in the same convent: "father and daughters leisurely strolled through the peaceful enclosure, all quite oblivious of the fleeting hours" (366). Zahm concludes his meditation on this relationship:

> although we have no record of this soul-communion between father and daughter on the occasion in question; although we are deprived of this invaluable letter which he wrote in reply to hers, we are, nevertheless, from the evidence at hand, justified in regarding this unique pair as being ever one in heart, aspirations and ideals, and comparable in their mutual influence on each other with any of those famous men and women who, through achievement on the one side and inspiration and collaboration on the other, have even been recognized as the greatest benefactors of their race (368).

This encomium could justly conclude the chapter, but Zahm goes on to note yet more candidates, some of them at first unlikely: Descartes with Elisabeth of Bohemia and Queen Christine of Sweden; Leibnitz with Sophia Charlotte, queen of Prussia and mother of Frederick the Great, couples like the Pasteurs and the Aggasiz, Isabella of Castile and Christopher Columbus, and yet other lesser known luminaries who have benefited from what Zahm identifies as a mode of "deduction"—we would rather call it *imagination* or *intuition*, which has ever been at the heart of discovery in science (384-85). "From the foregoing observations," Zahm concludes

> It is manifest that the best results to science are secured when men and women work together—men supplying the slow, logical reasoning power, women the vivid, far-reaching imagination; men generalizing from facts, women from ideas; men working chiefly by induction, women principally from deduction. [In this way] the two combined possess in a measure the elements which go to make up a man or woman of genius and which enable them to achieve far more for the advancement of science than would otherwise be possible (386-87).

He ends with unwitting corroboration of his view from the "biography of the late Professor Huxley," from which one might be led to infer "that his utterances on all subjects were utterly personal and entirely unmodified by suggestion or criticism from any quarter." Yet his son insists "that his father 'invariably submitted his writings to the criticism of his wife before they were seen by any other eye.' ... She was 'the critic whose judgment he valued over almost any, and whose praise he cared most to win'—the other self who made his life work possible" (388).

It seems natural to inquire, at this point, who the "great inspirers" in Zahm's own life might have been? Few letters from women are available, as one might expect, yet we do have Eurana Schwab's response to his dedication of this very book: *to Mrs. Charles M. Schwab as a slight tribute to her charming personality, goodness of heart and nobility of soul, this volume is respectfully dedicated with the best wishes of the author:*

> Dear Father Zahm:
>
> Please pardon my delay in acknowledging your beautiful birthday gift, and while the book itself is beautiful, the real surprise and pleasure was when I read the dedication. I surely do not deserve such commendation at your hands. Of course anyone must be immensely flattered and pleased, which I truly am.
>
> Dear Father Zahm, Charlie and I think of you as a very dear friend. We are honored in having you as such, and any other

words, than simple expression of pleasure is unnecessary. And
that I heartily give. Thank you again and sincerely.

Eurana Schwab

The Schwabs, associated with United States Steel in Pittsburgh,
had ever been his patrons, which ostensibly included his final
journey, destined for Turkey and Iraq. A participant in that
group was Marie Benzinger, from the Catholic publishing family (Weber 195), who signs her heartfelt letter to "Father Robinson" regarding Zahm's final days: "Marie Benzinger, E. deM
[="Enfant de Marie," a special honor awarded students who ex-
cel in character in schools of the Religious of the Sacred Heart].
She notes that "we have cabled his brother, and have written
Mr. and Mrs. Schwab who are good friends of ours. Outside
of these he often mentioned your name, telling us what a pity
it was you could not take the trip, as you would have made an
excellent traveling companion. ... When he really became very
ill he said, 'Well, I guess if Father Robinson can't go, I guess if
it's for the best that I can't go either.'" (Nov. 10, '21 letter–PA).
This last remark is redolent of Aristotle on friendship: friends
enhance our own enjoyment of what it is we both enjoy. There
is no doubt that Zahm enjoyed good friends, and understood
how central they were to his life; it is less clear who his women
friends were, and how they affected the "curve of his own life,"
which we have been following as best we can, through his writings. At the end of the next section, we can explore his relationship to Gilbert Français, his older brother, friend and superior
in Holy Cross, sometimes designated the "second founder of the
community." Français had called him from Rome to fill out the
term of Provincial in the congregation, in the wake of Corby's
sudden death, and confirmed his desire to enhance the intellectual strength of Holy Cross, so Zahm felt close enough to him
to engage, as we shall see, in a painful exchange.

Great Inspirers

We have already noted how this work was presaged by the penultimate chapter of *Women in Science*, and we are told at the outset of this volume that "some passages in this and the following chapter have appeared in an article I wrote some years ago, under a pseudonym, for the *Catholic World*" (3, note 1). Weber informs us that "chapter one of this book had been published earlier as 'Women's Work in Bible Study and Translation,' *Catholic World* 95 (1912) 463-77, under still another pseudonym, A. H. Johns!" (198, note 33). It is more informal in character than *Women in Science*, more heartfelt–if that be possible, though clearly written with an eye to historical accuracy as well. Its distinctive note may best be sounded in the choice of the two figures, Jerome and Dante, while the opening page of the initial essay may suggest why Jerome, since Zahm's manifest affection for Dante easily explains that choice:

> No period of history is more conspicuous for stirring and far-reaching events than is the second half of the fourth century of the Christian Era. It was this period that beheld the dissolution of the great Roman Empire, that witnessed the decisive combat between paganism and Christianity, and that rejoiced in some of the noblest achievements of Christian scholarship (3).

And as every sensitive person realizes, and Jung insists, great men and women will always live out their times in living their lives.

Jerome and His Companions

Already familiar with the status of Roman women, as we have seen, Zahm offers fresh perspective on those who assisted Jerome, helping us to realize that their assistance went beyond patronage to become (in some cases) collaborators in the work of translating the entire bible into Latin. But let us first trace his itinerary from his birthplace in the southern Alps to Rome, where he studied with the grammarian Donatus, only to be drawn by stories "of the monks of the Thebaid [Egypt]" to the east, to which he traveled overland "by way of the Danube, Thrace and Asia Minor," with "a desire to travel founded on the love of study," as Zahm quotes him approvingly (12-13)! In Syria, "in the torrid and inhospitable desert of Chalcis," he continued his study of Greek and took up Hebrew as well, landing in Constantinople where Gregory of Nazianzus was bishop, with whom he studied the scriptures and "the two became fast friends," as he made the acquaintance of Gregory of Nyssa as well (17-18). Returning to Rome (in 382) after ten years, for a plenary council called by Pope Damasus, "his somber habit and his intellectual features, bronzed by the fiery sun of Syrian deserts, where he had led the life of an anchoret, attracted special attention whenever he appeared in public," notably that of the pope, who appointed him "secretary of the assembled council," and later "secretary of the papal chancery" (9-10,21).

It was also at the pope's request that he undertook to instruct many of the noblest women of Rome "in a palace on the Aventine belonging to a distinguished patrician widow named Marcella. ... She was regarded by her contemporaries as the most beautiful of Roman ladies, but her talent and virtue were even more exceptional" (25). Yet she had transformed her "palatial abode [into] a house of prayer and a center whence ever radiates the most sublime deeds of Christian charity and sacrifice, [as well as] a home of learning" (32). Zahm notes how such a witness was altogether novel in ancient Rome. Among the auditors were Paula and her two daughters, Blesilla and Eustochium, descended from both Roman and Greek aristocracy. Blesilla undertook the study of Hebrew, as this entire group opened themselves to be taught and to assimilate the scriptures. It seems that the death of Damasus made things more difficult for Jerome in Rome, whose longing for study lured him east, where before long he was joined by Paula and Eustochium, after the early death of Blesilla. With Jerome as guide, they made their way to the Holy Land, by way of Antioch and then Egypt, visiting monastic sites there, only to settle in Bethlehem. Once there, Paula and Eustocium urged him to comment on the scriptures, especially the letters of Paul, at once goading and assisting him in his life's work of producing the Vulgate, translating the entire scriptures into Latin, as well as translating Origen's commentaries for the sisters in their convent. To underscore the point of this essay, Zahm summarizes:

> The intellectual activity of Jerome, while working under the inspiration of his two incomparable friends, was marvelous, and the amount of work which he accomplished under their benign influence, and with their efficient cooperation, was enormous. There were commentaries on both the Old and New testaments, translations from the noted Greek Doctors, and letters innumerable to all points of the compass. For, from all parts of the Roman empire, Jerome was appealed to as an oracle on all matters pertaining to scripture, or to traditions and doctrines based on scripture (65-66).

This was the context in which he undertook the translation of the entire bible from the original Hebrew. As Zahm indicates, Paula and Eustochium "read, compared, and criticized [his drafts from Hebrew]. And ... they frequently suggested modifications and corrections, which the great man accepted with touching humility and incorporated in a revised copy" (74). Yet Paula died shortly before their translation had been completed:

> Jerome was seventy-five years of age when the Vulgate was given to the world. [But] he had promised Paula, during her life, to write commentaries on all the Prophets. ... With the assistance of Eustochium, who was always near to sweeten his task and alleviate his sufferings, he labored on with amazing ardor. Paula in the tomb still animated him no less than when she was alive (87).

So Zahm can conclude: "Jerome is usually characterized as a man who was of an exceedingly stern and austere nature. ...

[Yet] no man, probably, was ever so completely under the sublime inspiration of 'the eternal feminine' as was this example of penance and mortification" (95-96):

> For Jerome, Paula, Eustochium, all three of whom are honored by the church as saints, constitute a triple star of the first magnitude—a star whose brilliancy will suffer no diminution so long as the world shall admire friendship and holiness and acclaim profound learning and supreme genius (108).

Beatrice and Dante

Before considering Zahm's way of delineating the fertile relation of Beatrice with his favorite poet, Dante Alighieri, it is worth noting how John Ireland, the archbishop of Saint Paul, responded to the gift of this book, in a letter to "my dear Father Zahm":

> I have read your new book from its first page to its last. I was enchanted with it. I wonder more and more of the fecundity of your pen—its erudition; its wise selection of the gems of many literatures: its skill in portraiture, its gracefulness of style. Your first part—St. Jerome—is perfect. Here his friends were truly inspirers. By 'inspirers' I mean not a passing glance or a fleeting word, but direct and continuous work. The second Part—Dante—meets less the general title of the book "The Inspirers." There was there no conscious, continuous inspiration. It is, however, a magnificent historical monograph and you hold well to your point that Dante['s] "Inspirer" was a real living person.

Nor can he resist signing off with a jocular barb: "I am not so sure of the book, including the Dante part, is just the thing for promiscuous convent reading" (14 Feb 1917–PA).

In fact, a good deal of the Dante book is preoccupied with questions raised by the plenitude of Dante scholarship, particularly regarding the "reality"—real or imaginary, of Beatrice, which Zahm turns deftly towards affirming her reality, as we have seen. Yet given that her untimely death assures that the *figure* of Beatrice prevails, the discussion is hardly baseless. In this respect, Zahm contrasts Dante's direct encomium to Beatrice in *La vita nuova* wih that of Petrarch for Laura, Aristo for his mistress, and Tasso for Leonora (142), each of whom focuses on their beloved's mouth and lips, whereas Dante

> Gives us an image of Beatrice's personal graces by telling us of the impression she made on him. He portrays the beauty of her soul as reflected in her deportment and in that *dolce riso*—sweet smile—which raised him above the things of earth. ... Dante's love, though deep and sensitive, was nevertheless as calm as it was pure and loyal. It was a love which, as he assures us, caused him to forgive everyone who had offended him and to make him feel that he no longer had an enemy in the world (142-43).

In the wake of her death,

> Dante's grief at the loss of the angel of his soul, and muse of his intellect, was as deep as the love which inflamed his heart when he first met her at the May festival in the home of her father, and when, nine years later, she saluted him with that generous smile which was to him as a beacon light during the whole of his extraordinary career (147).

In fact, that image would merge with Boethius' "lady philosophy" (150-51) to inspire him through an exile "banished from that Florence which he loved so tenderly and which he was never to see again," (152), during which he "prepared himself for his great life-work—for what was to be an imperishable monument to her who was to be the protagonist of his immortal masterpiece as well as its inspiring muse" (154).

In fact, "during Dante's twenty years of exile ... he felt that his loved one, still alive with the warmth of love and grace and beauty, as she was during her short existence on earth, was ever near him and presiding over this thoughts and life (166-67). Zahm will take this even further:

> It is safe to say that, after the death of Beatrice, the happiest days that Dante ever knew were when he was condemned to what was, in the eyes of the world, the lonely and joyless existence of an exile. For it was then that flashed upon his

inward eye those sublime conceptions which were to adorn
the magnificent monument which he had designed in honor of
the mistress of his soul—then that he could, in the words of
Wordsworth, refer to his angel Beatrice as one

> Who ever dwells with me, whom I have loved
> With such communion that no place on earth
> Can ever be a solitude for me—

then that he could declare with Shelley,

> In me communion with this purest being
> Kindled intenser zeal, and made me wise
> In knowledge, which, in hers mine own mind seeing,
> Left in the human world few mysteries (174-75).

Zahm culminates a long digression in response to "modern
critics" baffled by the way Dante interweaves levels of reality
in his *Divina Commedia*, with an astute hermeneutical contrast
between our age and his:

> modern writers have become so accustomed to passing every-
> thing—history, art, literature, religion—through the alembic
> of criticism that, by this forced analysis, they arrive at an ideal
> concept of woman and give it a certain nebulous appearance.
> ...But what is readily accepted now would not have been re-
> ceived in the time of Dante. For had a poet in the thirteenth
> century sung of an ideal woman in the style of modern symbol-
> ists, he would not have been understood. The medieval mind
> always demanded something real as a basis for the ideal. ...
> [And what is more, to them] the supernatural world was more
> real than the material: ... "the world of the living was but a
> shadowy appearance, through which the eternal realities of an-
> other world were constantly betraying themselves" (230-31).

Indeed, a recent book by Christian Moevs, part of a team at the
University of Notre Dame intent on realizing Zahm's dream of
a center for Dante studies at his university, details precisely this
observation of Zahm: *The Metaphysics of the Divine Comedy*
(Oxford: Oxford University Press, 2005). Moreover, the way
he elaborates Dante's "metaphysics" serves to illustrate Zahm's
central contention about the figure of Beatrice as well:

> Dante's Beatrice, then, according to the poet's habit of attrib-
> uting several meanings to one and the same thing, or person,

must, as D'Ancona has so conclusively shown, be viewed as existing in a threefold capacity—as a woman, as a living personification, and as an animated symbol. It was to her who, in all her transfigurations, was ever the same Beatrice, that Dante consecrated his verse and his affection (234-35).[63]

When we think that the writer of this animated prose was himself an exile, we may again inquire: who may have inspired him to "a desire to travel founded on the love of study," like Jerome; and buoyed his indomitable spirit through it all, as Beatrice did Dante? We have no records to answer that question, but the sensitivity with which he limns these transforming friendships should offer a hint of what shaped his own soul as well. The conventional portrait of John Zahm was (as he noted of Jerome) one "of an exceedingly stern and austere nature." Could his exile, together with his gift for writing, reveal a nature otherwise hidden, and often quite deliberately kept hidden, from his confreres as well as the bulk of his contemporaries?

---

[63]A communication from Cristina d'Ancona pinpoints this reference of Zahm: *La Vita Nuova di Dante Alighieri*, illustrata con note e preceduta da un discorso su Beatrice per Alessandro D'Ancona (Libreria Galileo, Pisa 1884). The "discorso su Beatrice" runs from p. xxiv to p. lxxxviii; I am copying here the passage which proves that Zahm was referring to this book (at his pages 234-5, as mentioned in your chapter):

E così è di Beatrice, che non è la donna in genere (...) ma una donna, vissuta al mondo, amata, celebrata, pianta da Dante, e da lui innalzata a rappresentare un'idea di sublime perfezione fisica e morale. Conforme all'arte di Dante, per la quale non vi ha nulla di vuoto, di vacuo, di sfumato, di vaporoso, Beatrice è donna prima di essere simbolo, e può esser simbolo appunto perché fu donna (p. xxxvi)

Alessandro D'Ancona is arguing against other scholars who contended that Beatrice was an ideal, the hypostatization of Faith, or Philosophy.

Chapter Six

FROM BERLIN, TO BAGHDAD, TO BABYLON

WE ARE NOW POISED TO ENTER upon the most enigmatic phase of John Zahm's enigmatic life, by way of his account of the celebrated and longed-for venture from, as he quaintly put it, Berlin to Baghdad to Babylon. The last of his South American travelogues–*The Quest of el-Dorado: The most romantic episode in the History of South American Conquests*–appeared in 1917, the same year in which Zahm addresses a letter to his friend and superior, Gilbert Français, C.S.C., stating his intent to "begin active work on my *Opus Maximum*–a book on which I have been laboring at intervals for more than a quarter of a century. It is on a subject which has profoundly interested me from my earliest youth—the lands of the Bible" (22 August 1917–PA). He then recounts the more recent stimulus: thirty years before:

> when I went to the Holy Land with good Father Sorin, I had very little opportunity for research, as I could not leave my venerable companion and he was unable to go beyond Jerusalem and Bethlehem. I saw enough, however, to inspire me with the resolve, if ever opportunity offered, to write a work on Bible lands that would incorporate the latest results of archaeological research in their bearing on the Bible and higher criticism. No sane investigator can deny that these results have all been in favor of the Sacred text, and that many of them have corroborated it in the most surprising manner.

His inveterate apologetic inclination directs him to undertake this work now, since "we have practically nothing in English that the Catholic readers can refer to when they wish information on the diverse questions raised by the higher critics and the enemies of revealed truth." He then confesses:

> my ambition for several decades has been to write a book on Bible lands that would be a material help to all Scriptural students, and to the general reader as well. My studies for many long years have specially prepared me for this undertaking, while my life-long interest in the subject will make the writing of the book a labor of love.

Then follows the shrewd assessment of this undertaking:

> but, as you know, a book of this kind will have few readers, and will have but a very short life unless it be pervaded by the true local color. My readers everywhere tell me that the secret of the success of my South America books lies in their genuine local color as well as in the facts embodied in the narrative. And my publishers—the oldest and largest publishing house in America—assure me that, by reason of my method of treating the subjects I have written about, they expect to sell more of my books a century hence than they are selling now. So far that has been said of no other writer on South America except the great savant, Alexander von Humboldt.

Now comes the request which necessitated this letter, according to Zahm's vows as a member of the Congregation of Holy Cross:

> but to carry out my plan as I have dreamed of it requires your cooperation. I cannot get the necessary local color without revisiting the lands of the Bible and writing many parts of the book while under the spell of the *genius loci*. You were good enough in a most cordial and encouraging way to make my last book possible–a book which many members of the hierarchy have assured me has vindicated the honor of the Church in South America–and I trust you will as graciously make it possible for me to succeed in a far more important undertaking by according me permission to visit the East as soon as the cessation of hostilities in the Old World shall make the contemplated journey prudent and profitable.

In the event, as we shall see, this request to imbibe and communicate "genuine local color" turns out to be ironic, yet Zahm is here impatient, and relying on his friends in government who "are hopeful that the Holy Father's peace proposal will soon be effective," wants to "have everything in readiness—books, maps and instruments—so that I can start on my journey as soon as an armistice is declared—which, in the opinion of keen observers here, may be before Christmas."

> And I wish also to converge all my reading on the history and archaeology of the places I shall visit so that I may be familiar, as far as books can help me, with the things and places I wish to visit and study.

There follows an assurance that "my journey will involve no expense to the community,"

> but it will, I trust, redound to its credit and to the credit of the Church. With God's blessing, it surely will, if interest and zeal and hard work and long, long years of serious preparation can achieve the results I have in view.

And he closes with a stipulation which casts some indirect light on his previous use of pseudonyms, at least for the travel books:

> Of course, as in the case of my letter to you about my South America trip, you will please regard this letter as strictly confidential. I do not wish anyone except yourself to know anything about my plans until I shall have actually started on my journey. I know you will guard the secret as sacredly as you did the last time, and I trust that *Deo Jarente* all will redound to the glory of God, His church and Holy Cross.

Was this coveted secrecy part of Zahm's character, or did he employ it to deflect possible envy from his confreres laboring away in Indiana while he was circumnavigating the globe? Français' reply (*en français*) makes no mention of this stipulation but endorses Zahm's project on the strength of his stunning record:

Reading your books on South America was like a revelation to me: I knew your genuine talent, but until that point I was completely unaware of your capacity of seeing things around you so well, expressing them in so fascinating a way, and of organizing them into so [striking] an historical context. All of that demands a detached view, as well as an immense capacity for work, and for that very reason your idea of composing an attractive book, in the excellent English of which you possess the secret, ... on the Holy Land and its incomparable memories, seems to me an authentic idea, useful, practical and honorable for all of us. (1 October 1917—PA—translation mine [DB]).

In other words, "permission granted." But at the same time, Français cannot resist bringing up something which had emerged at the very moment of Zahm's departure from Notre Dame in the wake of the provincial council elections: Bengal. Recall his own words to Français at that point:

What I would now suggest is that I be permitted to begin anew what I was prevented from accomplishing eight years ago [when he was abruptly recalled from Rome to take up the duties of provincial], that is, to go to Bengal and secure material for a series of illustrated articles on our Missions, to be written as soon as [soon] my health shall warrant, and published in the manner that shall be productive of the best results. ... I have already spoken to Monsignor [Hurth (vicar for East Bengal)] about the matter, and he gives it his cordial endorsement. Before undertaking such a journey, however, I should need a rest of six months or more abroad, preferably among my literary and scientific friends who for years have been inviting me to visit them (25 August 1906).

Français takes this occasion (eleven years later) to raise the issue anew:

This might be the place to return to our idea of beginning this [voyage] by way of Bengal. If a book written on [the subject dear to our heart] would also contain pages dedicated to the milieu and the work of our missions, it could have the ability to engender and encourage vocations. We could extract whatever concerned the missions and put that brochure in the hands of our young [confreres], to create an apostolic spirit in them. From India, given the way your work will have been carefully prepared, and once peace had been established, you could easily go to Jerusalem to realize the attractive book you have in you. ... Now I only had this idea today, but I am happy to open myself to you on this occasion. Do think about it yourself.

But Zahm was intent; he had the needed permission, so galvanized his friends—no doubt, Eurana and Charles Schwab, from whose home—"Immergrün, Loretto, PA"—the Foreword to this book had been composed and to whom the entire endeavor was dedicated, to begin to constitute a party for the trip.[64] We are never told who that was to be, and plans were doubtless made, yet the next communication we have, four years later (10 November 1921), is a poignant one from Marie Benziger (of the New York publishing family) to "Father Robinson," a confrere at Notre Dame whom Zahm had wished to accompany him on this valedictory voyage:

> Father Zahm came here on October 26th to visit us; as you know he was on his way to the Orient. In Dresden he had contracted a bad cough and the day after his arrival my father, Mr. Benziger, persuaded him to go to his doctor, a well-known physician. He said Father Zahm had bronchitis and should go to the hospital, but he would not hear of it (10 November '21—PA).

Given the influenza epidemic following the "great war" in Europe, Zahm may have had reasons to avoid hospitals other than standard male resistance, but as Marie Benziger relates, his resistance had the result that:

> for five days Mother nursed him here in the hotel, and one of our family was constantly with him. On November 1st the doctor called in a Red Cross nurse, who was Catholic, and four days and nights she never left his side. On the third he was

---

[64] "To the best of friends, ever loyal and inspiring Mr. and Mrs. Charles M. Schwab, in whose hospitable home every book I have written during the last quarter of a century has had either its inception or its completion, this volume is affectionately dedicated."

taken to the hospital where he received every care, after having
a slight hemorrhage and coughing up blood from 10 p.m. until
five [a.m.]. He was immediately given oxygen, and camphor
injections, and the doctor had every hope of being able to save
him. His nurse called in the priest, and told Father Zahm he
was to receive the Sacraments in thanksgiving because the day
before he had been very ill. ... There was every hope that he
might be saved; the difficulty lay in the fact that he had a very
weak heart and could not be given morphine as he would have
most likely fallen asleep ... never to awaken. ... At four thirty
this morning he fell into a peaceful sleep and passed away. ...
During his illness Father Zahm absolutely forbade us from telling anyone that he was ill. ... He was constantly talking about
his trip, and that his life work lay ahead of him. When he really become very ill he said, "Well, I guess if Father Robinson
can't go, I guess it is for the best that I can't go either." We
thank God that we had the privilege of being with him in his
hours of suffering, and that he was among friends. Science did
all it could to save him; the self-sacrificing devotion of Sister
Antoinette was almost superhuman, in her efforts to hold him
back from the arms of death, but He who is all-powerful called
and he went.

Marie Benziger concludes this difficult letter with "we wish
to condole with you the loss of one who called himself your
friend, and who during his sickness often spoke of you. Trusting this sad news of Father Zahm's death may not have any ill
effect on your health," she signs it "Marie Benziger, E. deM.
[*Enfant de Marie*]," testifying to her upbringing in schools of
the Religious of the Sacred Heart and the education which enabled her delicate narrative of John Zahm's final hours, itself
a testimony to his capacity for friendship as well. So the fact
of the matter is that he was caught in the deadly influenza epidemic following the great war, which reputedly took more lives
than that devastating war itself. And the saving grace is that
he was surrounded by friends who gave their utmost to care
for him, despite his reluctance to take the recommended steps
which might have saved his life.

We shall reflect on these last moments at the close of our appreciation, yet for now the bare fact of his sudden death can only elicit an enigma for us. For the book which emerged a year later had to have been printed from a manuscript already completed before venturing on this ill-fated pilgrimage: one which Zahm had requested to undertake since he would otherwise have been unable to "get the necessary local color, without revisiting the lands of the Bible and writing many parts of the book while under the spell of the *genius loci.*" Yet as we shall see, his descriptions are so vibrant and fitted to each particular context that the prospect of their having been composed at his desk in Washington D.C. boggles the mind. Moreover, we should cite an exchange with his publisher in the wake of the first South America book, occasioned by an accusation (aggravated by his use of a pseudonym) that Zahm had composed the entire travelogue before undertaking it! At the advice of their lawyers, "D. Appleton & Company" tendered the careful response: "We are acquainted with the author; ... we know him to be a man of reputation and a scholar of distinction, and we have every reason to believe that the experiences which he related in this book are based on actual fact" (24 February 1911—PA). Theodore Roosevelt, in a personal communication, was more direct: "You may be amused to know that yesterday a gentleman happened to mention that he doubted if Dr. Mozans were a real character, or had even been down where he stated he had been. I told him that I happened to know who Dr. Mozans was, and that he was a very real character, and most certainly had been down on the trip" (27 June 1911—PA).

In this case, however, we are presented not with conjecture but with a stark fact: the detailed itinerary which Zahm relates is one he never took! As we find ourselves reveling in his descriptions and analyses, this fact will appear all the more startling. One might suggest, of course, that his prior experience of attending closely to visual detail as well as to historical and political settings, and then weaving them into a seamless composition, may well have equipped him to prepare a manuscript that was virtually complete, even to its minute descriptive details, but the enigma remains. Doubtless the ethnographic sophistication of the earlier "travel" works—something which always set them apart in that amorphous genre (much like William Dalrymple's work in our time)—had demanded considerable preparatory work, as well as careful editing on return; but all we have here is Zahm's own attestation to "interest and zeal and hard work and long, long years of serious preparation," plus his desire to "converge all my reading on the history and archaeology of the places I shall visit," together with the more general observation that "my studies for many long years have specially prepared me for this undertaking." Doubtless his relatively sedentary situation during the years of the "great war" (1914-18), coupled with the excellent facilities of the Library of Congress (to which Français makes reference in his letter of approbation) gave Zahm abundant opportunity to prepare himself for the journey—indeed, so well, as we shall see, that there is little internal evidence that he never made it, except that (true to the title) it ends at "Babylon" yet with no indication of a return voyage. Moreover, the way back might naturally have included Jerusalem, and ideally an encounter with Marie-Joseph LaGrange, O.P. at the Ecole Biblique, whose ground-breaking forays into biblical criticism would have fascinated Zahm, while consummating his explicit desire to make this "a work on Bible lands that would incorporate the latest results of archaeological research in their bearing on the Bible and higher criticism."[65] There is, in fact, very little of that in the present text, though

---

[65]Bernard Montagnes, O.P., *The Story of Father Marie-Joseph Lagrange: founder of modern Catholic biblical study* (NY: Paulist, 2006).

a great deal on the civilizations that formed the matrix for the patterns of biblical thought.

But let us try to take the measure of his preparatory research by following the itinerary we are given, highlighting the grand themes of the work, notably those which break new ground for him, and sometimes for us as well. The narrative begins from "a comfortable hotel on the famous Unter den Linden in Berlin making final arrangements for my long journey

> *Romantic Baghdad, name to childhood dear,*
> *Where the sorcerer gloomed, and genii dwelt,*
> *And love and worth to good Al Rashid knelt.*

"Had I been in haste and been disposed to follow the most direct route, I should have taken the Orient Express which would have delivered me forty-nine hours later in the famed city of Constantinople on the picturesque Bosphorus. But that would have been too prosaic … " (2-3). So he follows the sinuous Danube through regions replete with history and "as rich in myths and legends as were ever the rivers and mountains and groves of ancient Hellas" (6), and which he recounts with his customary verve: Dresden to Ratisbonne [Regensburg], Passau, Vienna (where he "tarried hardly long enough to refresh my memory" [12] of frequent previous visits), on to "Pozsony—the capital of Hungary before it was transferred to Budapest" (15), thence to the still celebrated view of Budapest "to the traveler who enters it on the deck of [a] steamer" (18), on to Belgrade before negotiating "the celebrated Iron Gate at the confines of Serbia, Hungary and Roumania" (25).

At this point, his somber reflections on the Balkans call to mind the devastating "Balkan Wars," immediately preceding the "great war" during which he was doing his research and writing for this pilgrimage. They also introduce a tone of tolerance and instruction which will emerge full blown in his account of Turkey and of the Armenians:

> Few places have passed through more sieges or experienced
> more frequently the horrors of war than Belgrade. [Moreover,]
> the inhabitants had none of the gayety and animation of the
> people of Vienna and Budapest. Their cheerless faces were
> like those of a race that has witnessed many tragedies and is
> living in constant fear of impending disaster. And what coun-
> try, indeed, has passed through more and greater disasters than
> Serbia? (21) ... But it would be contrary to the teaching of his-
> tory to assert that all the disorders endured and all the cruel-
> ties suffered by the inhabitants of the Balkans during the long
> period when they were deprived of this independence were
> due to the Turks. Nothing is further from the truth. ... [He
> cites Nevill Forbes' *The Balkans: A History of Bulgaria, Ser-
> bia, Greece, Roumania, Turkey* (Oxford 1915).] It was not the
> Turks who taught cruelty to the Christians of the Balkan Pen-
> insula; the latter had nothing to learn in this respect" (22).

He spends the remaining time on the Danube, until its entry to
the Black Sea, at the Rumanian ports of Braila and Galatz, reflecting on the significance "of this historic waterway and of its
transcendent importance in the mercantile life of Europe" (31-
32). At the Black Sea the mythic journey begins in earnest.

In the next chapter, entitled "the Euxine and the Bosphorus
in story, myth and legend," Zahm regales us with stories celebrating "the Euxine" (or Black Sea) from Greek and Roman elegies,
as well as tracing the routes of early European explorers, like
Marco Polo, and trading exploits of the "Silk Road." The Bos-
porus itself unveils "countless myths, legends, traditions, and
historical souvenirs which cluster about its shores" (47), which
Zahm eschews canvassing, yet those he gleaned in his early introduction to Greek and Roman literature (at Notre Dame some
fifty years before) nourish his imagination and ours. Arriving
in Istanbul, he again eschews "even a brief description of Constantinople," citing "the scores of valuable books ... written on
this fascinating subject" (52). Yet to indicate his profound interest in it, he insists:

> I spent every available hour in visiting its churches, mosques,
> schools, museums and in contemplating its hoary, lichen-
> covered ruins, its battlemented walls and ivy-festooned tow-
> ers which, for long ages, cast their trembling shadows on the
> glimmering waters of the Sea of Marmora and served, for more
> than eleven hundred years, an effective bulwark against the
> fierce assaults of Avars and Goths, Arabs and Persians, Slavo-
> nians and Bulgarians and Mongols (52-53).

Now the fact that we must relegate this meticulous journey to
his imagination can either deflect our curiosity or enhance our
wonderment at the equally meticulous preparation which produced the descriptions we shall taste here.

His attention is riveted, of course, on Santa Sophia,
whose very structure imbeds pagan vestiges:

> Among the massive columns which support the great arches of
> the basilica are eight of verdantique which were brought from
> the celebrated Temple of Diana at Ephesus, [and] eight of por-
> phyry which belonged to the Temple of the Sun in Baalbek (54).

Ottoman whitewashing of "its matchless mosaic pictures"
has not kept the building itself from being "the delight of the
artists and architects of the world," nor has their effect been
any worse than the "mutilation ... of the exterior of the Par-
thenon by Lord Elgin" (57). He then recounts the signal attempts to capture the city, from the Muslims in 673, who "were
defeated but not crushed," only to effect its capture in 1435, to
the "forces of Russia, [which] for a thousand years continued ir-
resistibly to move towards the Bosphorus and the Dardanelles"
(61), punctuated by a conspiracy of Catherine the Great with
the Austrian emperor, Joseph II, to restore a "Greek Empire,
with Constantinople's its capital," and the plan of Alexander I
to divide sovereignty of the world with Napoleon, in exchange
for Constantinople—a scheme not even Napoleon could countenance: "Constantinople! That would mean the empire of the
world!" (61-62). Composing this narrative during the "great
war," Zahm cannot suspect the fate of this matchless city,

especially in the wake of Kemal Attaturk as the "new Turkey" arises from the collapse of five hundred years of Ottoman power, or Russia's transformation into the USSR. He then reflects on the strategic geo-political move from Rome to Constantinople, the splendor of the Byzantine court with its matchless array of theological talents, and the way in which "the occupation of Constantinople by Mohammad the Conqueror [in 1453] complicated the political, military, and economic conditions of Europe for nearly five centuries," forcing Europe either "to forgo its trade with the east [or] to discover a new route to the Orient which would be beyond the interference of Ottoman power," in Vasco da Gama and Columbus, thereby effectively removing Istanbul as "the nerve-center of the world's commerce" (73). Yet to Zahm's mind, this legendary city still holds the key to "securing a permanent peace in the Near East and achieving ... its spiritual and social regeneration" (75), much as geo-political strategists today focus on Turkey's axial role in East / West dynamics.

Yet Zahm resists focusing on Europe, and begins to instruct this audience in the way "Osmanli chieftains became the heirs of the Eastern Caesars [to gain] mastery of that portion of the world which from the dawn of human history has transcended all others in human interest" (106). Quoting Lane-Poole (1881): "No other dynasty can boast such a succession of sovereigns as those who conducted the Ottomans to the height of renown in the fourteenth, fifteenth, and sixteenth centuries" (107), calling attention himself to the role which certain women played in "Turkish politics and statecraft: the Muscovite Roxalana, who passed from a public slave market to the imperial harem to become the wife of Solyman the Magnificent, ... the Venetian Safia ... abducted at an early age from her home on the Grand Canal, ... and sold to the Sultan Murad III [only to become mother of] Murad II, and Aimée Dubuc de Rivery, born in ... Martinique, ... who eventually falls into the hands of Algerian pirates, ... sold in the slave market in Algiers, thence [given] as a present to the sultan, Abdul Hamid I, to whom she bore a son who became Mahmud II, the grandfather of the late Abdul Hamid II" (109-10). Beyond these charming vignettes, Zahm intends to alter the prevailing western impression of the Ottomans:

> from the day of Orkhan and Murad I, the Osmanlis have been classed as raiders like the devastating hordes of Timur and Genghis Khan. Nothing could be further from the truth. ... They were, from the days of their founder, a race of colonists and empire builders (113),

aided by the conflicting ambitions of Byzantine and other western sovereigns. He continues to instruct us:

> Nothing, probably, contributed more towards the rapid conquest of the Osmanlis than their spirit of tolerance in matters of religion. [Moreover,] to one who is familiar with the teachings of the Koran and the policy of Islam since the days of Mohammed, there is nothing surprising in this tolerance and religious freedom which the Osmanlis and Moslems have always accorded their Christian subjects. ... [Indeed,] the persecutions and harsh ordinances [which did occur] were not so much the result of religious antagonism as of political conditions at the time (116-17).

He closes this positive assessment of the Ottoman Islamic polity with a sidelong glance at the way Christian churches fared in the wake of the Muslim conquest, counting their very survival as further testimony to the religious tolerance of these rulers. Indeed, for five more chapters Zahm will continue his *apologia* for Islam, comprising a third of the book, with an appraisal of the Armenian massacre—a tragedy fresh in his mind.

Islam Past and Present

This sustained effort to enlighten his Western, largely American, audience about Islam marks John Zahm, the teacher, in an especially assertive way, even if all of the works we have examined display that zealous signature. What may be even more remarkable is that the fixed stereotypes he is determined to supplant remain imbedded in the Western psyche, only to be reinforced in the twenty-first century! Let us trace his pedagogical strategy. "Home life of the Osmanlis" (Ch. 6) links the fabled "harem" with celebrated Turkish hospitality, "In the footsteps of the Crusaders" (Ch. 8) takes us to Konya to meet Rum, "In historic Cilicia Campestris" (Ch. 9) uses a geographical rubric to enter into Kurdistan and the Armenian tragedy, "Islam Past and Present" (Ch. 10) offers an assessment of how Islam contributes to human history, while "Along the trade routes of the Near East" (Ch. 11) discovers Muslim shrines and the practice of the *hajj* [pilgrimage] in their life. The next two chapters—"From the Euphrates to the Tigris" (12) and "Churches of the East" (13)–treat the life and lot of Christians in the Islamicate, so Islam itself only indirectly. These chapters offer an ethnographic study displaying how Zahm's remote preparation for a journey he was not destined to take allowed him to enter deeply into a world he had but tasted a quarter century before, to bring us along.

Zahm begins strategically with the "home life" of the people, directly addressing Western prejudice:

> No people in the world, it is safe to say, have ever been more misunderstood or more misrepresented than the Osmanlis. For generations they have been regarded as a nation guilty of every crime and steeped in every vice, ... they have been denounced as cruel, bloodthirsty, treacherous, dishonest, intolerant, and fanatical in the extreme. ... But what is the truth about the Osmanlis (123)?

As against those who "have little or no personal knowledge of them," he notes how "those who have had any opportunity of becoming intimately acquainted with them find them to be thoroughly good, gentle, brave and loyal to the core." Indeed, "the better one knows them the greater is one's admiration for them" (124). Addressing the disparity in faith between them and his audience, he further notes:

> the piety and devotion of the Moslems, their gravity and solemnity and reverential attitude during prayer, whether in the mosque or elsewhere, are of such character as to make a deep impression even on the least religious[–citing Renan as a case in point!] (124).

He suspects that "many, if not most of these erroneous notions" stem from "ludicrous conceptions [of] harem life" as it has titillated Western male imagination. He first notes how rare in fact is polygamy in Anatolia, and then proceeds to offer the etymological origin of "harem" in the Arabic *haram*: "anything forbidden or a sacred thing or place" (126), noting how the Muslim *ethos* apportions sections of houses as well as trains and other public places to men and to women separately, yet "the inmates of the harem [do not] consider themselves as imprisoned in their houses like birds in a cage" (127). He cites liberally from reports of those who have lived extensively in Muslim lands, with special attention to "Lady Ramsey, the gifted wife of Sir W. M. Ramsey, the distinguished archeologist of Aberdeen, [who] frequently accompanied her husband on his expeditions ... to every nook and corner of the country" (129), noting how only women can have access to the harem. He takes up the usual complaints of male domination, only to find them no worse than England!

This allows him a segue into "the exceptional courtesy and cleanliness of the Osmanlis" (134) and their "very industrious habits" (135), concluding that "it would be difficult to find people who are more distinguished for natural virtues than are the Osmanlis who have not been debased by oppression or corrupted by power" (137). Knowing full well that he is straining against the grain of nearly universal public opinion, and since he cannot call on his own experience, he cites one authority after another, from Franciscans serving in Turkey to testify to the religious freedom they enjoy, to an enemy Serb who testifies that "the Turk was master of the Balkan nations for nearly five centuries. During all those centuries he consistently refrained from interfering with our national churches and with our village municipal life" (149). He does not hesitate to contrast the "remarkable spirit of tolerance which distinguishes the Ottoman government [with] the administrative bribery and corruption which have so long been the bane of Turkey, as well as of so many Eastern countries" (145), appealing to "the Great Powers to assist in its economic stress [and] help it to develop its marvelous natural resources, for the great trouble in Asia Minor today is an economic one" (149-50). To that end, he inserts a chapter on "the Baghdad railway," praising German initiative for undertaking what British, French, and Russian entrepreneurs had ignored, often for geopolitical reasons of their own, while the Anatolian Railway gave Anatolian peasants a market for their produce, yielding "twice to four times the prices formerly paid and the railways brought revenues to the [Ottoman] treasury" (157).

The chapter entitled "In the footsteps of the Crusaders" (Ch. 8) begins at Konya, the terminus of the Baghdad railway, which features the tomb of "Jelal-ed-din-Rumi, usually known as Mevlana, ... famed for knowledge and wisdom, and the founder of the dancing Dervishes" (172). Zahm notes that Rumi's "successors, as heads of the Dancing Dervishes, have ... the right and the privilege to gird each Ottoman Sultan, on his accession to the throne, with the historic sword of Osman" (173), so alluding to a political role for the Sufi orders. He also finds Konya to typify, along with Byrssa, "the manners and customs and simple pastimes of the genuine Turk," most of which center around "the coffeehouse [which] serves no food or alcoholic liquors of any kind" (177), yet the ever-present *nargile* [waterpipe] testifies that

> nothing more perfectly harmonizes with the temperament of the Oriental than the smoking habit, and it is doubtless this practice that contributes not a little to that remarkable patience and that wonderful repose which so distinguishes Turk and Arab from the nervous and overwrought American or European (179).

On leaving Konya Zahm reminds us that we are "on the route of the Crusades led by Godfrey de Bouillon and Frederic Barbarossa" (183) across the Taurus mountains, in the footsteps of Alexander through the "Cilician Gates, from time immemorial. …. The gateway between Syria and Asia Minor, between southwestern Asia and southeastern Europe" (188). Zahm concludes with a paean to the "weary and footsore Crusaders," only to arrive at Tarsus, the birthplace of St. Paul the Apostle" (190).

Historic Cilicia Campestris (Ch. 9) "comprised the triangle bordered by the Mediterranean and the lofty ranges of the Taurus and Amanus mountains" (193), an area of protracted conflict as well as a "field of romance, of myths, and legends innumerable" (194). Tarsus, the city of Saint Paul, was once "ranked as a center of Greek thought and knowledge with the world-famed cities, Athens and Alexandria" (201), so Zahm can speculate that "the future apostle came into close contact with the greatest teachers and scholars of his time, and was thus prepared to enter the intellectual arena with the keenest minds of Greece and Rome" (202). Eastern Anatolia provides the location for Zahm to make "a special effort to ascertain the truth regarding the

Armenian massacre that so stirred Europe and America to horror in 1909" (205). His Ottoman and Turkish predilections had already made him suspect that reports of "atrocities so frequently ascribed to the Turks were *ex parte* accounts of what had actually occurred and that most, if not all, of them were greatly exaggerated" (205-06). He cites "an English traveler who had exceptional opportunities for studying the question and who is well disposed towards the Armenians" to describe "the sudden period of liberty which followed the downfall of Abdul-Hamid, [leading] Armenians to give unrestrained vent to their aspirations [to establish] an Armenian kingdom of Cilicia [or] Lesser Armenia," which Zahm himself confirms and intensifies: "what is said here of the hot-brained revolutionaries of Lesser Armenia can with even greater truth be affirmed of their seditious compatriots of Greater Armenia" to the north (206-07).

The red flag "seditious" sets up his defense: after the Balkan wars of independence and European treaties designed to dismember it even further, what was left of the Ottoman Empire was fighting for its life, and Armenian aspirations to a separate state were the immediate internal threat to what territorial integrity it had left. Zahm allows another British traveler, sometime fellow of Oxford with several years in Armenia, David G. Hogarth, to outline the geopolitical situation, who finds a scapegoat in the Kurds:

> the Armenian, for all his ineffaceable nationalism, his passion for plotting and his fanatical intolerance, would be a negligible thorn in the Ottoman side did he stand alone, ... but behind Armenian secret societies ... it sees the Kurd, and behind the Kurd the Russian; or, looking west, it espies, through ceaseless sporadic propaganda of the agitators, Exeter Hall and the Armenian Committees. The Turk begins to repress because

we sympathize and we sympathize the more because he re-presses, and so the vicious circle revolves (209).

The picture Zahm goes on to paint, and in which he confesses himself to have been trapped, is of a veritable "clash of civilizations," where Western press and its readers do "not care to know anything which might be favorable to the Turks" (211). He denies being "a special pleader for the Turk; ... my sole desire is to make known the truth as I have found it" (212). Moreover, the issue far outstrips the Turkish-Armenian conflict:

> The present schemes of exploitation and conquest in Mohammedan lands now being executed by the Great Powers can, in the long run, have but one result: ... the result of still farther separating the Cross and the Crescent (213).

Zahm's instinctively scientific nose for sifting evidence, together with his voracious reading and passion for understanding, particularly the Middle East, has led him to see deeply enough into the events of the day to be able to speak prophetically of scenarios unfolding nearly a hundred years after this study appeared. At the outset of our appreciation we noted Jung's remark that conscious individuals live out their times as well as their lives, and this chapter and its sequel on "Islam, past and present," verify that once again for John Zahm. It is doubtful that his attempt "to make known the truth as I have found it" will settle this historical score, but what speaks powerfully is the Herculean task required to offset deep-seated prejudices which will not countenance listening to "the other side," with the way such pervasive "bad faith" persists in a touted "age of communication."

The next chapter (10) requires more than thirty pages to try to correct "the misrepresentations of Mohammad and his followers [that] have continued without intermission from the days of the Crusaders to the present time, [even] when their originators must have known that they had no foundation in fact" (232), and we can readily adjust his "present time" to our own! His historical soundings range from the *Chansons de Geste* to Voltaire, yet he remains baffled, for "in view of the clearness and simplicity of this creed, it is difficult to understand how the Western world has so signally failed to comprehend the real nature of Mohammed's teaching" (228). So he recaps the history of the Prophet's conversion of the tribes of Arabia to a high monotheism, and offers a fair appraisal of what Muslims believe, yet must illustrate their faith and practice for his readers by contrasting it with "Catholic teaching," usually negatively, as in asserting that "the mosque, unlike the church, is never the center of that kind of religious organization which we know as a parish; ... in the Ottoman Empire, the imam, so far as he is charged with special functions, is no more than a paid servant. ... There is none of that spiritual relationship which exists between the Catholic priest and his parishioners" (236). One wonders what might have ensued had he taken this pilgrimage, and met Muslims in their daily practice. But restricted to texts, to Western commentators and to his own devices, he can only compare the *Fatiha,* or the opening sura [chapter] of the Qur'an negatively to the "Our Father," insisting that "denying the Fathership of God, Moslem theologians maintain that it is impossible for men to love him" (238, citing from Duncan B. MacDonald, *Aspects of Islam* 1911). Yet he demurs as well:

> but in this case, as in so many others, the common sense—or shall we call it a special divine illumination?—of many in Islam has enabled them to arrive at a truer conception of God and of their relations to Him than was ever attained by Moslem philosophers and casuists, and incomparably superior to anything found in the Koran or in the traditional teachings of Mohammed. As proof of this assertion, I need only adduce the beauti-

ful prayer of the Persian imam, El Kachiri, who discarding the
cold and formal acts of praise prescribed in Moslem worship,
pours forth his soul to God (239).

Citing two other Sufi sheikhs, he can only exclaim: "How like
the language of a Christian speaking of the grace of our Savior,
Jesus Christ" (240)!

He then proceeds to challenge "the disposition everywhere
manifested in Europe and America to regard Islam not only as a
disintegrating organization but also as a decaying power" (240),
citing the burgeoning growth of Islam, especially in Africa. In
fact, he sees his task "to give an honest statement regarding the
actual tenets and status of Moslemism in the past as well as in
the present," all the while eschewing "to compare Moslemism
with Christianity as a means for attaining to a true knowledge
of our Creator or for realizing the highest spiritual ideal of this
our race is capable. ... Truth and justice, however, compel us to
admit that there are many, very many, things in Islam to extort
our admiration" (247-48):

Notwithstanding the long centuries of wars between the Cross
and the Crescent, Mohammedans are so far from regarding
our Savior, as is commonly supposed, with the hatred and
contempt which Christians have usually entertained for the
Prophet of Mecca, that they have for Him a reverence ...
inferior only to that with which He is regarded by Christians
themselves (249-50).

And were he asked why they remain Muslims, Zahm would cite

first and foremost, the selfish diplomacy and the unprincipled
aggressions of the European Powers, which nullify in advance
all projects of Christian propaganda, [as well as] the ruthless
conquests of Christian nations which have at times displayed
an utter disregard of the most elementary rights of humanity
and have often had recourse to the most cruel and barbarous
methods of warfare—these things have not helped to com-
mend to Moslems the religion of their conquerors (250).

This last confession allows him to direct the challenge to us:

what is needed more than ever before is a complete change of
attitude of the West towards the East; ... if we are to lead Islam
to a knowledge of Christianity and to an eventual acceptance
of the Gospel of peace and love, we, the followers of the Cru-
cified, cannot too soon abjure our accursed theory that might
makes right ... which has plunged the weak and the innocent
into such untold suffering ... (251-52).

He directs us rather to a "new Crusade ... inspired by ... the
ardent love of a Francis of Assisi, the flaming intelligence of a
Raymond Lully, the wisely tempered zeal of a Peter the Venerable, [replacing] the war cry [with] the peace cry–*Deus lo
vult*–God wills it" (252). Within a half-century, his church will
respond to this challenge in the Vatican II document, *Nostra
Aetate* (1965), even if Western geopolitical attitudes hardly
followed suit.

The next chapter, "Along the trade routes of the Near East"
(Ch. 11), returns to a travel mode to discover Muslim shrines
and the practice of the *hajj* [pilgrimage] in their life. "We left
the Cilician Plain by way of the Baghdad railway, which took us
over several well-constructed steel bridges and through a number of tunnels in the Amanus range" (255) to Aleppo, passing
"imposing monuments due to the Crusaders; ... crowning prec-
ipice-encircled heights and protecting strategic passes, they are
marvels of architectural beauty and massive grandeur" (257).
These monuments can only be contrasted with the countless
tombs and shrines celebrating holy men and women, a practice, Zahm reminds us, which is "totally at variance with the
teachings of the Koran and with the traditional doctrines of the
Prophet" (259):

> not only is the Moslem saint not dead, in our acceptation of
> the term, but his tomb is his house in which he continues to
> live and in which he receives the petitions of those who have
> recourse to him. There are countless dome-covered *tekkahs*
> [Sufi term for shrine] which stud the landscape—each with a
> Kiblah and frequently with a tomb and alighted lamp. Around

many of them we note small groups of women who have, presumably, come to make offerings of oil and fruit and coin to the
guardian and to implore the aid, if not the intercession, of the
local saint (260-62).

The railway soon brings them to Aleppo, in medieval times
"the great *entrepôt* of trade between the Orient and the Oc-
cident" (263). Yet while "the great camel trains which were
formerly so indispensable to the merchant of the Levant have
long given place to the lines of steamships that now connect the
East and West by way of the Suez Canal and the Cape of Good
Hope," caravans continued to exist for "transporting the countless thousands of pious pilgrims to annually visit the holy cities
of Mecca and Medina," though they now travel by the Hedjaz
Railroad, [whose] northern terminus is Aleppo, yet [thus far]
completed only to Medina" (267). It is here that he reflects on
Muslim piety, notably "the importance they attach to prayer and
the fidelity with which, five times a day, recite the orisons prescribed by their religion":

It is because of their profound religious earnestness, their abiding charity towards the poor and suffering and their many natural virtues that those who know them best have such good
reports to give of [them, citing those the fourteenth-century
Dominican Riccoldo da Monte Croce sent from Baghdad]. I
would fain to see them better known among our Western people, and will welcome the day when the prejudices and animos-
ities of ages shall disappear, when every soul-loving Christian
shall constitute himself a missionary to assist the followers of
Islam towards becoming members of the One Fold and finding
peace and happiness under the One Shepherd (271).

Yet from what he has intimated so far, we can justly hope that
he intends this desire follow the Qur'anic injunction of "No
compulsion in religion."

He ends this phase of his "journey" with an anthropological description of the "representatives of many lands whom I
met in the streets and mosques and bazaars" (271). But "out-

side of her people I found very little in Aleppo to attract attention [except] a small block of basalt which I saw in the south wall of a mosque" (273) with a Hittite inscription, which leads him to reflect on the "third civilization which was synchronous with those of the Nile and the Tigris and which, in the days of its splendor, prevailed from Nineveh to Smyrna and Ephesus" (274). He then takes leave of Aleppo and his "amiable Franciscan hosts [with] their charming and hospitable friends, with our faces turned toward the mysterious and spell-weaving Orient" (278). The train will take them along the "Euphrates as it flowed through arid wastes and washed barren rocks and hills of sand" (279), a terrain once efficiently irrigated so as to sustain a relatively dense human populace, but now what remains, beyond ruins, is hardly notable, except for Zahm's keen sense for history. "We interrupted our journey between the Euphrates and the Tigris by making a short side tip to Urfa, formerly the great city of Edessa" (284), in whose schools "the Syriac language and literature reached their highest degree of development," and whose "scholars translated many precious Greek works which otherwise would have been lost" (290). He is once more edified by the presence of Capuchins, whose arrival in the city in 1850 had incited the animosity of an array of other Christian groups, but whose "great self-abnegation, [and] abounding charity towards the poor and the distressed soon won all hearts" (292), as well as the Sisters of St. Francis from Lons-leSaulnier in France, whom he ranked among "the most buoyant and light-hearted beings I had ever met" (293).

The eastern terminus of the Baghdad railway is Nisibis, once "a literary center whose fame extended to Africa and Italy and whose schools were as celebrated for certain of their courses as those of Rome and Alexandria" (297). From there "to Mosul, about a hundred and fifty miles distant, we jour-

neyed on the backs of dromedaries" at a pace which appealed
to him. "I have spent many of the most peaceful and enjoyable
days of my life," he avers, in the desert, especially

> at the magic hour of refulgent sunset [when] its shifting sands
> and fantastically formed rocks ... are illumined by splendors of
> color and phantasmagorias of light which transform the most
> ordinary landscape into a veritable fairyland. ... Then there
> appears the wonderful, mystic afterglow which completely
> transfigures everything on mountain and plain, and lights up
> the scene with a light that rarely shines in our mist-enveloped
> clime (299-300).

As they camp each night, with

> the camels ... quietly browsing on the scanty broom and brush-
> wood ... , their Bedouin masters, seated in a circle, around an
> odorous camp fire, entertain one another by recounting past ex-
> periences and adventures, and by singing their favorite songs,
> most of which are in a minor key and characterized by the fre-
> quent occurrence of the terrible name of Allah, which gives to
> their doleful chant a note of sadness that once heard one can
> never forget (300).

Of all the chapters, it is both intriguing and challenging to think
this one was composed in Washington, D.C.!

As a segue to the chapter following, Zahm notes: "travel-
worn, we finally arrived at Mosul, the once famous emporium
on the arrow-swift Tigris" (302), where "I had a rare opportunity to complete observations which, during the greater part of
our journey, I had been making on the condition and influence
of what are known as the Eastern Churches [Ch. 13]" (303).
There is, however, less observation than there is delineation
for the reader of the many ecclesial bodies in "the east," with
special attention to what distinguishes them from "Rome." He
will identify these differences doctrinally, as has been customary, freely employing terms like "schismatic," which literally
means a group separating itself from the larger whole, so is
already a prejudicial descriptor, much like the "Shi'a / Sunni"

divide in Islam, where the key terms can be taken to mean "sectarian" and "consensus," respectively, intimating a valuation form the outset.

Beginning with the Nestorians, identified with "the assertion that in Christ there are two persons—the human and the divine—and the denial that the Mother of Christ is the Mother of God," Zahm notes that for "political and other reasons [they] soon became separated from the rest of Christendom, [and] banished from Edessa in 498 by the Emperor Zeno, they fled to Nisibis which then belonged to Persia, [where] the Persian King, learning that they did not profess the same creed as that held by the Byzantines, with whom he was always at war, took them under his protection" (305). With that impetus, by the thirteenth century "the jurisdiction of the Nestorian Katholicos [extended to] bishops at important points in Asia from Mosul to Malabar, and from Jerusalem to Java and Peking" (306). The incursions of Timur and later of the Tartars decimated the church, and of those remaining, "thanks to the untiring missionary labors of the Dominicans of Mosul, the majority of the Nestorians, after fourteen centuries of separation ... are now members of what is known as the Chaldean church which is in communion with Rome" (307). He then notes how the identifying doctrinal differences have often eroded, so that those in "communion with Rome" can effectively preserve their historic identity by retaining their "rites and liturgy" (308).

A not dissimilar story can be told of another community, the "Jacobites," after Jacob Zanzalos, who was an early and zealous propagator of the teaching "that there is in Christ but one nature and not two, the human and divine, as decreed in 451 by the Ecumenical Council of Chalcedon" (309). Once even larger than the Nestorians, Zahm is satisfied that "in consequence of the missionary labors of the Franciscans, Dominicans, and Capuchins the majority of the Jacobites are again in communion with Rome under the name of Melchites or Syrian Uniates [Catholics]" (310). This same doctrinal stance on the ontological constitution of Christ is held by the Armenian church as well as the Coptic church in Egypt, although each of these communities also have a subgroup in union with Rome. Yet on the issue of communion, Zahm shrewdly notes how "misunderstanding, national jealousies and aspirations had probably as much—if not more—to do with the separation of these churches from Rome as the particular heresies with which they are usually associated," citing the Coptic church in Egypt as a case in point:

> the decree of Chalcedon and the consequent deposition of their Patriarch gave occasion for a recrudescence of their hatred of Caesar and Caesar's religion and for an anti-imperialist outbreak in Alexandria, [so identifying] opposition to Byzantine imperialism with Egyptian nationalism" (315-16).

In an effort to depict this complex canvas accurately to his readers, he must first remind us that

> to envisage the State as separated from the Church, politics as distinct from religion, as we do in the West, is as alien to a Syrian or an Armenian patriot as it is to a Persian mullah or an Ottoman grand vizier. [Indeed,] the truth is that in all the Eastern Churches ... national loyalty and national pride count for more than religious conviction or dogmatic teaching. This, strange as it may appear, means that the nation comes before the Church; that politics takes precedence of theology (317-18).

Were Zahm's critical acumen in true form here, he would observe that the strange inversion which he notes infects his own country as well, despite the touted "separation" ethos. Nor would he be as lenient as he is with Rome's policies towards these churches, claiming that "she has, in her supreme wisdom, ever been ready to allow each church ... to retain its own laws and customs, rites and liturgy, language and hierarchy" (320). We have to charitably demur: not always.

What he has rightly done is to distinguish the "churches of

the East" from the "Orthodox churches," which have "their origin not in heresy but in schism, pure and simple" (321)—again, reminding ourselves that which one is in schism will be a matter of where one is standing! Zahm clearly stands with Rome, and with his Western predilection for separating state from church, locating the salient cause of the continuing schism with the Achilles heel of orthodox Christianity, as follows:

> during the Byzantine period which extended from the accession of Justinian to the throne to the fall of Constantinople under Mohammed II, ... the Emperors were unremitting in their efforts to make the Church a subject of the State. In this they had the ever-ready cooperation of the court bishops, ... whose ambitions were great and they counted on their imperial masters to help them realize their unholy aspirations (321).

He traces this collusion back to Constantine's scheme to elevate the bishop of his capital city to a Patriarch with "the primacy of honor after the bishop of Rome because Constantinople was New Rome" (323), which incipient rivalry "engendered and fostered that jealousy and friction that ever afterwards existed between Rome and Constantinople and which, more than anything else, led to the ever-regrettable schism that still separates East from West" (323). The tired rendition of that rivalry overwhelms the historical record of "reunions effected by each of the Councils [dedicated to that task] but in each case it lasted only a very short time" (328).

With the conquest of Constantinople, a new actor appeared on the scene to rally the Orthodox against Rome, and in time to divide the Orthodox churches in the Balkans, for to the extent that "the policy of the Phanar [the Vatican of the Orthodox Church] was identical with that of the [Ottoman Sublime] Porte, the enemies of the Sultan were unwilling to acknowledge any kind of dependence on the Byzantine Patriarch. [In fact,] no sooner had the different states in the Balkans freed themselves from Turkish rule than they proclaimed their independence of the

Ecumenical Patriarch" (330). Zahm's setting leads him to note how the Russians "are beginning to ask themselves whether the time has not yet come for the Holy Synod to assume the supreme headship of the entire Orthodox Church" (332)—an eventuality which Lenin subverted. At this point, Zahm cannot resist a triumphal prognosis on reunion of the Eastern Churches with the Holy See, confessing how "during my wanderings in the Near East, as during previous travels in Greece and in Russia, a question of ever-absorbing interest to me was that of the long-desired and often-attempted reunion of the Eastern Churches with the Church of Rome" (333). He canvasses once again the abortive efforts at reunion over the centuries, hoping that however ineffectual, "they set people ... to thinking, and that Church unity is now nearer realization than it has been for centuries" (336). Yet his formula is no less "Western" in its presumptions than most of Rome's efforts over the centuries and well into our own:

> comparing their condition before the Great Schism with what it is now, they find to their sorrow that they are suffering from arrested development; their boasted conservativism is but a euphemism for fossilization; that they have long ceased to be a living, active force, and that their only hope of regaining their erstwhile power and prestige is to be reunited with the Apostolic See (336).

Zahm could hardly hope, speaking in such fashion of the "Eastern Churches," to rectify the trail of failed attempts. Nor could the actual pilgrimage have improved that voice, if they had persisted in lodging with religious communities of the Latin church.

For the last five chapters, Zahm dons his archaeological hat, and beginning with the excavations at Nineveh, proceeds to show, from site to site, how

> science, whether it appears in the guise of geology, or Assyriology, or of what has falsely been called the science of evolution, can never invalidate a single one of the fundamental teachings either of Scripture or of the Church of Christ (367).

To illustrate his point with regard to deciphering inscriptions at Nineveh, the combined efforts of nineteenth-century orientalists allowed them to gain "a knowledge of Old Persian ... by comparing it with Avestan, Pahlavi, and Sanscriit, [so] that it could serve as the long-sought key to Assyro-Babylonian" (360). Building on this example, he will generalize:

> we now know incomparably more about the history, the social and economic conditions of the ancient Assyrians and Babylonians than we did before the explorer brought to light the literary treasures of Nippur, Telloh, Abu-Habba, and Nineveh; but we have discovered nothing which is competent to discredit any of the eternal verities on which our faith is founded (368).

So long as he rests on the bedrock of "eternal verities," Zahm's contentions could be repeated in good faith today, yet he was not saddled with a "doctrine of scriptural inerrancy," which his Protestant fellow inquirers sought to confirm from archaeology. One could hardly be so sanguine, say, of efforts to corroborate the conquest narratives in the book of Joshua from "archaeological evidence."

He begins this portion of the narrative by crossing "the shaky and crowded pontoon bridge that connects Mosul with the long-buried city of Nineveh" (341), and his exploration of the tale will carry him back to a Dominican who had "first awakened my interest in Nineveh ... more than three score years ago. ... As a consequence of the repeated reading of the book which he had placed in my hands, ... I never lost my early love of sacred history or of the history and geography of the Near East" (342). This chapter brims with the history of explorers, some of whom turned to inscriptions at Persepolis to find the key to developing the "science now known as Assyriology" (358), detailing the multiple converging steps needed to decipher what they found. He celebrates their decision to travel to Baghdad "by a peculiar kind of raft which had been in use on the Tigris since the time of the early Assyrian kings" (371), a *kelek*, both for the way it returned them to the time they were studying as well as entailing "at least a week of absolute rest" (372), guaranteeing uninterrupted observation and reading:

> on our writing table we placed some of our favorite books. Among these was a small copy in India paper of the Bible which was in constant use during our journey in the Orient. Another was a small pocket edition of the *Divina Commedia* which, for years, had been my companion to the most distant parts of the world. Here were also small editions of the *Soliloquia* of St. Augustine and of the select works of St. Teresa. ... To these were added copies of Xenophon's *Anabasis*, Arrian's *Anabasis of Alexander*, and the *Oxford Book of English Verse*" (374).

Zahm allows that those will suffice, "as I expected to spend most of my time on our way down the river in contemplation of the many objects of interest with which both banks were everywhere studded" (374).

They stop to investigate the ruins of Nimrod and of "Assur, the first capital of ancient Assyria" (379), where Walter "Andrae's superbly illustrated reports of his careful and methodical excavations" had not "prepared [him] for the wonderful ruins which greeted my vision when I first surveyed them from one of the imposing ziggurats of the great temple of Anu and Adad—one of the architectural wonders of western Asia, ... as reconstructed by Andrae," beginning in 1903. Here again, we need to remind ourselves that his vision had to rely completely on the books which he "had read with exceeding interest shortly after their publication" (1909, 1913). He devotes some pages to "the fascinating romance of [the legendary queen] Semiramis because it is so interesting an illustration of the extraordinary progress which the new science of Assyriology has made during the last few decades" (387). Returning to the travel mode, he notes that "during the entire journey between Mosul and Baghdad one is never long out of sight of ruins of some kind or another" (390). They pass "the little town of Samara, as celebrated for its romantic history as for its remarkable monuments," described by a well-known archeologist, Gertrude Bell:

> the spiral towers of Samara and Abu Dulaf are an adaptation of the temple pyramids in Assyria and Babylon which had a spiral path leading to the summit; the technique of arch and vault was invented by the ancient east and transmitted through Sassannian builders to the Arab invaders; the decoration is Persian or Mesopotamian and almost untouched by the genius of the West (398).

Then "the domes and minarets of Baghdad hove in sight and our week's happy floating on a *kelek* was at an end. We were at last within the gates of the world-renowned metropolis of the Abbasside Caliphs" (401).

The final three chapters focus on Baghdad and its environs: "the famous city which, during five hundred years, was the capital of the Abbaside Caliphs, [and] which, during a half millennium, was to Islam what Rome is to Christendom" (409). Would that Zahm's compatriots a century later had the sense of history that animates this account! He connects first with the Carmelite friars, relating their work in its Ottoman context, under protection of the French, with that of French sisters who find that "the children of Baghdad are very bright and very eager to learn," and who arrived–to Zahm's utter amazement–from Beirut after "twenty-four days in the saddle" (406-07). He then proceeds to sketch Baghdad's five hundred years of splendor, with its palaces and gardens, focusing on the "reception accorded the Greek ambassadors who were sent to Baghdad, A.D. 917, by Constantine Porphyrogenitus. Before being introduced to the Commander of the Faithful, the envoys were conducted in state through the various buildings within the palace precincts. Each of these buildings, of which there were twenty-three in number, was a separate palace" (414). Yet characteristically, Zahm wants to tell us:

> it was, however, the colleges, of which there were more than thirty—"each more magnificent than a palace"—that gave Baghdad its greatest fame in the medieval world (416).

The caliph who especially promoted education, al-Mamun, collected books and manuscripts from the subject provinces of Syria, Armenia, and Egypt; and when he "dictated terms of peace to the Greek emperor, Michael the Stammerer, the tribute which he demanded from him was a collection of Greek authors" (421). Yet Zahm is insistent that Muslim intellectuals "were borrowers and not originators" (423), a view which prevailed when he was writing, but which closer attention to the manner in which they both adapted and translated Greek classics has been modified considerably.

The brutal destruction of this glorious city, first by Mongols under Hulagu Khan, and again, less than a century and a half later, by Mongols under Timur, leads Zahm to decry:

> when, in addition to all these atrocities, one recalls the deeds of violence and savagery which afterwards followed the successive storming and occupation of the unfortunate city by Turkomans, Persians, and Turks, one must conclude that the proper epithet for Baghdad would have been not Dar-as-Salam–City of Peace—but Dar-al-Harb—City of War" (427).

And we can echo his foreboding words a century later. The fulsome descriptions which follow will be baffling to us who know that the journey never took place. Identifying denizens of the bazaar by their garb:

> every style of headdress, [from] fezes, tarbooshes, keffiehs, turbans, the brimless hat of the Baktiari, the long felt hats of the Lurs and the Kurds, the black astrakhan caps of the Russians and the Persians. . . . The vesture of the women is even more variegated and costly and resplendent. ... Some are garbed in rich silks of all the tints of the autumn leaf. Some are veiled, others unveiled, according as they come from the Moslem,

Jewish, or Christian quarter of the city. ... [Finally,] my attention was directed to the large numbers of Jews who had shops in the city and stalls in the bazaars (432).

His valedictory to this array of humanity and of history is even more poignant today:

one cannot but feel that there is a brilliant future in this celebrated region of the two rivers, but only when a stable and enterprising government shall have been established ... that is willing to guarantee to the people the blessings of peace (436).

The last two chapters return to the biblical theme, to canvass theories about the location of the "Garden of Eden," with the most likely candidate being in the vicinity of the current Baghdad (Ch. 17), and a visit to the site of Babylon (Ch. 18). In the first of these, "Motoring the Garden of Eden," he reminds us of the close relationship between Bedouins and their horses and camels, describing an encounter with "pilgrims on their way to the sacred shrines of Nejef and Kerbela—the holy cities of the Shiites" (444). His clearly second-hand descriptions of Shi'ite "occasions of rejoicing such as weddings or the birth of a child" being accompanied by the "sobs and lamentations" associated with the death of Hasan (*shura*) leads him to conclude that "Shiites are born, live, and die in the midst of tears and moans and lamentations, [which] during the first ten days of the month of Moharram and every day during the pilgrimage to Nejef and Kerbela ... are obligatory" (447). It can often be the case that people who have broken through Western stereotypes about Islam, as Zahm certainly did, can still find Shi'ite Islam "beyond the pale." Lacking any tangible leads to the site of "Eden," Zahm concludes the chapter with a poetic allusion to his early childhood fantasies about it, stimulated by "the stately trees and ravishing shrubs and blooms of ... a beautiful garden adjoining the home where a kindly and well-to-do Arab gave us hospitality while we visited Babylon and its vicinity." But of course the fantasy has been compounded in this composed narrative.

The final chapter "narrates" their visit to the fabled site of Babylon, surrounded by "magnificent groves of date palms" (471), which leads Zahm to catalogue the manifold benefits of this tree and its fruit, repeating the "Eastern saying: 'the palm is the camel and the camel the palm of the desert'" (472). They come upon "a group of happy, laughter-loving children" as they set out for the ruins of Babylon, which elicit his "surprise to find that the favorite games of these sunburnt children ... were just the same as the games that are popular among the boys and girls of America, [or those] played by Indian children on the plateau of the Andes and in the wilds of Brazil" (474). A parent could only repeat: surprise, surprise! He then regales us with the vista from the summit of the famed tower, named Babil after the original name of Babylon, yet often associated with the "Tower of Babel" in Genesis 11:

> from its summit, which towers seventy-one feet above the surrounding plain, one has a magnificent view not only of the ruins as a whole but also of many notable features in the immediate vicinity. [Indeed,] this prospect is absolutely thrilling ... when, at the hour of sunset , the long amethystine shadows cast on the dun-colored plain, bring out into bold relief the rich golden lines of the spell-weaving ruins of that great city which, in her glory, ruled over the kings of the Eastern world" (471).

His extensive canvassing of quite recent archaeological findings pertinent to the Babylonian civilization includes "advances made by astronomy at different periods of Babylonian history, [thanks to] the persistent labors of three Jesuits, Fathers Epping, Kugler, and Straszmaier" (502). Moreover, Zahm considers that the discovery of Hammurabi's Code, "more than five hundred years earlier than that of Moses" (506), "completely demolishes a favorite argument of certain Biblical critics respecting the laws of Moses, [contending that they] must have been the work of the Jewish priesthood in the later days of Israel, who, in order to give it the necessary sanction, falsely attributed it to Moses" (505-06). Moreover, "in proportion as the cuneiform inscriptions continue to disclose their long-withheld secrets, so also, we may feel sure, will they, in all essential matters, be found to verify and corroborate the declarations of the Sacred Text" (506). Lest we associate this hope with a purely positivistic view of the worth of archaeological results, however, we should note how Zahm the logician wisely inserted the qualifying phrase "in all essential matters." Is the Mosaic origin of the "law of Moses" essential? Writing somewhat earlier, his Dominican contemporary, Marie-Joseph Lagrange, contended *no*, to the dismay of Vatican authorities at the time, so temporarily jeopardizing the fledgling Ecole Biblique in Jerusalem, where Lagrange was the founding director.

The chapter concludes the book with a series of biblical prophecies predicting how "that broad wall of Babylon shall be utterly broken," all thematically similar to Qur'anic readings of desert ruins as divine punishments. One can only surmise how this desk-bound narrative might have been enhanced were its detailed descriptions, gleaned from extensive reading in ancient literature and contemporary reports, able to have been checked against eye-witness testimony, as well as actual encounters with the peoples whom he describes, often with such verve and acuity.

EPILOGUE
Assessment of John Zahm in a Larger Context

ATTEMPTING TO TAKE THE BALANCE of this endeavor to "appreciate" a living individual, an older confrere in the Congregation of Holy Cross by nearly a century, I must register my own appreciation of the encouragement given by contemporaries in Holy Cross whose talents for history kept me from many egregious errors, and especially that given by Ralph Weber, Zahm's sole biographer to date, who was startled and gratified that someone would pick up his trail of fifty years to find it so fresh and inspiring. To recap, my original intent had been two-fold: first, to show how a person of faith responded at fifty-five years of age to a personal and institutional setback, instigated by members of his own religious community; second, to illustrate how that same religious community would shepherd his embracing vision for the University of Notre Dame, and undertake, at the hands of some younger confreres whom Zahm had inspired, to create the conditions needed to implement that vision within thirty years of his untimely death. In short, by the quality of his response to this personal setback, which represented a severe setback for the University as well, his own life blossomed into that of an adventurer and writer, whose talent for teaching and for "promoting good things" appears to be boundless, with his genius for friendship animating his peripatetic inquiries, as it inspired some key younger confreres sharing his place of residence at the house of theological studies which he had founded in Washington, D.C. In this way a "setback" became an opportunity, assisted by the insistent counsel of his medical doctor who assured the "travel for recuperation" prescription which was to guide his new life after fifty-five. Indeed, the reaction of his own body to the role of Provincial, which occasioned the doctor's response, must have taught him that he needed to answer the call to serve God through his religious community in ways more amenable to his own psychic constitution.

To be sure, he took the "complete rest" prescribed in a way peculiar to his temperament, yet anyone reading his initial travel narratives through South America cannot help but be impressed at the way in which contemplative dimensions became increasingly evident in this very active personality. In short, relieved of responsibilities of an academic or religious kind, he was given ample room to develop his intellectual and spiritual capacities, nourished by his studied way of responding to the diverse worlds into which he so heartily entered. His boundless dedication to intellectual inquiry, shaped by a firm classical education at the University which he had quickly adopted as his home, then deliberately directed to researches in the world of science, extended well beyond the classroom from the outset, through extensive lectures and subsequent publications. Indeed, ever the publicist and apologist for things Catholic in a decidedly Protestant milieu, he invariably sought to disseminate his reading of the "signs of the times" in which he lived so intensely and gregariously. Perhaps that helps us see how the "setback" became the opportunity it did, for his attachment to Notre Dame had always been one of promoting the *good* of the University rather than seeking personal rewards, so when he found events there had made him *persona non grata*, he could continue working for its good in a larger context, trusting that his extensive work as a Catholic intellectual and publicist would redound to the larger world of education and in time to his own University as well. Whether he ever entertained reflections of this sort we can only suspect, but we now know that it turned out that way, thanks to confreres whom his witness had inspired. That thesis has been at the heart of this appreciation.

That he never ceased thinking of ways to enhance Notre Dame can be gleaned from two letters early in his period of exile: one to Mathew Schumacher, C.S.C., Director of Studies, who had asked Zahm's advice regarding University expansion (1913), and the other to Paul Folk, C.S.C., Director of Libraries (1915). In the first, he is thinking in the mold of a Provincial, responding to the needs of young candidates for Holy Cross: "a special building for them after they have left the novitiate, [yet] are not ready to go to Holy Cross College"; "the second building ... should be the library," while "the next buildings in order would naturally be dormitories," and finally, "a building that has long been needed ... is a large dining hall." The letter ends characteristically:

> But more important by far than buildings is the proper preparation of our young subjects for their work as teachers. What every university needs and what every community needs above everything else is scholars and specialists, as well as devoted religious. Large and imposing buildings have little value unless those in charge of them and teaching in them be thoroughly educated and properly trained to teach the special classes which may be assigned to them (Zahm to Schumacher, 30 August 1913—PA).

The letter to Paul Folk begins:

> My desire always was to have for Notre Dame the best, most beautiful, most up-to-date fire-proof library in the country— one that would be a convenient and inspiring literary workshop for the University and the Community as well. To secure such a library I spent four years in examining the best libraries in Europe and South America and the plans I left at Notre Dame

were drawn only after consulting the most eminent librarians in the United States. ... I hope provision has been made for a special room for the Dante collection, [for] from the fact that the world's greatest poet was a devoted son of the Church, if for no other reason, Notre Dame should have the largest and most complete Dante library in America (Zahm to Folk, 12 December 1915—PA).

As it turns out, these latter recommendations, including the classical frame of the building, were carried out faithfully in 1917, when the library was constructed, while the "Dante room" became the seedbed of the Devers Program in Dante Studies in 1995 (www.dante.nd.edu). What does seem clear, however, from the absence of further correspondence in this vein, is that he forswore any anxiety regarding the execution of the suggestions he had made.

A 1960 in-house study by Philip Moore, C.S.C., a medievalist (Ecole de Chartres) specializing in old French, then serving as Dean of the Graduate School, expounds the negative effects for the University of Zahm's exile:

Father John Zahm had joined the Faculty in 1873 and by 1883 was Professor of Physical Sciences and Curator of the Museum. His zeal for scholarship and the intellectual life are well known. He was himself a scholar devoted constantly to research and he strove to stimulate superiors, colleagues and the students toward scholarship especially in science, and to raise the over-all intellectual tone of the school. His writings and lectures brought prestige to the institution. During his twenty some years on the Faculty, and later as Provincial (1898-1906) he exercised an influence and left a stamp on Notre Dame that perhaps has not been equaled by any other man. [Yet] after difficulties with Father Andrew Morrissey, who became President in 1893, and two years in Rome, where he came to know first hand European university life, his eyes were opened and he was assailed with bitter disillusionment (http://archives. nd.edu/moore/moore00.htm).[66]

---

[66] As expressed in a letter to his brother, Dr. Albert Zahm, written on December 12, 1897:

Philip Moore's retrospective view is telling, especially in revealing the perspective of a confrere hard at work to realize the vision that he found in Zahm. Yet as we have seen, Zahm's own development in the wake of these setbacks evidenced less "bitter disillusionment" than the unfolding of an omnivorous desire to learn, while communicating its results in such as way as to serve "the glory of God, His church and Holy Cross" (as expressed in his letter to Français requesting permission to undertake what was to have been the journey "described" in our final chapter). Moreover, Philip Moore himself was clearly inspired to carry out the work he did by the vision of John Zahm, expressed in a life of inquiry which embodied everything to which both of them aspired for Notre Dame. So the last word is rather of one who, despite personal and institutional reversals, fulfilled the promise of that One who called him to be his friend, "sending him out to bear fruit, fruit that will last" (Jo 15:16); and last it has.

A final word on John Zahm's continuing relationship with Gilbert Français, as evidenced in their correspondence over the crucial years between 1906 and 1921. Sometimes referred to as "the second founder of Holy Cross," Gilbert Français was elected coadjutor superior general at the 1892 general chapter because Sorin's health was precarious. When Sorin died on

---

It would indeed be a trial for me to return to the dull, humdrum, unintellectual, dwarfing environment where I spent, or rather, wasted, the best years of my life. What a pity it is that our people do not realize the necessity of a higher culture for their members, especially those who are here to devote their lives to the enobling work of education. With possibly one or two exceptions among the younger priests, not one at Notre Dame has the faintest conceptions of the wants of a university, and the demands of the age in which we live. I look forward to the young men now being educated at the Catholic University in the hope that they will effect eventually the much deserved change, but this will require time and patience. The old generation must die out before any real progress can be made. Notre Dame ought to be one of the first educational institutions in the land, whereas it is in reality nothing more than a large boarding house for elementary students (cited in Weber 105).

The publication by Philip S. Moore, entitled "Academic Development, University of Notre Dame : past, present and future," was published for University distribution in 1960.

Oct. 31, 1893, Français succeeded him, serving in that role from 1893 until 1926. We saw (in Chapter 3) how Français' questioning of Zahm's stewardship so hurt him that it occasioned a twelve-page heartfelt exculpatory response detailing the tangible results of his years in office as well as delineating the goals which had elicited them, culminating in:

> What I have written would, I am sure, be endorsed by all the intelligent members of this province who know anything about the aims and ambitions of the administration during the last eight years. I wish now, however, to speak only for myself, and to reiterate, respectfully but positively, that I have given you no reason for writing such a letter as your last. Such a letter is a strange recognition, indeed, of the many toilful days and sleepless nights spent during the many long years in the work of upbuilding this province, in securing for it the stability it now possesses and in commanding for it the prestige it now enjoys. Suspicion, distrust, curtness, unkindness, the implication of squandering Community funds and in this exhibiting a lack of ordinary common sense, are the acknowledgement you make of the results achieved—results which may have extorted the admiration of the phlegmatic and indifferent and of those far less interested in them than you should be—results of which you, of all men in the world, should be the first to recognize the value and importance. ... The implication in your letter that I have not told you the truth ... is as unwarranted as it is cruel and so unlike you that I make no attempt to explain it. I leave that to you (13 January 1906–PA).

This letter is clearly composed to one whom he felt to be his friend, as well as the person to whom he was accountable by his vow of obedience. He doubtless suspects that others have actively undermined his standing with his superior general, so tries to let the facts stand for themselves, trusting in the intelligence and probity of his friend.

Subsequent correspondence between them would indicate that the trust had been restored, first in Zahm's own sharing his medical reports with him, seven months later (August 1906), in the wake of the chapter which freed him from the onerous office; as well as a series of letters some years later, from Français to Zahm, between 1914 and 1917, culminating in the exchange seeking permission for the Middle East voyage, which we have seen. The first available letter from Français, in April 1914, begins auspiciously:

> I am very touched at the delicate and heartfelt attention which prompted your lovely letter hard upon your return to Washington—thank you very much! This journey will have been very good for you, in giving you the repose you needed.

He goes on to remark on the clear profit of his South American journey to "the honor of Catholicism," and then assures him:

> Know very well that I am acutely interested in your work, and that I am going to pray for the full and lasting success of your efforts. Take heart for your great work; know that I am very affectionately yours in Our Lord (27 April 1914–PA, my translation).

A second letter, of February 1916, praises his "four magnificent volumes" on South America, remarking at length on his capacity to overcome deep-seated prejudices to bring north and south into conversation, and his splendid powers of observation, closing with

> I detect in you more and more, and better and better, the prodigious worker and exceedingly intelligent person whom I have known and esteemed. ... Once again, my very dear brother, thank you, and [I am] cordially all yours in Our Lord (19 February 1916–PA, my translation).

Expressions of affection between men were inevitably restrained in that epoch, yet their friendship appears to have weathered Zahm's exile from Notre Dame, to find expression in the mutual respect in which they held one another. It appears that the interior bond with his religious community, here in the person of his superior and friend, together with his residence among young men preparing for ordination in Holy Cross

College in Washington, offered a homing path for him in the midst of friends and professional colleagues in Washington, and one which he treasured.

A Comparative Conclusion

Writing on a person inevitably invites identifications between author and subject, nor can this appreciation be an exception to that rule. Yet I would rather deflect that inveterate tendency by comparing Zahm with two near contemporaries, both French and each a *Grenzgänger*: Marie-Joseph Lagrange, O.P., and Louis Massignon, in a way that only a later appreciation could even attempt, considering these distinct persons in a stereoscopic view suggested by their cognate concerns and their shared Catholic faith. We have already noted (in Chapter 1) the potential contact points between Zahm and Lagrange, notably that they were both participants in the fourth Catholic Scientific Congress in Fribourg in 1897, as well as their cognate concerns to relate the study of the Bible to scientific inquiry, though in opposite directions: Lagrange, to incorporate historical-critical methods into the study of the biblical texts; Zahm, to illustrate the compatibility of the disparate genres–biblical and scientific–in expounding cosmological and anthropological issues. Given the climate of the times, that the work of each elicited concern on the part of Roman authorities was doubtless inevitable as well, yet neither allowed that to deter their commitment to faith or to scientific inquiry. Moreover, their relative removal from the epicenter (Rome), as well as their adherence to their respective religious communities, did give each of them a relatively protected space to continue their inquiries, though Zahm was constrained to alter his original field of inquiry.

The second figure, Louis Massignon, relates to Zahm's final *opus maximum*, incorporating "more than a quarter of a century" of intermittent work, two-fifths of which is devoted to a sustained effort to enlighten his Western, largely American, audience about Islam. Yet this passion to supplant stereotypes fixed in the Western psyche about Islam had also animated, in another key, his intensive studies of Latin America, though in that case the corrective impulse was directed to a Protestant North American psyche. A similar passion can be found in the life of Louis Massignon (1883-1957), a French Islamicist whose life and work, like Zahm's, was devoted to crossing boundaries, and whose dedication to the Muslim mystic and martyr, al-Hallaj, led him to "revert to faith in the God of Abraham" in such a way as always to think of the revelations of Bible and Qur'an together.[67] We owe the prescient phrase, "Abrahamic faiths" to Massignon, and there is little doubt that his longtime friendship with Pope Paul VI expedited the reconciling lines in the Vatican II document on the relation of the Catholic Church with other religions: *Nostra Aetate*. But what drew me to this comparison was the way their respective Catholic faiths impelled them to direct their co-religionists to ways of appreciating the Muslim "other" without in any way diluting their own faith-commitment. To be sure, Massignon was far more instructed in Islam than Zahm, blessed with a bevy of Muslim friends plus fluency in Arabic, as well as enjoying a rich family background and intellectual formation at the Sorbonne; yet their instincts converge in an instructive way. Catholic faith cannot be "exclusive" in the sense of our having nothing to learn from others; in fact, quite the opposite, it is encounter with persons of other faith–in their case, Islam– which opens us to the reaches of our own. What Massignon's mysterious encounter with the subject of his study, Husayn ibn Mansur "al-Hallaj" (857-922) allowed

---

[67]Mary Louise Gude, C.S.C., *Louis Massignon: The Crucible of Compassion* (Notre Dame IN: University of Notre Dame Press, 1995), Louis Massignon, *The Passion of al-Hallaj: Mystic and Martyr of Islam*, tr. Herbert Mason (Princeton NJ: Princeton University Press, 1982) Vol. 1: Foreword to the English edition, by Herbert Mason; citation in text is at xxv.

him to overcome were nineteenth-century French intellectual prejudices against anything related to Catholic faith, whereas Zahm's inherent desire to understand, together with an education in the classics and a subsequent sojourn in Rome carried him beyond his virtual frontier origins in western Ohio in the mid-nineteenth century.

Yet in Zahm's case, his openness to Islam is nearly as baffling as the composition of the account of the Middle East, without having taken the journey itself, for nothing in his background can plausibly account for that. So we must look to a more generic principle of explanation, already exhibited in his documented travel through South America: an inveterate recoil from narrow or provincial ways of seeing anything, perhaps in gratitude for the liberation which his early education and the opportunities for travel and friendship as a Holy Cross priest had afforded him, first in service of the fledgling University which had become his home, and then of a far larger public: "the glory of God, His church and Holy Cross." Others had received the same education, however, and were content simply to pass it on, much as Massignon belonged to a burgeoning group of "Orientalists" in the early twentieth century, responding to the opportunities afforded them by European colonization. Yet Edward Said will identify countless ways in which his work eludes the distorted construction of "Orientalist" he finds so offensive.[68] So it must be said that "something else" influenced intellectuals like John Zahm and Louis Massignon, something which cannot be identified unilaterally with their Catholic faith, since many who profess that faith have responded to "others" in disdainful ways. Indeed, it is that "something else" which attracted me to attempting an appreciation of John Zahm's life through his works, as well as suggested this *prima facie* far-fetched comparison with Louis Massignon. Can we suspect that there is

---

[68]Edward Said, *Orientalism* (London: Routledge and Kegan Paul, 1978) 266-74.

"something else" in each person which, were we able to identify it and reach to express it, would give us the individual image of the creator in each human being? Yet that unique person is born, reared and educated in a family and a community, and as our shared experience of family life tells us, may be unable to express their uniqueness within that otherwise nourishing context. That has certainly been the case with John Zahm in the Congregation of Holy Cross, and I can only hope that this "appreciation" may open his bothers and sisters in that religious family to cherish the unique witness that is his..